Law in Society Series

DECISIONS IN THE
PENAL PROCESS

other titles in the series

The Social Control of Drugs
PHILIP BEAN

Lawyers and their Public
COLIN M. CAMPBELL and R. WILSON

The Factory Acts: A Sociological Perspective
W. G. CARSON and BERNICE MARTIN

Pollution, Social Interest and the Law
NEIL GUNNINGHAM

The Politics of Abolition
THOMAS MATHIESEN

Social Needs and Legal Action
PAULINE MORRIS, RICHARD WHITE, PHILIP LEWIS

The Search for Pure Food
INGEBORG PAULUS

Knowledge and Opinion about Law
ADAM PODGORECKI, WOLFGANG KAUPEN, J. VAN HOUTTE,
P. VINKE, BERL KUTCHINSKY

Deviance, Crime and Socio-Legal Control
ROLAND ROBERTSON and LAURIE TAYLOR

by the same author

Prison Before Trial (1970)

Decisions in the Penal Process

A. KEITH BOTTOMLEY

Lecturer in Criminology, University of Hull

Law in Society Series

edited by
C. M. CAMPBELL, W. G. CARSON,
P. N. P. WILES

MARTIN ROBERTSON

First published in 1973 by Martin Robertson and Company Ltd, 17 Quick Street, London N1 8HL. Reprinted 1975

ISBN 0 85520 047 2 (case edition)
ISBN 0 85520 046 4 (paperback)

Text set in 11/12 pt Photon Times, printed by photolithography, and bound in Great Britain at The Pitman Press, Bath

CONTENTS

Introductory Note *by Editors*   vii

Preface   xi

Acknowledgements   xii

Introduction   xiii

1   CRIMINAL STATISTICS AND SOCIAL ATTITUDES   1
    The Meaning and Validity of Statistics 2; Social Attitudes:
    Defining and Reporting Crime 8; Recording Crime: the Role of
    the Police 21; Conclusions: the Purposes of Criminal Statistics
    26; Notes 31

2   POLICE DISCRETION IN LAW ENFORCEMENT   35
    The Need for Discretion 37; 'On-the-Street' Discretion: the Deci-
    sion to Arrest 43; Disposition Decisions and Police Cautioning
    61; Police and the Criminal Justice System 73; Notes 77

3   PRE-TRIAL DECISION-MAKING   84
    The Granting of Bail 85; The Decision to Plead Guilty 105;
    Notes 124

4   THE SENTENCING PROCESS   130
    Evidence of Disparities 133; The Human Element in Judges'
    Decisions 143; Sentencing and the Community 155; The Selection
    and Use of Information 163; Notes 170

5   PRISON CLASSIFICATION AND PAROLE   175
    Aims of Imprisonment 175; Classification in Theory and Practice
    179; Parole Decisions 194; Notes 212

6   CONCLUSIONS: SOCIETY AND THE PENAL   217
      PROCESS
        *Conflict and Consensus in the Penal Process 217; Social Values
        and Penal Aims 225; Notes 227*

Select Bibliography   229

Index of Authors   245

Index of Subjects   249

INTRODUCTORY NOTE

The 'Law in Society' series was established to help foster the growth of the sociology of law in the United Kingdom. All those interested in this field like to think that their work is breaking radically new grounds, and we are sensitive to the utility of the excitement which such a belief engenders. However this should not blind us to the facts that some of the questions we are now asking have been posed, at least tentatively, and that some of the information needed to answer them has been collected. Often all that is different is the precise formulation of the questions. In this sense, the present activity is a development rather than a radically new departure in itself.

Nowhere is this more true than in the work that has been carried out in what has traditionally been called 'criminology' and 'penology'. Increasingly, researchers in these fields have been asking questions, the answers to which are dependent upon the development of satisfactory work in the sociology of law. This reorientation in criminology and penology has involved a massive stock-taking exercise of the existing literature: so much so that some people have complained that this has been at the expense of pushing forward empirical research. But this is to misunderstand what is happening. We must first re-evaluate our existing knowledge in the light of the kinds of questions now being asked, in order to define the place of empirical research in the new order of things. This process of re-evaluation has at times been brutal, leading to schisms and open hostility. Sometimes however we may discover that a careful examination of existing work provides a good basis for beginning to answer our new questions.

Keith Bottomley's *Decisions in the Penal Process* is an excellent example of this kind of work. The book is not a report on a particular empirical research project, nor is it simply a catalogue of the work of others. Instead the concern is with asking at what stage in the process of dealing with offenders decisions are being made, and what are the nature of these decisions. The attempt is to discover how far our existing knowledge is adequate for answering these questions. However, this is not merely stock-taking, but a constructive and systematic analysis with explicit purposes. The objectives are firstly to discover at what point our knowledge is inadequate to the task of answering pertinent questions, and how these deficiencies may be remedied; and secondly to spell out the extent to which our existing, if limited, knowledge may help us to achieve those goals at which we believe the penal process ought to be aiming.

Dr. Bottomley is aware, as any student of the penal process must be, of the ambiguities and confusions involved in the way in which we deal with offenders: hence his insistence that we talk about process rather than system, with its connotations of order and coherence. It is precisely these confusions and inconsistencies which must be spelt out if we are ever to understand the decisions taken about the future of those who have transgressed against the law.

C.M.C.
W.G.C.
P.N.P.W.

To my mother and father,

and Denise

PREFACE

This book has emerged from my experience, during the last few years, teaching criminology and penal policy to students in the Department of Social Administration at Hull University. My main debt of gratitude, therefore, is to the University and, more especially, to my Head of Department, Ronald Drinkwater, who provided me with this opportunity to develop my ideas with the greatest freedom and flexibility; I warmly appreciate the teaching and learning experience enjoyed during this time. As for the students, I can only hope that their exposure to my ideas has whetted rather than blunted their appetite for this book.

Academically, the book would not have been possible without the large number of scholars, from Britain and overseas, whose work I have drawn on extensively, in my attempt to integrate and develop a great deal of previous thinking and research in the penal process. Specific references to authors and researchers will, of course, be found fully documented in the text and notes, but I feel that it is important to acknowledge in a more personal way the invaluable part played by all those who have contributed to the body of knowledge from which my work has derived.

Finally, in the actual production of the book, my main thanks are due to the publishers, particularly to David Martin, for their personal concern throughout the process; to Mrs Pauline Keel, for typing the entire manuscript in a most efficient and tireless way; and to my wife, who helped to compile the index, and inevitably had to put up with considerable disruption of home life during the final stages of my writing.

Keith Bottomley

University of Hull,
March, 1973

xi

ACKNOWLEDGEMENTS

Grateful acknowledgements are due to the following authors and publishers for permission to use material from their publications in the tables for this book: E. Cumming, I. M. Cumming and L. Edell 'Policeman as Philosopher, Guide and Friend', *Social Problems*, Vol. **12** (1965) p. 276; I. Piliavin and S. Briar 'Police Encounters with Juveniles', *Amer. Jo. Soc.*, **70** (1964) p. 206; L. W. Shannon 'Types and Patterns of Delinquency Referral in a Middle-sized City', *Brit. Jo. Crim.*, Vol. **4** (1963) p. 24; R. M. Terry 'The Screening of Juvenile Offenders', *Jo. Crim. Law, Crimin. and P.S.*, Vol. **58** (1967) p. 173; J. G. Somerville 'A Study of the Preventive Aspect of Police Work with Juveniles', *Crim. L. R.* (1969) p. 472; N. L. Weiner and C. V. Willie 'Decisions by Juvenile Officers', *Amer. Jo. Soc.*, Vol. **77** (1971) p. 199.

M. King *Bail or Custody*, Cobden Trust 1971; President's Commission on Law Enforcement and Administration of Justice *Task Force Report: The Courts*, U.S. Government Printing Office (1967); A. S. Blumberg *Criminal Justice*, Quadrangle Books (1967); H. Kalven and H. Zeisel *The American Jury*, Little, Brown and Co. (1966); E. Gibson *Time Spent Awaiting Trial*, H.M.S.O. (1960).

K. W. Patchett and J. D. McClean 'Decision-making in Juvenile Cases', *Crim. L. R.* (1965) p. 699; F. J. Gaudet 'The Sentencing Behavior of the Judge', in V. C. Branham and S. B. Kutash (Eds.) *Encyclopaedia of Criminology*, Philosophical Library (1949); J. Hogarth *Sentencing as a Human Process*, Toronto University Press (1971); R. G. Hood *Sentencing the Motoring Offender*, Heinemann (1972); S. S. Nagel 'Disparities in Criminal Procedure', *U.C.L.A. Rev.*, Vol. **14** (1967) p. 1272; R. G. Hood *Sentencing in Magistrates' Courts*, Stevens (1962); F. V. Jarvis 'Inquiry Before Sentence', in T. Grygier *et al.* (Eds.) *Criminology in Transition*, Tavistock (1965).

V. O'Leary and D. Glaser 'The Assessment of Risk in Parole Decision Making', in D. J. West (Ed.) *The Future of Parole*, Duckworth (1972); K. O. Hawkins, 'Parole Selection: the American Experience', unpublished Ph.D. thesis, Cambridge University Library (1971).

INTRODUCTION

The penal process can be studied in various different ways and for a variety of reasons. Traditional textbooks about 'the penal system' tend to concentrate upon describing the structure and operation of a particular country's system from a legal and administrative viewpoint: on the other hand, to a growing extent in recent years criminologists and sociologists have been developing an entirely different and much more radical approach to the study of society's response to criminal behaviour, of which the major elements include a fundamental questioning of existing social responses and the development of more truly sociological theories of crime and deviant behaviour. The student or practitioner who seeks to understand the penal process often finds the traditional textbooks somewhat uninspiring and uncritical in their approach to the problem, but is often equally alienated by the kind of radicalism and social attitudes implicit in much of modern sociological writing about the penal process. Accordingly, a preliminary attempt has been made in this book to fill the gap between the purely descriptive account, with its official, administrative and national bias, and the purely sociological critique, with its theoretical and radical concerns. The starting-point of this study is a belief that the penal process in any country can best be understood not simply by looking at its formal structure and legal basis, but by closely examining the various pressures and constraints which influence the *actual operation* of the process, as it is only through a greater awareness of these underlying influences that a society can make the crucial value judgements as to the appropriate definition and response to the deviant behaviour of its members.

The particular perspective, which has been chosen to provide a framework for understanding the penal process, is one which focuses attention on the decisions which are taken at different stages of the process, from the point at which members of the public report crimes to the police, through the enforcement decisions taken by the police and magistrates, to those decisions which determine the date of a man's release from prison on parole. This perspective is by no means original, but owes much to the formative ideas of Leslie T. Wilkins, whose writings first introduced the author to the idea of 'decision-stages' in the penal process; similarly, in the United States of America, the major research programme sponsored by the American Bar Foundation adopted a very similar approach in its study of the processes of criminal justice, so that many of the resulting publications, particularly those by Wayne LaFave, Donald Newman and Robert Dawson, have provided invaluable sources of comparative data. This research enterprise clearly influenced the official report of the President's Commission on Law Enforcement and Administration of Justice (1967), which analysed the working of the American criminal justice system according to an 'information systems' framework. Apart from these major sources and developments of the perspective, numerous other criminologists and sociologists, both in Britain and America, have carried out research into particular aspects of the penal process, which either explicitly or implicitly has been informed by similar thinking. What this book will be attempting to do, therefore, is to bring together much of the relevant research and ideas to see how they can illuminate our understanding of the penal process. Inevitably, much of the source material comes from the United States, but wherever possible relevant British research findings are used to full advantage, as this has been somewhat neglected by many scholars who advocate this perspective; nevertheless, it is the author's view that the understanding of any particular penal system can be usefully enhanced by theories and research carried out in countries other than the one of prime concern, so that the comparative element has a real contribution to make to the accumulation of knowledge and the development of methods of study for more general application.

Many different but related themes will recur throughout the decision-stages studied; any single one of these themes could have provided the main focus for the book, but it was thought that more would be gained at this stage by a rather broader-based approach to the chosen subject, instead of being constrained by a narrower focus on certain aspects of decision-making, as the aim is *not* to develop a theory of decision-making, illustrated by examples from the penal process, but to further an understanding of the penal process in its relationship with society, from a perspective in which the framework is provided by a series of decisions. The themes include the fundamental one of the nature and extent of the *exercise of discretion* in criminal justice, which has recently been subjected to a penetrating analysis by K. C. Davis, in his book *Discretionary Justice* (1969); in addition, there are the recurring issues of the *ambiguity of penal objectives,* and the *availability of information,* which may (or may not) be relevant to any of these objectives, but which clearly influences the 'quality' of decision-making and the practical exercise of discretion. Another major theme is that of the connexion, or lack of connexion, between the different stages of the penal process; the very choice of the term penal *process,* instead of the more usual penal *system,* is meant to indicate the problematic nature of the relationship between different parts of the criminal justice system, and to raise questions about the degree of integration which obtains in practice. A further significance which is intentionally attached to the idea of 'process', relates to the role of the people who are being dealt with as suspected or convicted offenders; the idea of a 'system' implies an emphasis upon a bureaucratic structure, in which there is little room for considering the interests of individuals, where these might conflict with the interests of the system; this, of course, may well be the most accurate image of a society's handling of suspects and offenders, as Abraham Blumberg has forcefully suggested in his important work, *Criminal Justice* (1967). However, when it is sought to focus attention upon the importance of 'individual' factors in criminal justice, whether relating to those who make the decisions or those who are on the receiving end, the concept of 'penal process' seems more appropriate; thus, in this book, its use is meant to signify an *awareness* of the fact that a major link between all stages of the penal process is the transmission or 'procession' of individual suspects and offenders from one stage to the next, so that for these people there *is* a vital connexion between each and every part, as *they themselves are that connexion;* secondly, its use is meant to reflect a major focus on the individuals who make the decisions, who are influenced not only by their role in the 'system' but also by other factors deriving from their individuality and idiosyncrasies. The main emphasis, in practice, upon the second of these aspects of the process is in no way intended to underrate the importance of understanding the penal process from the perspective of those who are actually 'processed', and it is hoped that the fine example set by John Irwin's study, *The Felon* (1970), will be followed by many other studies of a similar kind.

There are so many different points in the penal process at which decisions are made that any study of this length is bound to be selective, if it is to treat each decision-stage in appropriate depth. This study, then, reflects a *selection* of the possible areas which could have been examined in this way, and naturally reflects the personal interests of the author; but also the selection does, to some extent, reflect the differential amount of attention paid to various parts of the process by researchers, and was influenced by the contemporary relevance of certain issues. Some of the major omissions include aspects of decision-making in the formulation of criminal legislation, decisions taken by defendants about legal aid and representation at trial, the decision to acquit or convict taken by judge or jury, and many decisions taken by the penal agents who deal with offenders after sentence, involving aspects of community supervision and institutional treatment. Clearly, there is plenty of scope for a second edition of this book!

Finally, a brief comment needs to be made about the relationship between theory, empirical research and social values. This book relies heavily on the findings of empirical research, in its development and illustration of the decision framework of the penal process; only in the discussion of prison classification (chapter 5) is the evidence not mainly of an empirical kind, but based on a complementary historical approach. It is hoped that the use of empirical research findings in the analysis will be seen to be directed and informed by the more 'theoretical' considerations which underlie the general perspective; a major intention of the study is to bring together as much of the relevant research as possible, to substantiate and illustrate the chosen approach, not in the belief that empirical findings are necessarily valuable *per se,* but with the firm conviction that any theory or perspective upon the penal process must ultimately be supported (and not contradicted) by the available empirical evidence; thus, the value of empirical research has always to be considered in relation to a particular theory or theoretical perspective being developed. From this point of view, it is unfortunate that much empirical work in criminology has been 'social accounting' of a purely descriptive nature, uninformed by any theoretical considerations; so much so, in fact, that 'empiricism' itself has tended to get a bad name and to be used mainly as a pejorative term. There is a great need, therefore, for a reassessment of the relationship between theory and empiricism in criminological research, so that empirical work may become more informed by theoretical considerations, and theories may be seen to depend ultimately on the degree of support they receive from empirical findings of one kind or another.

In the study of the penal process, as in so much of social science research, the ultimate significance of any findings, however apparently well-attested, is crucially affected by the major role of social and political values in their interpretation and implementation; this vital relationship between the penal process and wider social values is perhaps the most important (if not always very explicit) underlying theme of this study. 'Crime' is itself a socio-political concept, which reflects and is the product of the structure of social values and attitudes in a society, at any particular point in time; in a very simple fashion, this is shown by the analysis (chapter 1) of the role of social attitudes in the definition and reporting of 'crime' to the police in the first instance. This means that all decisions in the penal process are both influenced by and reflect a variety of social and political values, although with varying degrees of awareness of this fact by those directly involved. Research is vital to the proper *understanding* of the operation of the penal process, but it is a fundamental mistake to believe that understanding necessarily brings about *social change*, let alone change in the direction favoured by the researchers themselves. In the final analysis, society (or certain groups within society) decides what should be regarded as 'crime' and what measures should be taken against those detected and officially labelled as 'criminals'; all that research can do is to indicate a number of contradictions and ambiguities in the process, in the hope that the uncovering of such a situation may render it unacceptable to many of those in a position to do something about it, and will make it less easy for society as a whole to close its eyes to what is being done in its name.

1 CRIMINAL STATISTICS AND SOCIAL ATTITUDES

Official criminal statistics are the main source of routine information about the extent of criminal behaviour and the operation of the penal system. For England and Wales, these statistics include a record of the number of crimes which become 'known to the police' in each year, the proportion of crimes 'cleared-up' by the police, and extensive details of the ways in which the persons proceeded against for alleged offences are dealt with at Magistrates' Courts and Crown Courts. Because of their regular appearance each year, enabling comparisons to be made with previous years, and because of the apparent objectivity and accuracy of totals such as that of 'crimes known to the police', it is inevitable that these statistics should be used by the press and television, by laymen and politicians, and even by many self-styled experts in criminology, as a measure of the moral state of society and the effectiveness of the penal system, without any serious word of warning about the many notorious pit-falls of interpretation affecting their reliability and validity.

One of the main reasons for this general unquestioning attitude towards official criminal statistics is a failure to recognize that they are not just simple mathematical counts of events that happen, and which can be recorded with complete accuracy and objectivity, but rather they are the product of a complicated process, involving a variety of social attitudes towards criminal behaviour, and discretionary patterns of law enforcement and decision-making by the police, courts and other penal agencies. Comprehensive descriptions and critical discussions of the form of English criminal statistics are available elsewhere,[1] so it is intended in this first chapter to present a view of the statistics from a perspective which concentrates on the nature of the processes producing some of the most important statistics, and to

1

suggest ways of increasing our understanding of the meaning of criminal statistics in the context of a wider study of the penal process.

THE MEANING AND VALIDITY OF STATISTICS

It is traditional for criminologists to question the validity of criminal statistics and to speculate about the extent and nature of unreported criminal behaviour. The most often quoted statement of the traditional position is that made by Thorsten Sellin:

> Generally speaking, all criminal statistics are in fact statistics of law enforcement, in the broad sense of that term. Our problem is to discover whether or not these statistics can also be employed for measuring criminality. In view of what has been said above, it is obvious that for such a purpose we cannot use the *total* recorded criminality.... Therefore, we may suggest as a second principle that the value of criminal statistics as a basis for the measurement of criminality in geographic areas decreases as the procedure takes us farther away from the offence itself.[2]

Early post-war studies of English criminal statistics served to emphasize the fact that there are several different kinds of criminal statistics. Thus Radzinowicz drew the now obvious distinction between statistics recording the number of crimes reported, the number of persons tried or convicted and the number given different sentences. He also pointed out that 'what makes every study of criminal statistics so difficult is the fact that each one is based on a different statistical unit, is compiled by different authorities, and according to different criteria'.[3] In a similar tradition, Grünhut outlined the various possible factors influencing the size and constancy (or otherwise) of the 'dark figure' of unreported criminal behaviour, and described the regressive nature of statistics in terms similar to those of Sellin:

> With every further stage in the process of criminal administration the 'dark figure' increases and the figures obtained become less symptomatic of the actual crime position. Crimes known to the police, persons arrested, charged, tried, convicted, and prisoners

received in penal institutions are a regressive scale in the representation of the volume and forms of crime.[4]

The underlying conception of the processes of law enforcement and criminal justice as a sequence of events or decisions, reflecting various stages of the interaction between the community, the suspected offender and penal agents, has been developed by contemporary criminologists in Britain and the United States, and has also been the focus of special attention from the developing school of sociologists of deviant behaviour.

The most important contribution to the development of this approach to criminal statistics in Britain has been that of Leslie T. Wilkins. In one of his earliest writings on the subject, in 1962, he presented a 'flow-chart' showing the different stages in the English penal system.[5] Wilkins emphasized that criminal statistics are static representations of situations and processes which are essentially dynamic; there are many stages between the commission of an offence and the reconviction of a sentenced offender, and criminal statistics attempt to intercept persons and events at different points along this 'process continuum' and make counts.[6]

Up to this point, Wilkins' analysis was more or less an extension and elaboration of the traditional view of the sequential nature of criminal statistics; but it was with his introduction of the 'decision-stages' concept that he began to break rather newer ground. He discussed the various kinds of statistics, *not* in relation to whether they were 'reliable' measures of different aspects of criminal behaviour, but in relation to the kind of decisions which they reflected, which could have an independent influence upon the future progress of individuals through the criminal justice system:

At all these points decisions are made *regarding* people, *by* people in authority, *resulting* in an action which is describable and which takes into account preceding known facts. Most of these points refer to decisions resulting in the diversion of the individual subject from one track of the process to another within whatever system is concerned. These points of decision may thus be looked upon as 'gates', and these 'gates' may be given some sort of counting mechanism. . . . It will be apparent that different statistical data which are often loosely said to relate to the concept of 'crime' in

3

fact relate to figures from counting mechanisms at different 'gates' in the system.[7]

Statistics relating to the movement of persons through the 'gates' of the decision network of any system can usually be accurately determined—as Wilkins says, it is a matter only of technical efficiency; but for what purposes it is valid to use these decision-gate counts is a different matter and will be discussed at greater length in the final section of this chapter. It is sufficient, at this stage in the discussion, to note that Wilkins' model of the system greatly clarifies our understanding of the issues, without necessarily solving the problem of the valid purposes for which different statistics can or ought to be used.

At about the same time as Wilkins was putting forward his ideas in this country, Newman published a short and relatively neglected paper in the United States along very similar lines, in which he not only talked about decisions and criminal statistics but in which he particularly emphasized the element of *discretion* surrounding many of these decisions.[8] Newman indicated the points in the penal process where discretion is formally allowed, such as the discretion of the prosecutor as to how or whether to charge a suspected offender, and the discretion of the judge in his choice of sentence; but, perhaps more importantly, he showed that discretion operates where it is not officially permitted. He concluded that a failure to recognize criminal procedures as a complex pattern of decision-making and discretionary choices of administrators resulted in fundamental errors in basing conclusions upon statistics of convictions or even upon statistics taken from any point in the process. A careful analysis of how the system operates, and how it records its business, was seen as a vital prerequisite for the use of any data gathered from it.

This new focus, turning away from the traditional concern with the *unreliability* of statistics for assessing the extent of criminal behaviour, towards a new concern with the *processes* whereby official statistics are produced, attracted the attention of the newly developing school of sociologists of deviant behaviour. In an important paper, modestly entitled 'A Note on the Uses of Official Statistics', Kitsuse and Cicourel elaborated their sociological perspective upon the meaning and validity of statistics.[9] In the same way as Wilkins and Newman, they stressed that statistics are the results of decisions and actions taken by

4

persons in a social system which defines, classifies and records certain behaviour as deviant. The process is therefore, crucially affected by the subjective attitudes of individuals, within a particular social and cultural setting, and by how they define and interpret behaviour as criminal. It was suggested that criminologists need to study both the explicit and implicit definitions which precede and underlie the 'objective' statistical categories:

> Thus, the questions to be asked are not about the appropriateness of the statistics, but about the definitions incorporated in the categories applied by the personnel of the rate-producing social system to identify, classify, and record behaviour as deviant. . . . Rates can be viewed as indices of organisational processes rather than as indices of the incidence of certain forms of behaviour.[10]

Cicourel expanded these same ideas in his later study, *The Social Organisation of Juvenile Justice* (1968), in which he illustrated, from extensive fieldwork observation, how law enforcement personnel and penal agents define and process juveniles largely on the basis of their existing expectations and stereotypes of deviant behaviour.[11] Official statistics, he claimed, can never accurately reflect the ambiguous decisions, discretion and accommodations of law enforcement personnel, nor the important role of the victim of criminal acts and the family or subcultural group of the suspected offender. The picture presented by official statistics and accounts must be examined in the light of a detailed knowledge of 'the networks of social action by which the actor becomes officially known as a delinquent or criminal'.[12]

Cicourel's views have perhaps even more important implications for traditional theories of the *causes* of criminal behaviour, which have almost without exception been based on data relating to officially defined and processed criminals:

> . . . the use of such [official statistical] data to document conventional theories of individual delinquency obscures the view that official statistics reflect socially organised activities divorced from the sociological theories used retrospectively for explaining the same statistics. Members of the community, law-enforcement personnel, attorneys, judges, all respond to various behavioural or im-

5

puted symbolic or reported acts and events by juveniles with commonsense or lay conceptions, abstract legal rules, bureaucratic procedures and policies.[13]

What is needed, therefore, is a comprehensive theory of social organization which would not only explain, or help in the understanding of behaviour which contravenes criminal or social norms but also equally explain the processes and operational characteristics which produce the official statistical records of that behaviour and society's response to it.[14]

The impact of this recent theorizing by criminologists and sociologists on the subject of criminal statistics has not been entirely confined to academic circles. In particular, the President's Commission on Law Enforcement and Administration of Justice (1967) used a detailed model of the various stages in the criminal justice system to illustrate its overall view of that system, and commissioned an operational research exercise into the cost effectiveness of criminal justice in the United States.[15] The main Report of the President's Commission discussed the different parts of the system and the crucial interrelationships between the parts, in terms very similar to those used by Wilkins and Newman, although implying rather more order and coherence in the progression of an individual through the system than was suggested either by Wilkins' network of 'decision-stages' or by Newman's emphasis on discretion and accommodation patterns.[16]

A convincing attempt to integrate the practical and theoretical significance of the new approach to understanding criminal statistics was made by Stanton Wheeler (1967). His article, 'Criminal Statistics: A Reformulation of the Problem', brought together many of the main issues which have been dealt with in this section, and provides a useful link with the subsequent discussion.[17] Wheeler attacked the traditional assumption that statistics were the 'passive' response of official penal agents to the active behaviour of criminals, and that the problem of criminal statistics was simply a matter of improving the efficiency of crime reporting and detection. The alternative, which he put forward in his reformulation of the problem, was to conceive of criminal statistics as the result of interaction between (a) the offender who commits an illegal act, (b) the members of the public who may witness or

6

be the victims of the act, and (c) the police responsible for law enforcement. Each of these three elements should be seen as a 'legitimate and inherent part of the model of criminal statistics, rather than conceiving of them as external and unwanted sources of error and unreliability'.[18] In this way of looking at the problem, the decisions and actions of members of the public and the police become important events *to be explained*, just as traditional criminology seeks to explain why some persons commit crimes and others do not:

> The actual justification for treating crime statistics as a result of three-way interaction between an offender, victims or citizens, and official agents, is that deviation itself is increasingly recognised as a social process that depends heavily on social definition. Acts become deviant when they are so defined by members of the collectivities in which they occur. Whether a given pattern of behaviour will be labeled deviant is itself problematic, and is likely to vary from community to community, or even from policeman to policeman. ... A model stressing the social definition of crime, and especially the actions of other social agents as well as those of presumed offenders, is pragmatically useful as well as being highly realistic.[19]

The practical consequences for empirical research, which Wheeler derived from his theoretical position, included (i) a closer study and understanding of public attitudes towards criminal behaviour and social control; (ii) improved understanding of police and official agents along the lines of studies carried out by James Q. Wilson (1968), by studying the dynamics of police systems in relation to offenders rather than simply regarding the police as 'mere reactors' to the actions of criminals;[20] and (iii) the development of consumer-oriented statistics, detailing characteristics of victims and the social circumstances of offences as well as details of offenders. We can in fact go even further than this and, as Wiles has suggested, extend our study to include the process of law-making:

> What must be done, to complete our understanding of the meaning of criminal statistics, is to explore the effects of formal law on the process. We need to know precisely how and why a particular law was made, how it relates to differences in the wider social structure,

7

how it relates to the distribution of normative structures, and what kind of typifications of meaning it includes.[21]

An examination of the information available in official criminal statistics is invariably the starting point for any student of the penal process, who wishes to discover the extent and nature of the 'crime problem' and to study the working of a country's penal system. To such a student, many glaring deficiencies soon become apparent, relating particularly to the technical aspects of collecting and presenting the different kinds of criminal statistics; it is hoped that these introductory comments have shown that, although considerable improvement is possible and desirable to increase the reliability of statistics, yet a more fundamental problem is a true understanding of the essential nature of criminal statistics as the product of a series of interrelated decisions and interactions between society, its deviant members and the agents of social control and criminal justice.

SOCIAL ATTITUDES: DEFINING AND REPORTING CRIME

Most indictable crimes 'known to the police' are not discovered as a result of the direct initiative and detection work of the police themselves, but are reported to the police by members of the public who have witnessed or have been the victims of the crimes concerned.[22] The attitudes of members of the public towards reporting criminal behaviour must therefore be studied in order to analyse the relationship between crimes committed in the community and those crimes which become officially known to the police. A broad framework needs to be constructed, which goes beyond simply cataloguing the many and various factors influencing the reporting of crime. For this purpose, an important distinction can be drawn between factors influencing the way members of the public *define* certain acts or events as criminal, and, on the other hand, factors influencing whether crimes, once defined as such, are then *reported* to the police. This distinction between problems of *definition* and problems of *reporting* seems a useful aid in the analysis of the problem, but, like so many useful distinctions, it is often a rather artificial one, and it will be seen in the subsequent discussion that there is sometimes an overlap between the two categories.

8

Leslie Wilkins has expressed the basic issues surrounding the definition of crime in a perceptive and stimulating fashion. Putting himself in the place of the ordinary member of the public who witnesses or is the victim of a 'potential crime' incident, Wilkins shows that the first step must be for the person to define the incident as 'something that the police ought to do something about';[23] he claims that it is unrealistic, at this stage, to talk vaguely about the concept of 'crime', because the layman might in fact be ignorant about the details of the law, and be witnessing or experiencing an incident which is perfectly legal, although possibly regarded as 'wrong' from a moral standpoint. Equally, of course, a layman's interpretation or knowledge of 'crime' may exclude (i.e. regard as legal and/or merely immoral) behaviour which is actually illegal. Wilkins therefore suggests an operational definition of crime as 'any event known to the citizens of an area and *thought* by them to be worthy of notification to the police in the expectation of police action regarding the matter'; this definition incorporates an important qualitative element, reflecting the 'level of disapprobation on the part of the public, such that they actively seek the assistance of the forces of social defence'.[24]

It is clear, therefore, that the definition of behaviour as criminal is primarily influenced by broad socio-cultural factors, which can be studied both from a national and from an international or cross-cultural perspective. It is not intended here to pursue the interesting cross-cultural study of the definition of crime, which has recently received attention from Gibbens and Ahrenfeldt[25] and Lopez-Rey;[26] but even in a country like Britain, at a relatively stable stage in its socio-cultural development, there are likely to be changes in social attitudes towards criminal behaviour between one generation and the next, and also changes in attitudes about the appropriate boundary between criminal and immoral behaviour, with important implications for the initiation of the process of law enforcement by members of the public. Such changes in social attitudes and social definitions will obviously be reflected in the kinds of crime regarded as something that the police ought to do something about, and thereby introduce new bias into the official statistics of 'crimes known to the police'.[27] A fundamental need for criminological theory and research is the development of techniques for measuring the relevant social attitudes and definitions, so that changes over periods of time can be accurately assessed and related to trends in the number of different crimes reported to the police. Until such time as these techniques have been successfully developed and applied, the importance of being fully aware of these influences must be stressed, but for the present we are left to speculate on the effects with more or less informed guesswork.[28]

Closely related to the broad cultural changes which may influence the public's view of the relative seriousness of different forms of criminal behaviour and also its view of the appropriateness of criminal or moral sanctions with respect to certain activities, is the role of legislation in shaping and being shaped by social attitudes. Traditional arguments about law, crime and society, have tended to assume that most members of the public are reasonably well acquainted with the legislation of their own country, if not in minute detail at least to the extent of knowing which broad categories of behaviour are against the law. This assumption was central to the Devlin–Hart debate about the role of law in relation to morality and sexual offences,[29] and it is a minimum requirement (i.e. without necessarily knowing typical *sentences* passed) for proponents of the deterrent principle in the penal system. However, it seems that general knowledge of legislation is much less common and less accurate than has sometimes been believed, and therefore the relationship between law and social behaviour must be questioned, not only with respect to an individual's own behaviour but also with respect to attitudes towards the behaviour of other people, which a person may be in a position to report to the police.[30] Changes in criminal legislation must therefore be studied carefully, not with an oversimplified expectation that they will automatically change or reflect the attitudes and behaviour of the members of that society, but with the knowledge that they are a crucial variable in the understanding of social attitudes towards defining and reporting crime.

Mannheim, in his classic study of crime in England between the wars, summarized the issues and implications well:

The passing of a new statute may signify social changes of a much more general and far-reaching character. It may be the outcome of a prolonged state of public anxiety and excitement caused by actions, punishable or not, of certain undesirable elements among the population. In such a case it is clear that subsequently the general

10

public as well as the police will do their best to carry out the law as strictly as possible. Private persons will be inclined to act as informants, prosecutors, and witnesses. Consequently, there is likely to be an increase in the number of prosecutions and convictions, even in spite of a decrease in the actual amount of crime.... This, of course, will happen only in those cases where public opinion agrees with the course taken by the legislator. It is quite different when both move in opposite directions or when there is a dissension among the various social groups of the community as to the merits of a certain change in the law.[31]

Mannheim's final sentence indicates the second main aspect involved in understanding the problems surrounding the definition of criminal behaviour: not only must broad *cultural* factors be studied, which are based on the working assumption of cultural homogeneity in a particular country, but, perhaps more importantly, it is necessary to make a careful study of the influence of *subcultural* factors. In this context, the term 'subcultural' is being used rather loosely to describe factors deriving from commonly held attitudes or behaviour within different communities or institutions, which affect the way members of those communities or 'subcultures' define behaviour as criminal. Three related groups of factors will be briefly considered: (i) *subcultural toleration* of behaviour as 'normal'; (ii) *subcultural antipathy* towards those in authority, especially the police; and (iii) *institutional immunity* from the normal processes of law enforcement and criminal justice.

It hardly needs criminologists or sociologists to spell out the fact that in most societies there exist different levels of social toleration of behaviour which is, strictly speaking, illegal. The very avoidance, by particular groups within a society, of the adjective 'criminal' for illegal behaviour which they themselves accept as normal might suggest an internalization of Wilkins' concept of crime as 'something that the police ought to do something about'. The idea of subcultural toleration of criminal behaviour as 'normal' has usually been applied to working-class areas where violence and aggression are thought to be more common and, therefore, allowed a greater degree of 'tolerance' before it is thought appropriate for the police to intervene. In their study, *Crimes of Violence*, McClintock and his colleagues suggested several factors which might contribute to the 'dark figure' of unreported crimes of violence: these included situations where the violence involved adults known to each other, in working-class areas where a certain amount of violence was accepted, and also amongst juveniles in similar areas and certain schools.[32] McClintock went on to suggest, however, that there appeared to have been a general decrease in many neighbourhoods in the amount of violence that was tolerated as normal, which had led to a greater tendency to report such crimes to the police:

> The fact that more of the 'dark figures' are now coming to the notice of the police indicates a new situation: namely, that among certain strata of the community violence is nowadays tolerated much less than in the past, and that local inhabitants and others affected by incidents of violence feel that some form of public action has to be taken.[33]

Changes of this kind, affecting the level of toleration of offences of violence in such areas, could have a considerable impact upon statistics of violence known to the police, because it seems likely that these areas of traditional tolerance of violence are the very areas where the greatest proportion of violent 'offences' are committed; so the whole argument becomes rather circular, inasmuch as definitions of 'normality' are closely related to frequency as well as to values.

In addition to this common application of the concept of sub-cultural toleration to behaviour in certain working-class communities, there is a need for a more explicit and systematic application of the concept to other forms of behaviour which are accepted as 'normal', particularly by those who indulge in them. Two obvious examples are (i) occupational 'perks', usually referring to middle-class or professional occupations, and 'pilfering', usually referring to working-class jobs, and (ii) traffic offences. In his Reading survey of employers' attitudes towards crimes committed by their employees, Martin (1962) included an interesting discussion of the distinction drawn by different firms between 'pilfering' and 'stealing'.[34] Definitions often differed according to the type of firm concerned: thus, in banks, no line was drawn between 'pilfering' and 'stealing', because neither was ever condoned; whereas, in building firms, 'pilfering' of nails, wood off-cuts etc. was entirely tolerated, but a line was usually drawn at some point with reference to items of greater value. Martin concluded that it was vir-

12

tually impossible to assess the 'dark figure' of unreported crimes committed by employees at work—although the significance of the term 'dark figure' in this context (and many others) is questionable, as what the firms recognized as 'pilfering' was by this definition not perceived by them as a 'crime problem'. A minority of employers took a strictly legal view and condemned any unauthorized taking, but the majority seemed to exist in a rather vague state 'where a blind eye is turned on 'pilfering', which, however, merges at an ill-defined point into 'theft'.[35]

Traffic offences and social attitudes towards motoring offenders have only recently become the focus of serious attention from criminologists and social scientists in Britain.[36] It might be argued that relatively indifferent or tolerant social attitudes towards this type of behaviour are becoming part of our national culture, but because of its uneven social class distribution, it can still be usefully included within the framework of subcultural toleration. The toleration is shared generally among the driving public but, as MacMillan has shown (1970), a more specific toleration towards motoring offences is exhibited by those who have themselves committed similar offences.[37] The practical implications for law enforcement and the reporting of crime are rather more complex in this instance, because the police necessarily assume a more direct role in discovering and reporting traffic offences than in most other forms of crime, with a relatively less important part played by initiative from members of the public, even though they may witness or be the victims of traffic offences or accidents.

The list of examples of 'subcultural toleration' could be extended to a great length, although there is an unfortunate dearth of systematic studies of different kinds of social definitions of crime. Whole categories of so-called 'white-collar' crime would almost certainly be included in such a list, together with some of the examples to be included in the discussion of 'institutional immunity', below. A major task for criminology is to identify and describe the characteristics and extent of such toleration, and, of equal importance, to relate it to detailed study of the actual behaviour which is being tolerated, so as to provide the raw material for comprehensive sociological theories which can go beyond apparently explaining away or explaining 'into existence' phenomena by concentrating exclusively on questions of social definition.

13

Closely linked to subcultural toleration, which mainly affects the *definition* of criminal behaviour, is subcultural *antipathy* towards the police, which mainly affects the *reporting* of crime. This factor could more accurately be termed 'contra-cultural', to reflect its origins and expression in more negative and hostile attitudes and behaviour towards the police, in their capacity as law enforcement agents of society. Antipathy of this kind is often, but not necessarily, accompanied by a wider toleration of criminal behaviour, and is often therefore to be found in the same working-class areas, where violence and petty crime are common; Wiles (1971) has correctly pointed out that the development of contra-cultural ideologies may encourage the commission of offences at the same time as it discourages the reporting of them by others in the community.[38]

In the survey of crimes of violence, mentioned above, McClintock suggested that two of the factors contributing to the number of unreported crimes were the offences of violence between persons of the criminal classes with an understandable lack of sympathy and willingness to cooperate with the police, and also those offences where the victim was a member of a 'minority' group such as coloured people, Irish immigrants, vagrants or prostitutes, who might feel that the police were prejudiced against them and would not therefore act very positively on their behalf.[39] The attitudes of these minority group members, who have been the victims of crimes, is rather different from the attitudes of hostility on the part of the more dominant 'offender' group within a subculture, but the key variable remains the same, so that it should be possible to measure the strength of feelings of antipathy in both cases and relate this to attitudes towards the reporting of crimes.

Just as the concept of subcultural toleration can be usefully extended to the behaviour of wider middle-class and occupational groups, so it is possible to speculate on the possible application of the concept of antipathy, to other groups besides the working-class and minority groups already mentioned. It would seem that the development of hostility towards the police among any group in society derives mainly from the fact that the group's past and present experience of interaction with the police has been largely of a negative kind and in conflict situations; this accumulated experience may at some stage be fully incorporated into the subcultural group norms and

14

may then become very resistent to change, even in the light of more positive interactions in the course of future experiences. For example, the increasing involvement of middle-class driving members of the public in negative interaction with the police (despite the important traffic-warden 'scape-goats'), might soon cancel out the more traditional positive attitudes towards the police. In fact, in dealing with traffic offences and in many other areas of discretionary law enforcement, the police may find themselves enmeshed in a process of diminishing returns, not only in the specific area of immediate concern but also extending to social attitudes towards reporting other forms of criminal behaviour.

Confirmation of the potential of research along these lines, is to be found in the recently published findings of research carried out by Shaw and Williamson (1972). They found that public attitudes towards the police differed in four areas of an English city, particularly according to the social class characteristics of each area, and the age distribution of the respondents.[40] They also found that the *type of contact* between the police and the public contributed directly to variations in attitudes: the proportion of respondents who reported 'negative' contacts with the police (viz. being stopped and questioned) varied from less than 2 per cent in Area B (mixed social class) to more than 20 per cent in Area C (working class). When the respondents were divided into those with 'negative contacts' and those with 'positive contacts', the former not only expressed more critical views of the typical characteristics of the police but indicated much less 'cooperative' attitudes towards the police in practical situations, such as helping them to handle drunks or disorderly crowds, or agreeing to act as witnesses. The authors' conclusion that 'the social class composition of an area thus becomes an important indicator of the nature and quality of police–public contacts' is of obvious significance in understanding the way different publics initiate the reporting of crime.[41]

The final factor to be considered is rather different from the preceding two, and will be termed *institutional immunity*. Chapman has used a similar concept, but in a wider sense with particular reference to the immunity accorded by membership of the middle—or upper—classes.[42] Its present inclusion in the subcultural category seems justified because of its connexion with the earlier factor of subcultural toleration in the occupational context. The main illustrations

15

of institutional immunity will be drawn from studies of employers' attitudes towards offences committed by their employees at work, and shoplifting; but the concept is equally applicable to many other 'institutions', ranging from the relatively closed community life of the army or a university hall of residence, to membership of a professional occupational group, such as medicine, law or the church. The common feature of all these social institutions is that to a greater or lesser extent the functions of social control and law enforcement have been taken over by the institution itself so that the definition of crime as 'something which the police ought to do something about' has become adapted into a series of alternatives, ranging from 'something which *no one* ought to do anything about' (in this particular social context), through 'something which the *institution* ought to do something about' (for its own good), to, but only as a last resort, 'something which the police ought to do something about'. The institution rarely demands a lower standard of social behaviour from its members and, in fact, often requires a much higher standard, but its main concern is with ensuring the required behaviour as effectively and appropriately as possible, rather than automatically resorting to the official processes of law enforcement through the police and the courts, which may not only be less effective in ensuring the desired control of the behaviour in question but will almost certainly have important negative consequences for the institution concerned.

Martin's study of firms in Reading again provides valuable information, not only about the extent to which employers 'take the law into their own hands' but also about some of the reasons for their policies.[43] In the larger firms, only four out of ten of the offences connected with employment were brought to court, and in the smaller firms less than a quarter of offences resulted in prosecution. In no case was a man prosecuted when his firm did not want him to be, and Martin concluded that 'if an offence is concerned with a man's work, then the employer's definite opinion on what should be done is likely to correspond very closely to what actually happens'.[44] The main reasons for firms not taking official action against offenders were that the offence was not regarded as serious enough, that it was not worth the publicity or internal repercussions that would accompany a prosecution, or that the person concerned was a 'decent worker' or a 'good chap', presumably on the assumption that this was a lapse unlikely to recur. Thus the policy of these firms seemed to be the result of a balance of several different concerns, especially that of direct or indirect self-interest on the part of the firms, who in fact dismissed a large proportion of those men not prosecuted. Martin's conclusions on the relationship between employers and law enforcement are worth quoting:

> This evidence emphasises one fact of fundamental legal and sociological importance. It is that an employer, more perhaps than any other civil person (policeman excepted), is in a position where he has to decide whether or not to put a man in the hands of the law. The extent of this power and responsibility has tended to go unrecognised. . . . To the layman one question stands out. How far is it a good thing for standards of the law enforcement to vary as widely as they do between different sections of the community or between different social situations?[45]

A second example of institutional immunity is that of shoplifting, in which there is even less empirical evidence on questions of policy and practice in Britain than in the first example. Gibbens and Prince (1962) briefly recorded some information derived from unstructured interviews with thirty chief store-detectives;[46] but one of the best surveys is that carried out for the President's Commission on Law Enforcement and Administration of Justice in the United States, and reported by Hood and Sparks.[47] This survey of businesses in Boston, Chicago and Washington, found that two thirds of the wholesale and retail businesses claimed to have been the victims of shoplifting, but that, even when the offender was known, the stores called the police in a minority of cases—58 per cent never called the police and only 37 per cent said they usually did. Most shopkeepers felt that nothing was to be gained from police action, and therefore preferred to take informal non-legal action. In three quarters of the cases where the police were not called in, the shoplifter was required to pay for the stolen goods, and in most of the remaining cases the offender was warned not to return to the store in future.[48]

It seems a reasonable hypothesis to suggest that the policy of many stores in Britain towards shoplifting involves a similar combination of humanity and expediency as that found in studies of employers' attitudes towards employees who commit offences at work. Given a certain level of seriousness of the offences involved, policy seems to be determined by a desire to prevent the behaviour from taking place, as effectively as possible, and also to reduce the consequences for the firm, either in short-term loss of goods or more long-term loss of reputation and attraction for potential customers. Many firms achieve these aims by an efficient internal security system, without involving the police in any but exceptional cases, and conversely, other shops rely on an essentially deterrent policy of automatic prosecution; perhaps the majority operate an uneasy combination of these two approaches, so that any 'immunity' provided by their internal and often *ad hoc* decisions is unpredictable and unjust. Moreover, these and many other examples of institutional immunity clearly pose additional problems for knowing what significance to attach to official statistics, when they are based on such subjective and often inconsistent definitions of what situations require police intervention, and whether the possible advantages of official action outweigh the many practical disadvantages and inconveniences.

Having outlined the influence of cultural and subcultural factors upon the definition and reporting of crime, the last group of factors to be discussed in this section relate rather more specifically to reasons for the *non-reporting* of behaviour defined as criminal. It was suggested earlier that the distinction between problems of *definition* and problems of *reporting* was to some extent artificial, but for purposes of clarification it nevertheless seems useful to consider these last factors as relating mainly to the *reporting* problem.

There are a variety of factors, detailed particularly by Walker,[49] which are mainly 'technical' reasons why certain crimes are most unlikely to be reported, and which derive their significance from the central fact that the majority of crimes which become known to the police are reported primarily by the victim or, less frequently, by members of the public who are witnesses. Included in this category are offences which are known to no one other than the offender (e.g. motoring and other 'regulatory' offences), offences where there is no 'victim', in the usual sense of the word (e.g. 'public order' offences), or where the 'victim' is a willing party (e.g. drug offences, abortion and other sexual offences), and circumstances in which the victim is directly or indirectly intimidated from reporting the crime (e.g. embarassment or blackmail in relation to sexual offences) or does not know that an

18

offence has been committed against him (e.g. child victims of sex offences or victims of confidence tricksters).

An important reason, not included in the previous paragraph, for not reporting many of the more common crimes is a belief that the police will be able to do little or nothing about it. This is a different belief from those discussed earlier, where it was not regarded as the job of the police to intervene, or where a firm or institution believed it was primarily their own internal responsibility to control social behaviour and enforce the law. The view that the police will be able to do little about a reported crime may be an entirely realistic assessment of the situation, and does not question the theoretical appropriateness of the role of the police in dealing with the problem, only their likely effectiveness in practice.

For direct information about the extent to which this reason contributes to the non-reporting of crime, it is necessary again to refer to data collected by the so-called 'victim studies' in the United States.[50] In a nation-wide study carried out by the National Opinion Research Center of Chicago University (N.O.R.C.), one of the two major reasons for victims not reporting offences to the police was because it was believed that the police could not be effective or would not want to be bothered; this reason applied to six out of ten unreported cases of larceny and burglary, half the unreported sexual offences (excluding rape), 45 per cent of the robberies, and more than a third of unreported cases of fraud and false pretences.[51] Ennis noted that the reasons for not reporting crimes varied both by type of crime and by the social characteristics of the victim, but it was clear that there was strong resistance to invoking the law enforcement process even in matters that were clearly criminal, and in particular there was considerable scepticism as to the effectiveness of police action.[52] He discovered an important clue to this scepticism when he examined the sequence of events following a call to the police and found tremendous 'attrition' as the cases proceeded from the stage when the police were notified right through to conviction and sentence: in a quarter of the cases in which the police were notified, they did not even come to the scene of the crime to investigate the report; when they did come to investigate, the incident was not regarded as a crime in a further quarter of the cases; in only a fifth of the recorded crimes was any arrest made, of which less than half came to trial; and only half of those tried

19

were convicted, and given a sentence which the victims considered appropriate in all the circumstances—so that from a total of 1,024 crimes originally reported to the police, only 26 offenders were satisfactorily dealt with (from the victim's point of view), giving an amazingly low 'pay-off' rate of $2\frac{1}{2}$ per cent! If this high level of 'attrition of justice' were to be typical and if it were generally known to members of the public, would anyone ever think it worthwhile to report a crime?

It seems undeniable that there is a strong relationship between the perceived effectiveness of the police, with regard to different crimes, and the proportion of those crimes which are reported to them by victims or other members of the public. Glaser (1970) has pointed out that vicious circles can develop here, but that so too can 'beneficent' circles:

> Beneficent circles, however, can also occur: the more successfully the police cope with crime, the larger the proportion of offences of which they will be told. This may be one reason why improved police work leads to higher police-reported crime statistics: more crime is reported to good police forces, in addition to better records being kept by them. Regularly collected victim survey crime rates could break this particular circle of higher apparent crime rates with improved policing, due to lower discrepancy between police-reported rates and actual rates.[53]

A final reason for a reluctance to report crime is an unwillingness to become involved in the formal judicial procedures likely to follow a report to the police. This has been hinted at, as an underlying reason, in some of the earlier discussion: for instance, it is often the inconvenience of police interviews and court proceedings which encourages firms and stores to deal with shoplifting or offences committed by their employees as an internal matter; equally, this is an important influence upon the attitudes of members of the public who witness traffic offences or accidents. In the N.O.R.C. victim survey in the United States, between 5 and 10 per cent of unreported crimes were not reported because the victim did not want to spend the time that would have been involved, including 9 per cent of the unreported robberies and 16 per cent of offences involving false pretences or fraud.[54]

20

In a rather different way, many female victims of sexual offences, ranging from indecent exposure to rape, are too embarassed to face the necessary process of a detailed rehearsing of the incident for statements to the police and in court, so that they often may decide not to report an offence for personal reasons of this nature. Similarly, in the case of sexual offences committed against children, parents may be unwilling to submit their children to the potentially more harmful experience of reliving the incident in the overdramatized setting of a court of law or police station.[55]

The combined result of the various social attitudes towards criminal behaviour, which have been surveyed in this section, would seem to reinforce the view put forward in the first part of the chapter, that the important question in understanding the meaning of statistics is not the accuracy with which they describe the extent of criminal behaviour or illuminate the 'dark figure' of unreported crime, but rather the way in which they reflect the complex relationship between society and criminal behaviour, with the result that official criminal statistics provide a barometer of society's attitudes towards its deviant members rather than an objective measure of its social behaviour.

RECORDING CRIME: THE ROLE OF THE POLICE

In the first section of this chapter it was seen that, despite serious doubts about the validity of all official criminal statistics, criminologists have tended to compromise for practical purposes by using the statistic of 'crimes known to the police' as being nearest in time to the commission of an offence and therefore less subject to the distortion of the later stages of the penal process. When it refers to official statistics, the term 'crimes known to the police' more accurately means 'incidents known to the police and *recorded as crimes* by them'; this section will outline some of the essentially technical problems surrounding the decisions of the police to record incidents as crimes, and indicate some necessary cautions in interpreting the statistic of detected or 'cleared-up' crimes, leaving broader issues of the exercise of police discretion for more detailed consideration in the next chapter.

In his important study of crime in England between the wars, Mannheim discussed the influence of police activities and police methods upon criminal statistics.[56] He gave examples of the effects of changes in police policy and methods of crime detection upon the incidence of recorded offences, such as the decrease in the number of prosecutions for speeding after the introduction of uniformed (instead of plain clothes) motor patrols in 1936, but he paid particular attention to those changes in police organization and methods which might bring about fluctuations in the figures of crime statistics without any corresponding changes in crime itself. The classic example, which is mentioned in most discussions of English criminal statistics, was the effect of the discontinuation of the use of the *Suspected Stolen Book* by the Metropolitan Police in 1932, resulting in an artificially inflated increase in the number of larcenies recorded as known to the police in that year, compared to 1931.

More recent evidence and examples have been provided by the studies carried out by the Cambridge Institute of Criminology. In *Crimes of Violence,* McClintock questioned the assumption that all the *prima facie* crimes of violence reported to the police were automatically recorded as such by them.[57] Day-to-day observation of police work showed the complicated problems that could arise in the apparently straightforward matter of recording a reported incident as a crime of violence. There were problems relating to the number of crimes that have been committed on any one occasion by different numbers of persons, as well as problems relating to unreliable or uncooperative victims and witnesses, particularly common in incidents of domestic or subcultural violence.

McClintock also analysed the effects of a change, in 1950, of Home Office instructions as to the way in which the police should compile their annual statistics of indictable offences against the person. Basically, this change involved the recording of these crimes according to the initial assessment of the police following their preliminary inquiries, with no subsequent alteration in the light of any judicial findings, such as conviction on a lesser charge. Applying this change retrospectively to the statistics of crimes of violence in the Metropolitan Police District for 1938 and 1949, it was shown that the new method of recording would have resulted in approximately 7 per cent more crimes of violence being recorded. Thus, this is one more

22

example of a purely technical change which serves to emphasize the caution that is necessary when drawing comparisons between the criminal statistics of different periods of time, even in the same country.

In the same study, it was found that in the decade 1950 to 1960 greater emphasis had been placed by the police on recording crimes of violence in a more uniform and comprehensive way, leading to a further increase in crimes of violence 'which was purely statistical in character and quite independent of any *real* increase'. McClintock concluded:

> The overall effect of these two administrative changes—the one relating to the publication of the data, the other to greater uniformity in police recording—means that there has been an appreciable increase in crimes of violence recorded which is statistical rather than real. Comparing 1938 with 1960 it can be calculated that the combined effect of these two changes means that for every 100 crimes of violence recorded in the *Criminal Statistics* in 1938, there will be at least 113 so recorded today. On technical points alone, therefore, any comparisons of data between recent and earlier years are likely to be extremely misleading.[58]

Despite the importance of such changes in police methods of recording and presenting criminal statistics, it would seem likely that there have been even greater changes in social attitudes towards defining and reporting criminal behaviour since before the last war, which render such comparisons even more misleading.

In addition to their responsibility for recording 'crimes known', the police are directly involved in the statistic which records the number of crimes 'cleared-up', often referred to as the 'detection rate'. This particular statistic is of crucial significance in the study of a country's penal system, not only because it is usually taken as the best measure of police efficiency, but also because it serves as a necessary reminder that the 'official' criminals processed in the rest of the penal system are persons thought to be responsible for this minority of 'cleared-up' crimes, and not necessarily representative of persons responsible for the crimes known to the police but not cleared up. It is not intended here to enter into a detailed discussion of detection rates as a measure of police efficiency, but even at a superficial level of analysis it is clear

23

that a detection rate, which expresses cleared-up crimes as a *propor-tion* of all crimes known to the police, must be translated into *numerical* terms, and then related to the strength of particular police forces. McClintock and Avison carried out such an exercise for the decade 1955 to 1965, and reached the conclusion that the number of crimes detected per policeman in England and Wales went up from 3.3 to 5.3, even though during the same period the official 'detection rate' went down from 49 per cent in 1955 to 39 per cent in 1965.[59] Another important consideration in using detection rates to measure police efficiency is the strong possibility, mentioned above, that more crimes will be reported to efficient police forces, thereby making it harder for those forces to maintain their apparent success, if judged only by the detection rate.

A related but more important issue, in the context of the present discussion, is the extent to which the so-called 'detection rate' is a product of direct 'detection' work on the part of the police. Empirical surveys, mainly those carried out by the Cambridge researchers during the last decade, have gradually disentangled the various elements which contribute towards the overall detection rate statistic.[60] These surveys not only have emphasized the large and consistent differences between the detection rates of different categories of offence, but also have shown that, within the high clear-up category of offences against the person, if the offender is not known or not related to the victim, the clear-up rate is very much lower than the overall average for the category.[61] In other words, a high clear-up rate in any particular offence group is only partly due to the operational priority which may be given to its detection by the police, and perhaps a more important factor is that in many such offences there is no real problem of detection, as the offender will have been identified by the victim.

In an excellent survey of the issues surrounding crime detection rates, McClintock and Avison summarized their views about the importance of knowing the extent of actual detection involved in the clearing up of any crime reported to the police:

Such studies on crime detection rates indicate the need for a knowledge of the extent to which the police are faced with genuine problems of detecting unidentified offenders at the time when the offence is reported to them. Such cases have to be contrasted with

24

those crimes that are automatically 'solved' when reported to the police or when the offenders are caught by the police in the course of committing the crime, so that no problem of detection arises. . . . Obviously detection rates as indicators of the effectiveness of police work are of less value when such distinctions are not made in relation to the crimes that are recorded as cleared up.[62]

The overall clear-up rate not only includes crimes reported to the police with very different degrees of detection involved, but also crimes which an offender asks to be 'taken into consideration' by the court when he is being sentenced. These offences may have only come to light during police questioning of a suspect, or they may include offences already known to the police, to which a suspect confesses during interrogation. McClintock and Avison emphasized the important contribution made by these offences to the detection rate, and suggested that there exists considerable variation in the extent to which different police forces conduct such interrogations leading to additional charges or further offences 'taken into consideration'.[63]

In his Birmingham police study, John Lambert investigated the various components of the clear-up rate for a sample of 2,000 recorded property offences: 16 per cent were cleared up directly by the arrest or summons of a suspect, with an additional 12 per cent cleared up indirectly by being admitted by suspects and 'taken into consideration' by the sentencing court.[64] In some categories of offence, such as thefts from houses and parked vehicles, many *more* offences were cleared up by being 'taken into consideration' than by direct arrest or summons. In fact, two thirds of the clear-up rate of four categories, accounting for almost half of all recorded property offences, was due to crimes 'taken into consideration'. Lambert rightly questioned the appropriateness of using, as a widely publicized measure of police efficiency, one that was dependent upon 'the whim of offenders declaring their interest in previous exploits in the probably groundless hope that they will receive better treatment in court'.[65]

In an attempt to draw comparisons between the detection rates of different police forces, McClintock and Avison were very much aware of the problems created by the different ways in which crimes were cleared up, particularly as a result of the police questioning offenders about other offences they may have committed. They suggested that in the large urban areas, where greater anonymity was afforded

25

criminals and law-abiding citizens alike, there was less likelihood that criminals would admit offences out of fear of future detection and identification; to overcome this difficulty, they formulated the concept of a 'relative detection rate', which was calculated by excluding those crimes cleared up by 'indirect' methods, both from the total of crimes known to the police and from the total of crimes 'cleared up'. Using such a formula, more meaningful comparisons could be made between the detection rates of different police forces, and it was found that there was a significant correlation between high crime rates and low 'relative detection rates'.[66]

It should be clear from the preliminary discussion in this section that the police play an important role in the recording and presentation of criminal statistics. At the present time, there seems to be too much variation resulting from individual and local policy differences in the many police forces throughout the country. If official statistics are to be of even limited use, especially for comparisons over a period of time or between different areas of the country, there must be greater uniformity in the way crimes are recorded, and for any real meaning to be attached to the statistic of crimes cleared up, routine information must be collected to distinguish between 'direct' and 'indirect' methods of police detection and to indicate the circumstances surrounding offences with very different clear-up rates. The recommendations of the Report of the Perks Committee on Criminal Statistics,[67] for standardized Crime Report and 'Result of Case' forms, would enable the official statistics to include details of how each offence was cleared up, and would provide basic data for calculating the 'relative detection rates' suggested by McClintock and Avison. Until such changes are introduced, the general public and even the police themselves will be in as much dark as ever as to how they should interpret changes in the proportion of crimes known to the police which are cleared up each year.

CONCLUSIONS: THE PURPOSES OF CRIMINAL STATISTICS

The general conclusion and guiding principle of the Report of the Perks Committee on Criminal Statistics in England and Wales was that 'the statistics should serve as fully as possible the needs of all persons and organisations concerned with legislation, law enforcement and the treatment of offenders, as well as the more general interests of Parliament and the public, and that in order to do so they should extend to cover the whole process of law enforcement'.[68] At the beginning of the Report, the practical implications of this view were spelled out in more detail:

24. The subjects on which information is required can be divided into four categories:
(a) The nature of crimes and the circumstances in which they are committed.
(b) The extent and seriousness of crime, and whether it is increasing or decreasing.
(c) The persons who commit crime, their previous records and general background.
(d) The action taken to deal with offenders and its consequences.
25. This information can be used to help in:
(a) Measures to prevent delinquency: for example, in the social and educational field.
(b) Police procedure in the prevention and detection of crimes.
(c) Legislation concerned with the scope of the criminal law, the definition of offences and the sentencing and treatment of offenders.
(d) The administration of the penal system.
(e) Criminological study.[69]

It was acknowledged by the Committee that many offences do not come to the notice of the police, and that various factors affect the reporting of offences; but they concluded that the study of such unreported offences must be left to research workers, although the variation in reportability would need to be taken into account when dealing with the classification of offences (paras 26–27, pp. 6–7).

The main improvements which were thought necessary, in the collection and presentation of the statistics, in order to fulfil the functions outlined above (see 25a–25e), included (i) comprehensive cover of the different stages of law enforcement, involving continuous records linking the chain of events from the first report of a crime to the subsequent history of the criminal, (ii) additional information about the circumstances in which offences occur, to supplement the present almost exclusively legal classification of offences, and (iii)

27

more information on the characteristics of offenders, beyond the present sex and age-group. Most of the Report was devoted to a detailed examination of these aspects and recommendations for their practical implementation. Thus, given that the terms of reference of the Perks Committee were limited and virtually restricted to concrete issues of practical administration, it can be seen that some of their recommendations apparently derived from an awareness of some of the issues which have been presented in the course of this chapter. Their recommendations for linked records throughout the law enforcement process reflect, to some extent, the ideas about 'decision-stages' and the sequential nature of criminal statistics, and would enable investigations to be carried out not only of the persons being dealt with, but also of the officials and agencies making the 'processing' decisions; similarly, further information about the characteristics of offenders and the circumstances in which offences occur would go some way towards meeting Wheeler's demand for statistics which are more 'consumer-oriented'. However, the basic concern of this chapter has been on a rather different level from the primary concern of a Government Committee of this kind; because of this different concern, it is possible, on the one hand, to agree with Perks that much more information of various kinds is desirable, but, on the other hand, seriously to question whether this extra information will automatically improve the effectiveness of penal policy, police detection, the administration of the penal system or theoretical research in criminology. Unless the administrative and technical improvements in the collection and presentation of criminal statistics are accompanied by a fundamental reappraisal of the meaning and validity of any such statistics, and of the crucial importance of social attitudes towards defining and reporting criminal behaviour, then the gain will be either only superficial or possibly only result in an even more misleading situation than before.

The scope of official criminal statistics has traditionally been so limited and biased towards exclusively *judicial* statistics that it has been easy to show how inadequate they are for providing an accurate picture of criminal behaviour, as opposed merely to a record of the annual business of the criminal courts. However, if and when much more routine information were to be provided about crimes known to the police, details of the clear-up rate, and linkage between different sentences and the subsequent behaviour of convicted offenders, then it would be much more important for members of the public, laymen and experts alike, to be aware of the complex problems of interpretation in order not to draw completely inaccurate conclusions from the statistics or make vital administrative or policy decisions on the basis of misleading information. From earlier discussions in this chapter, it should be clear in general terms what are seen to be the main problems of interpretation relevant to the different purposes outlined in the Report of the Perks Committee: for example, social or educational measures to prevent delinquency need to be based on an accurate assessment of the extent and nature of criminal behaviour among different groups in the community, rather than on a simple acceptance of the traditional picture of 'official' delinquency, which is a product of the formal steps taken by members of the public and law enforcement agencies; measures of the success of police policy and methods of detecting crime need to be based, at the least, on a more rigorous examination of the so-called 'detection rate'; penal legislators must be fully aware of their possible roles as moulders or mirrors of contemporary social attitudes towards different forms and styles of behaviour; those directly involved in the sentencing or the treatment of offenders need to be constantly examining their own decisions, particularly in the light of their part in the whole process of society's response to criminal behaviour; and, finally, criminologists, who construct theories of criminal behaviour or study the working of the penal process, must take into account any or all of the foregoing issues which may be relevant to the subject of their investigation.

The recent development of the construction of a 'crime index' provides a good example of how a certain branch of 'technological' criminology has advanced in blinkers, with little regard for basic questions about the purpose of criminal statistics in general, or of a crime index in particular. The idea for developing a crime index stemmed from a quite proper dissatisfaction with the way existing criminal statistics were often crudely used as a measure of crime in a country or state; it was claimed, rightly up to a point, that using a single numerical total (e.g. indictable offences known to the police), to assess the crime situation, concealed all kinds of variations in the seriousness of different types of offence. The main pioneers in the United States, Sellin and Wolfgang (1964), attempted to devise an index of crime which would accurately reflect not simply the *numerical* changes in criminal behaviour but, more importantly, the *qualitative* changes in the degree of seriousness of the crimes being committed.[70] The result of several years of research was a model for a crime index which incorporated different weightings for the various elements of a crime incident contributing towards the seriousness with which it was regarded by a sample of the population. In fact, the gain in usefulness from an annual crime index, incorporating a calculation for seriousness as well as for frequency, seems to be more than out-weighed by the loss of descriptive information included even in existing criminal statistics based on questionable legal classifications.

It is a little difficult to explain the rise of the cult of the 'crime index'; it is clearly an attractive concept for criminologists who have a par-ticular interest in statistical techniques, and, as Wilkins has stated, in-dex numbers have an attraction in the way that they seem to simplify complex problems—but they do only *seem* to simplify them:

> Society is dynamic, and the problem of the extent to which an index of crime should reflect the changing attitudes of the culture is a thorny one. If events were to be defined in such a way that the classification of a crime indicated very precisely the nature of the action and the role of the actors in such a situation, some sort of fixed base index might be meaningful, but the purposes of social defence are doubtless best served by definitions which can be inter-preted in slightly different ways in order to take account of the changing attitudes of society without the necessity of completely revising the legal structure at very frequent intervals.[71]

Even the Perks Committee dismissed the ideas of Sellin and Wolfgang in a short paragraph, expressing doubts both about the technical construction of a crime index and about its appropriateness as an official measure of crime as a whole.[72] They thought it would be better to construct a small number of different indicators relating to relatively homogeneous groups of offences, such as organized robbery, homicide, breaking and entering and drunken driving. Clear-ly such offence-specific indicators would be much more meaningful, for most purposes, than an overall 'blanket' index, particularly if these indicators were linked to new classifications of offences based on the circumstances in which they were committed.[73] Even those readers of

30

criminal statistics, who are mainly concerned with changes in the seriousness of the crimes being committed, are not likely to be interested in this aspect in such an abstract way as to be satisfied with a simple numerical expression of the seriousness, but rather, they are likely to be interested in what types of offence contribute towards the index of seriousness at any one time or in any one country, so that they can more accurately assess changes in social behaviour or the differential risk of being a victim of particular criminal offences.

If then, from the general public's point of view, a crime index appears to conceal many important aspects of the crime situation, would such an index be useful for policy makers, administrators or researchers? Once again, the answer seems to be a categorical negative. The very real problem of the lack of knowledge relevant to decision-making throughout the penal process and to the construction of valid theories of criminal behaviour, cannot be solved by the kind of narrow oversimplification represented by attempts to develop a crime index of the Sellin–Wolfgang type but, if in any way, by greater *elaboration* of the information which currently constitutes the raw material for official statistics, so that at every stage in the penal process data becomes available which is directly relevant to the needs of the persons taking the decisions and to other members of the general community who wish to gain a fuller understanding of such decisions, taken on their behalf. In the subsequent chapters of this book, it is hoped to illustrate certain aspects of the 'information base' underlying selected 'decision-stages' in the penal process, and, at the same time, to relate the practical and administrative constraints upon the penal agents to the wider social framework in which the process operates.

NOTES

1. N. Walker *Crimes, Courts and Figures* Harmondsworth (1971); L. Radzinowicz 'English Criminal Statistics: a critical analysis' in Radzinowicz and J. W. C. Turner (eds) *A Modern Approach to Criminal Law* London (1948); H. Mannheim *Social Aspects of Crime in England between the Wars* Part I London (1940).
2. T. Sellin 'The Significance of Records of Crime' *Law Quarterly Review* Vol. **67** (1951) p. 489.
3. Radzinowicz, *op. cit.*

4. M. Grünhut 'Statistics in Criminology' *Jo. Roy. Stat. Soc.*, **Series A,** Vol. **114** (1951) p. 139.
5. L. T. Wilkins 'Criminology: An Operational Research Approach' in A. T. Welford *et al.* (eds) *Society: Problems and Methods of Study* London (1962) pp. 305–31. For subsequent development of his ideas see Wilkins 'The Measurement of Crime' *Brit. Jo. Crim.* Vol. **3** (1963) p. 321; Wilkins *Social Deviance* London (1964); and 'New Thinking in Criminal Statistics', *Jo. Crim. Law, Crimin. and P.S.* Vol. **56** (1965) p. 277.
6. Wilkins 'Measurement of Crime'.
7. Wilkins *Social Deviance*, p. 148.
8. D. J. Newman 'The Effects of Accommodations in Justice Administration on Criminal Statistics' *Sociology and Social Research* Vol. **46** (1962) p. 144.
9. J. I. Kitsuse and A. V. Cicourel 'A Note on the Uses of Official Statistics' *Social Problems,* Vol. **11** (1963) p. 131.
10. *Ibid.* pp. 135–7.
11. Cicourel *The Social Organisation of Juvenile Justice* New York (1968).
12. *Ibid.* p. 28.
13. *Ibid.* p. 37.
14. For a recent good discussion of sociology and the interpretation of English criminal statistics, see P. N. P. Wiles 'Criminal Statistics and Sociological Explanations of Crime' in W. G. Carson and P. N. P. Wiles (eds) *Crime and Delinquency in Britain* London (1971); also, from a broader perspective, S. Box *Deviance, Reality and Society* New York (1971) chs 3 and 6; and J. D. Douglas *American Social Order* New York (1971) chs 3 and 4.
15. President's Commission on Law Enforcement and Administration of Justice *The Challenge of Crime in a Free Society* Washington, D.C.(1967), and *Task Force Report: Science and Technology,* pp. 55ff. Along similar lines, see V. O'Leary and D. J. Newman 'Conflict Resolution in Criminal Justice' *Jo. of Research in Crime and Del.* Vol. **7** (1970) p. 99; F. W. Howlett and H. Hurst 'A Systems Approach to Criminal Justice Planning' *Crime and Delinquency* Vol. **17** (1971) p. 345; M. W. Klein *et al.* 'System Rates: An Approach to Comprehensive Criminal Justice Planning' *Crime and Delinquency* Vol. **17** (1971) p. 355.
16. President's Commission on Law Enforcement *op. cit.* pp. 7–10.
17. S. Wheeler 'Criminal Statistics: A Reformulation of the Problem' *Jo. Crim. Law, Crimin. and P.S.* Vol. **58** (1967) pp. 317ff.
18. *Ibid.* p. 317.
19. *Ibid.* pp. 319–20.
20. J. Q. Wilson *Varieties of Police Behaviour* Cambridge, Mass. (1968).
21. Wiles *op. cit.* p. 187.
22. For detailed empirical evidence from the United States, see Sellin and M. E. Wolfgang *The Measurement of Delinquency* New York (1964) ch. 11.
23. Wilkins *Social Deviance* p. 144.
24. Wilkins 'Measurement of Crime' p. 325.
25. T. C. N. Gibbens and R. H. Ahrenfeldt (eds) *Cultural Factors in Delinquency* London (1966) esp. ch 1.
26. M. Lopez-Rey *Crime: an analytical appraisal* London (1970).
27. Wilkins 'Criminology' p. 308.
28. A typical example of informed speculation is found in F. H. McClintock *et al. Crimes of Violence* London (1963):

    It was clear, therefore, from an examination of all the records and from the various discussions which took place with the police, that the increase shown in the statistics on crimes of violence does not give an accurate assessment of the *real* increase in such crimes. For in addition to any actual increase it first of all reflects a greater readiness on the part of the police to record incidents as crimes of violence. . . . Thirdly, the increase reflects a greater readiness on the part of victims and other members of the public to *notify* or report incidents of violence [pp. 70–1].

29. See, for example, P. Devlin *The Enforcement of Morals* Oxford (1965), and H. L. A. Hart *Punishment and Responsibility* Oxford (1968).
30. N. Walker and M. Argyle 'Does the Law Affect Moral Judgements?' *Brit. Jo. Crim.* Vol. **4** (1964) p. 570; and H. D. Willcock and J. Stokes *Deterrents to Crime among Youths aged 15 to 21* (Government Social Survey Report) London (1968).
31. *op. cit.* p. 50.
32. McClintock *et al. op. cit.* p. 71.
33. *Ibid.* p. 73.
34. J. P. Martin *Offenders as Employees* London (1962) pp. 114–19 and 125–8.
35. *Ibid.* p. 125.
36. For example, T. C. Willett *Criminal on the Road* London (1964); M. H. Parry *Aggression on the Road* London (1968); F. A. Whitlock *Death on the Road* London (1971); R. G. Hood *Sentencing the Motoring offender* London (1972); and J. A. D. MacMillan 'The Social Pathology of Motoring Offences and Accidents' unpublished M.Phil. thesis, University of Reading (1970).
37. MacMillan *op. cit.*
38. P. N. P. Wiles *op. cit.* p. 183.
39. McClintock *et al. op. cit.* p. 71.
40. M. Shaw and W. Williamson 'Public Attitudes to the Police' *The Criminologist* Vol. **7** No. 26 (Autumn 1972) pp. 18. Tables 8 and 9.
41. *Ibid.* p.32.
42. D. Chapman *Sociology and the Stereotype of the Criminal* London (1968) ch 3.
43. Martin *op. cit.* pp. 84ff.
44. *Ibid.* p. 87.
45. *Ibid.* p. 106.
46. Gibbens and J. Prince *Shoplifting* London (1962) pp. 146–50.
47. A. J. Reiss *Studies in crime and law enforcement in major metropolitan areas, Field Surveys III*, Vol. 1 (President's Commission on Law Enforcement and Administration of Justice) pp. 84–102, as quoted in Hood and R. F. Sparks *Key Issues in Criminology* London (1970) p. 19 and Table 1.1, p. 21, see also M. O. Cameron *The Booster and the Snitch* Glencoe (1964).
48. Hood and Sparks *op. cit.*, Table 1.1, p. 21.
49. N. Walker *Crime and Punishment in Britain* 2nd edn, Edinburgh (1968) p. 12, and *Crimes, Courts and Figures* Harmondsworth (1971) pp. 15–16.
50. Hood and Sparks *op. cit.* London (1970) ch 1; and P. H. Ennis *Criminal Victimisation in the United States: A Report on a National Survey* (President's Commission on Law Enforcement and Administration of Justice, Field Surveys II), Washington, D.C. (1967); also D. Glaser 'Victim Survey Research: Theoretical Implications', in A. L. Guenther (ed.) *Criminal Behavior and Social Systems* Chicago (1970) pp. 136–48.
51. Ennis *op. cit.*

52. Ennis 'Crimes, Victims and the Police', *Trans-Action*, Vol. 4, No. 7 (June 1967) p. 36.

53. Glaser *op. cit.* p. 144; note also the similar, well-known argument that more efficient and appropriate sentencing measures lead to a greater willingness to report crime, e.g. juvenile crime after the 1933 Act, discussed in H. Mannheim *op. cit.* ch. 3.

54. Ennis *op. cit.*

55. For evidence of the potential harm to children in these circumstances, see Gibbens and Prince *Child Victims of Sex Offences* London (1963).

56. Mannheim *op. cit.* pp. 68–78.

57. McClintock *et al. op. cit.* London (1963) ch III.

58. *Ibid.* p. 66.

59. McClintock and N. H. Avison *Crime in England and Wales* London (1968) p. 119.

60. See particularly McClintock and Avison, *op. cit.* ch. 4; also McClintock *et al. op. cit.* ch IV, and Radzinowicz (ed.) *Sexual Offences* London (1957) chs. II and VI.

61. McClintock *et al. op. cit.* Table 34, p. 80.

62. McClintock and Avison *op. cit.*

63. *Ibid.* p. 104.

64. J. Lambert *Crime, Police and Race Relations* Oxford (1970) Table 12, p. 43.

65. *Ibid.* p. 43.

66. McClintock and Avison *op. cit.* pp. 113–17.

67. *Report of the Departmental Committee on Criminal Statistics* Cmnd. 3448 London (1967) ch. 6.

68. *Ibid.* §131, p. 39.

69. *Ibid.* p. 6.

70. Sellin and Wolfgang *op. cit.*

71. Wilkins *Social Deviance* p. 174.

72. *Report of the Departmental Committee on Criminal Statistics* Cmnd. 3448 London (1967) §128, p. 37.

73. For an example of such a classification, applied to crimes of violence against the person, see McClintock *et al. op. cit.* ch. 2.

2 POLICE DISCRETION IN LAW ENFORCEMENT

If, as has been argued in the previous chapter, the penal process can usefully be viewed as a linked series of decision-stages through which an offender (or suspected offender) passes, then it is clear that the early stages of the process are of crucial significance in selecting the persons who thereby become 'eligible' for processing by the later stages. Thus the police, who are in the very vanguard of the law enforcement process, play a vital role in determining the boundaries within which the subsequent stages of the penal process largely operate. Joseph Goldstein noted the significance of this role in his discussion of police discretion *not* to take formal action against individuals:

> Police decisions not to invoke the criminal process largely determine the outer limits of law enforcement. By such decisions, the police define the ambit of discretion throughout the process of other decision-makers—prosecution, grand jury, judge, probation officer, correction authority, and parole and pardon boards. These police decisions, unlike their decisions to invoke the law, are generally of extremely low visibility and consequently are seldom subject to review.[1]

The police are therefore key 'middle-men', in their role as mediators and interpreters of the necessary action to be taken on the basis of reports from members of the public. Their strategic position in the criminal justice system means that they are particularly vulnerable to having their decisions either implicitly or explicitly criticized or overruled by the courts and penal agencies, in ways which will be further discussed at the end of this chapter, but it also means that the early police decisions can have an irreversible influence on the subsequent handling and experience of processed offenders. Piliavin and

Briar have described the potential consequences of the apparently simple and limited decision by the police as to whether or not to arrest a suspected young person:

> As the first of a series of decisions made in the channeling of youthful offenders through the agencies concerned with juvenile justice and corrections, the disposition decisions made by police officers have potentially profound consequences for apprehended juveniles. Thus arrest, the most severe of dispositions available to police, may not only lead to confinement of the suspected offender but also bring him loss of social status, restriction of educational and employment opportunities, and future harassment by law-enforcement personnel.[2]

Having already considered, in the first chapter, certain aspects of the role of the police in producing the statistics of the number of 'crimes known to the police' and the proportion 'cleared-up', this present chapter will focus on what are probably the two major areas of the exercise of police discretion: firstly, 'on-the-street' discretion, when an immediate decision has to be made whether or not to arrest an individual, and, secondly, police disposition decisions, in which there is a range of choices between different kinds of formal and informal action that can be taken against those who have been arrested. Throughout the discussion, it is important to keep in mind two recurrent themes: those individuals, in whose cases the police decide that arrest and formal action is necessary, will then proceed to the next stage of court appearance (with its own range of possible outcomes), with the police decisions now forming a potentially important part of their personal and social experience; and, secondly, although at the time the police might appear to exercise their discretion in relative isolation from any wider context, in fact their decisions can be better understood by relating them to other parts of the penal process, such as the social context and attitudes which lead to the reporting of a particular incident or the later sentence which might be passed by a court, if the case goes to trial.[3] Before examining the empirical evidence on the exercise of police discretion, brief consideration will be given to the various arguments put forward in support of the claim that there actually is a *need* for discretion on the part of the police.

36

THE NEED FOR DISCRETION

The claim that there is a need for the police to exercise discretion in law enforcement follows logically from the various arguments used to show that *full enforcement* of the law is impossible or undesirable, from both theoretical and practical viewpoints. Criminologists and commentators in Britain and America have suggested several kinds of reason which go far to explain the lack of full enforcement in police policy and practice.[4] This preliminary discussion will be focused around the framework suggested by Quinney in *The Social Reality of Crime:*

> Full enforcement of criminal law, however, is not a realistic expectation. Numerous limitations and circumstances preclude the possibility of enforcing the law to the fullest extent. First, *procedural* restrictions prohibit the enforcement of the law beyond the lawful rights of the individual citizen. Second, *interpretational* latitude, resulting primarily from ambiguity in the wording of many statutes, permits considerable discretion as to what constitutes a criminal offence. Third, *technical* difficulties confound law enforcement, such as limitation of police time, personnel, and equipment in the detection and investigation of crime. Fourth, *organisational* demands of local police departments provide guides for both the enforcement and non-enforcement of criminal law. Fifth, *ideological* orientations or values of policemen provide a basis for selective law enforcement. Sixth, numerous *societal* pressures prevent full enforcement of some criminal laws.[5]

Procedural restrictions

The inherent ambivalence of society towards the law and its enforcement comes to the surface in those situations where the means of enforcing a particular law (which may itself have general social support) conflict with other social values concerning the rights of individual citizens to be protected from undue invasion of privacy by agents of law enforcement. The concept of 'institutions of privacy' was used by Stinchcombe as the central element in his analysis of police practices, which sought to show how police policy was deliberately determined

37

by considerations of the differential immunity afforded to certain types of offender.[6] It is possible to accept the central importance of the private rights (and differential powers) of individual citizens, as illustrated by Stinchcombe, without necessarily imputing the same degree of motivation and deliberateness to the police as he does. These 'means-ends' conflicts are particularly likely to arise in crimes relating to sexual behaviour or other illegal activities, where there is no 'victim' in the usual sense of the word and where enforcement is mainly initiated by the police.

Interpretational latitude

Although Quinney seems to imply that the 'interpretational latitude' of many criminal law statutes is due to an ambiguity which could be removed by rather more careful initial drafting, it is probably a fundamental characteristic of criminal legislation in most democratic societies that laws usually leave open a certain degree of latitude for interpretation. The subtleties of legal definitions and the great variety of circumstances in which behaviour can take place mean that an exact formulation which will cover every possible alternative is unattainable for most practical purposes.[7] As it is, even when the police have decided to enforce the law in a situation and subsequently bring formal court proceedings against individuals, there is often a series of verbal battles in court between lawyers on both sides, disputing points of law, with a more or less explicit reflection upon the police interpretation of the law which brought the defendant to trial. Finally, after a finding of guilt, the court often has the difficult task of choosing an appropriate sentence, in the light of all the circumstances, so that the individualized sentencing decision has features very reminiscent of the police officers' 'individualized' interpretation of the requirements of the law at the very earliest arrest stage. In their study of police and the administration of justice in Oslo, Cressey and Elgesem (1968) made some very perceptive comments on the conflicting demands upon the police; on the one hand, there is an expectation of absolute consistency and equality in the process of law enforcement, and, on the other hand, there are the ideals of modern justice, with its concepts of individualization and the exercise of discretion:

38

According to the law enforcement ideology, policemen must, as indicated, be 'honest' and 'incorruptible', thus symbolizing justice of the kind requiring uniform and equal punishments—a government of law, not of men. But according to what we shall call the 'adjustment ideology' police must also be 'kind', 'fair', and 'understanding', thus symbolizing the system of taking similarities and differences into account. The policeman is being 'just' when he behaves in terms of his duty to invoke the penal process whenever he observes a violation, regardless of the consequences to the offender, for punishments are to be distributed equally. But, he is also being 'just' when he overlooks offences by using discretion, for in doing so he is symbolizing a system of justice which takes 'mitigating circumstances' into account.[8]

Technical difficulties

The most direct and obvious constraint upon a policy of full enforcement is that provided by the limited resources of police manpower normally available. When limited resources rule out the possibility of anything approaching total law enforcement, all police policy and administration must be a matter of the allocation of priorities, with the inevitable consequence that there will always be individuals or groups of individuals who either refuse to accept the need for priorities or whose own priorities are different from those of the police. In his study of Birmingham police, John Lambert rightly emphasized this problem, indicating some of the areas where conflicting priorities are likely to emerge:

> This is perhaps the most important of all aspects of discretion, that which derives from police organisation itself in determining what level of policing to apply to what areas, how to deploy personnel, and what significance to attach to certain specialised police duties in enforcing 'non-complainant' infringements whose prosecution depends entirely on police initiative. Commonly these special duties relate to prostitution, drugs, illegal gambling and gaming clubs, and infringements of licensing laws.[9]

Other essentially 'technical' constraints relate not so much to the problem of the allocation of police resources in the general task of crime prevention but more to issues surrounding police methods of crime detection. As part of the understood *modus vivendi* and 'bargaining' relationship between the police and the criminal fraternity, some laws are not enforced against certain individuals because of some future expected 'pay-off' for the police in the enforcement of other laws (or against other individuals) which are regarded as of higher priority. The most well documented example of this is the use of narcotic law 'informers' against more serious violators, in the United States.[10]

Organizational demands

There are at least two kinds of organizational constraint upon the exercise of discretion by the police. Quinney uses the term to describe the specific demands placed upon an officer by the policy of his local police department, which may take the form of very explicit guidance on the enforcement of a particular law over a specific period of time, or be in the shape of a much less explicit set of 'expectations' of law enforcement behaviour. In Britain, Ben Whitaker illustrated the effects of a change in the policy of Manchester police in enforcing the law against male importuning, which resulted in a 1,000 per cent increase in prosecutions for this offence over a four year period, following the appointment of a new chief constable;[11] and in his summary of the factors influencing police discretion in Britain, he placed the local organizational factors at the top of the list.[12] The President's Commission on Law Enforcement and Administration of Justice felt very strongly that police departments had a responsibility to the community and to their own officers to formulate explicit guidance on the exercise of discretion. The Commission regarded it as both 'inappropriate and unnecessary for the entire burden of exercising this discretion to be placed on individual policemen in tumultuous situations', and one of their major recommendations on the police was on this subject:

> Police departments should develop and enunciate policies that give police personnel specific guidance for the common situations requiring exercise of police discretion. Policies should cover such

matters, among others, as the issuance of orders to citizens regarding their movements or activities, the handling of minor disputes, the safeguarding of the rights of free speech and free assembly, the selection and use of investigative methods, and the decision whether or not to arrest in specific situations involving specific crimes.[13]

Only by a specific formulation of policy along these lines was it thought likely that a proper and consistent exercise of discretion could be achieved in a large organization like a police department, and even then there would still be an element of 'risk-taking' in many decisions made by individual police officers.[14]

The second kind of organizational constraint relates not to internal features, within a police department or particular police force, but to wider organizational features of the criminal justice system in which police decisions form a part of the total network. This aspect has already been mentioned earlier in the chapter, but it seems appropriate to refer to it again at this point of the discussion. In the same way that the police have been seen to operate a system of selective non-enforcement of certain laws to conserve their limited resources, to deal with crimes which *they* believe are more deserving of their attention, so they may sometimes exercise their discretion in the light of their knowledge of the priorities of later decision-makers in the process. Whatever their own views of the importance of particular crimes might be, if it is common knowledge that local magistrates take a very different view which is reflected in their sentencing decisions, the police will often not wish to 'waste' time on arresting individuals who may subsequently be given a merely nominal sentence by the court. Police knowledge of the way offenders are likely to be handled in other parts of the system does not always, of course, work to the advantage of an offender, as *informal* police action might sometimes have more serious consequences for the offender than the more formal alternative of court proceedings.

Ideological orientations

In addition to the more or less external factors, so far discussed, which all militate against a police policy of full enforcement, research findings and common sense alike stress the vital contribution of a

41

policeman's personal values and moral standards to the way his job of law enforcement is carried out. Even if a society could be envisaged with a system of law enforcement and social control exhibiting none of the procedural, interpretational, technical or organizational pressures towards the exercise of discretion, it is still more than likely that the essentially subjective and human elements would undermine any attempt to maintain a rigorous policy of total enforcement:

> The fact is, the human being does get out whenever the policeman exercises his considerable discretionary powers to evoke the law. What he decides is frequently coloured by his ideological values, his moral standards, his beliefs about the causes of criminal behaviour and his stereotypical conceptions of criminals.[15]

In order to understand fully the complex set of personal variables which affect the way individual police officers reach their decisions, Box has indicated that it is necessary to consider their social class and educational background, political and moral beliefs, job conceptions and the comparative social isolation experienced in the course of a policeman's life.[16] At a time of rapid changes in social structure and social attitudes, it is even more imperative to examine the background and personal values of the police, and for these to be related to the wider society in which they function.

Societal pressures

Many of the societal pressures which are included in Quinney's final category of factors indicating the need for police discretion can be extrapolated from or derive directly from the analysis, in the first chapter, of the social attitudes affecting the defining and reporting of crime to the police. In other words, many of the same kind of factors that make members of the public reluctant to report certain illegal activities to the police, in the first instance, often play a crucial part in determining the extent and nature of police discretion in dealing with crimes which come to their notice. Thus Quinney cites such factors as the lack of correspondence between particular criminal statutes and current norms, the failure of 'victims' to report offences, and the harmful social consequences that might follow the rigorous enforcement of certain laws.[17] On this basis it could be convincingly argued that these general societal pressures have probably the greatest combined effect upon the exercise of police discretion, operating at two levels, by affecting the way members of the public report crimes to the police, and also by affecting the police decisions as to how to handle those crimes that are reported to them.[18]

The purpose of this introductory section has been to outline some of the arguments used in support of the claim that police discretion is necessary, but it should have become clear that there is no strict dividing line between the factors affecting the *need* for police discretion, and those affecting the *way* in which it is exercised, so that although the rest of this chapter will be more directly concerned with evidence about the factors affecting the way in which police discretion is exercised, many of these same issues will reappear in later stages of the discussion.

'ON-THE-STREET' DISCRETION: THE DECISION TO ARREST

The last decade has seen a growing interest, especially on the part of social scientists, in the activities of the police; largely for political and social reasons much of this interest has centred around the face-to-face contact between the police and the public, with the result that there is now available a considerable amount of empirical evidence about the way police exercise their 'on-the-street' discretion in interaction with members of the public, especially from the United States. Although it could be argued that the police in different countries face very different problems of law enforcement and social control, yet the accumulation of research findings seems rather to show how the broad constraints upon police decision-making are essentially similar, at least in Western industrialized democracies. Many of the research studies which have examined police decisions to arrest suspected offenders have tended to concentrate on detailed analyses of the characteristics of persons arrested compared with those against whom no such formal action is taken by the police, and on the personal interaction which surrounds the arrest decision; alternatively, other studies have focused on the organizational and occupational pressures

43

upon the police to exercise their arrest discretion according to certain expectations. However, it seems important to start by considering the broader aims and social purposes which shape police behaviour, in the belief that much of the empirical data will make more sense in the light of an increased awareness of how police functions are perceived.

Peace-keeping v. law-enforcement

So far in this chapter the phrase 'law-enforcement' has been used as a blanket term to describe the context in which our present concern about the use of police discretion is located. It is now time to treat directly one of the central issues in the understanding of the problem, namely the question of whether (or when) an alternative phrase such as 'peace-keeping' would more accurately describe the function and aims of the police in their dealings with members of the public.

The common use of phrases such as 'law-enforcement' and 'social control', to typify the nature of police work and the function of police in society, reflects an image of the police as agents of a powerful source of authority (e.g. 'law', or 'society'), imposing the demands of that authority upon a more or less subservient or unwilling populace. Although this image has some basis in the realities of much social and political life, it can also be an oversimplification which hinders and distorts a full understanding of the exercise of police discretion in the arrest decision. In the first place, as has already been stated, most police activity is 'citizen-initiated'; in Reiss' observational study of police activity in three American cities, 87 per cent of all police patrol mobilizations were initiated by members of the public:

> Thus it becomes apparent that citizens exercise considerable control over police patrol work through their discretionary decisions to call the police. This is very important in terms of the legitimacy of police authority. When police enter a social setting, it is usually based on the assumption that at least one citizen believes the police have both a legitimate right and an obligation to enter that situation.[19]

Until we have more information about the social and other characteristics of the persons who initiate police activity in this way, it could still be argued that the police only act on behalf of or in response to a politically powerful section of the community, but the little evidence we do have suggests, to the contrary, that the people who summon the police are typically from the *less* powerful and privileged sections of the community.[20] The second important point is that most contacts which the police have with members of the public relate to entirely neutral 'services', ranging from giving street directions or telling the time, to calling ambulances in an emergency:

> The police, then, can be said to have, in addition to their obvious responsibilities with respect to law enforcement, a tremendous number of service duties, which in themselves constitute an important and essential part of their function in the ongoing life of the community. In an emergency of almost any type—of human relations, of health, of nature—the police are among the first to be called in, and generally people expect them to do something about it.[21]

In the light of these and other similar considerations, a shift of emphasis has occurred in many writers about the police, away from the concept of 'social control' towards the concept of 'social support', with a control-support dichotomy (or continuum) being used to provide a framework for describing police activities. In an important study by the Cummings, published in 1965, an analysis of the calls to the complaints desk of a metropolitan police department showed that half were calls for support (Table 2.1).[22] The concept of 'social support' must obviously attempt to relate police behaviour to the society or community in which they operate; if the police are to provide effective social support in any situation, they must know what kind of support is needed, be fully aware of the norms and values of the community in which they seek to provide support, and also themselves *receive* the much wider support of the community for what they do.[23] It is just because most modern industrialized societies are far from being homogeneous communities with shared norms and values that the concept of 'social support' runs into difficulties which do not arise in the same way for the more usual concept of 'social control', which conceives of subcultural norms as being directly suppressed or ignored by the agents of law enforcement. Quinney has suggested that the

45

degree of homogeneity in any community is a key variable in explaining the degree and nature of police discretion:

> The consequences for law enforcement is that the police in a homogeneous community operate as an integral part of the community, enforcement of the law being guided by the way such enforcement relates to the order of the community. In a heterogeneous community, in comparison, the police must operate

TABLE 2.1: *Classification of calls to the complaints desk of a Metropolitan Police Department, during 82 selected hours in June–July 1961.*

Type of call	No.	%
Total	801	100.0
Calls included in analysis	652	81.4
1. Calls about 'things'	255	31.8
2. Calls for support	397	49.6
Persistent personal problems	230	28.7
a. Health services	81	10.1
b. Children's problems	83	10.4
c. Incapacitated people	33	4.1
d. Nuisances	33	4.1
Periodic personal problems	167	20.9
a. Disputes	63	7.9
b. Violence	43	5.4
c. Protection	29	3.6
d. Missing persons	11	1.4
e. Youths' behaviour	21	2.6
Calls excluded from analysis	149	18.6
Information only	33	4.1
Not police business	28	3.5
Feedback calls	88	11.0

Source: E. Cumming, I. M. Cumming and L. Edell 'Policeman as Philosopher, Guide and Friend' *Social Problems*, Vol. 12 (1965) Table 1 at p. 279.

more by the formal law than by community expectation. The police in a homogeneous community may detect more law violations than those in a heterogeneous community, but the police in a homogeneous community handle the cases informally rather than through the formality of an arrest. . . . Invocation of the law may be the only means of maintaining order in the heterogeneous community.[24]

Translating this argument into our present terminology, it would mean that just as general community support is necessary for the police to carry out a function of 'social support', so, if community support is lacking, then the police are more likely to adopt a strictly 'law enforcement' role, which itself would probably increase the lack of community support and make the whole process spiral. An example, which shows a typical complication, is the combination of circumstances, instanced by Lafave (1965), where a member of a subcultural or minority group, who has been seriously injured in an assault, calls the police *not* as law enforcers, to arrest the offender, but in order that they can summon the necessary help to take him to hospital.[25] Thus, despite its initial usefulness as a direct counterpoise to 'social control', the concept of 'social support' does not by any means solve all our problems.

It will be seen (below) that many of the empirical studies of the personal interaction involved in situations of police intervention suggest that police decisions are more than anything else influenced by the extent to which an officer feels that he is not being afforded the respect he deserves and his authority is being challenged. This evidence points to an interpretation of the aims and functions of the police in 'on-the-street' encounters as focusing on immediate, face-to-face, 'situational control'. If, therefore, control of the situation can be seen as the basic and perhaps rather obvious aim of the police in their use of 'on-the-street' discretion, then it is clear that in many situations this control has to be gained 'against the odds', often on the basis of an individual officer's own personal authority in the public situation. Without wishing to anticipate the detailed empirical data to be presented in the following section, it will be useful here to cite some of the general observations and conclusions drawn by the researchers, which are of direct relevance to the present discussion of the relationship between 'situational control' and the police concern for their authority and the respect felt to be due to them.

47

In *Justice Without Trial,* Skolnick (1966) talked in slightly different terms about police competence and 'craftsmanship', but the underlying ideas seem very similar to the emphasis in later studies on authority and respect:

> In sum, neither philosophical principle nor personal prejudices should be taken as the most significant factors for understanding police conduct on the job. Their actual behaviour seems to be influenced more than anything else by an overwhelming concern to show themselves as competent craftsmen. An obstreperous prostitute symbolizes an affront to a policeman's competence. Measures are therefore taken to create instruments for punishing those who interfere with the policeman's goals—ultimately survival; immediately, appearance of ability—and for rewarding those who contribute to their achievement. The relationship of these measures to implanting or undermining the rule of law does not seem to be a matter of great concern.[26]

In his interview survey of police attitudes to the use of force in the arrest situation, Westley found that the highest proportion of respondents (39 per cent) gave 'disrespectful behaviour' as the reason for force being thought to be necessary in the situation, directed particularly against the 'wise guy' who thinks he knows more than they do, who talks back, or insults the policeman:

> Fundamental to all rationalisations about the maintenance of respect as the basis for the illegal use of force is the idea of the interactional situation in which the offender insults and tries to demean the policeman. . . . The listing of maintenance of respect for the police as a basis for the use of force by 39 per cent of the men interviewed indicates that this is a prime value of the police. It is a value oriented to the experience of the policeman, experience that consists primarily of interaction with a public that is conceived to be hostile, in a role that is unpleasant to the public. In terms of this experience, the value gains meaning. It represents a form of individual and group action in opposition to a threat of personal and group degradation. That it operates normatively, as a regulator of conduct, is apparent in the way in which the police define their actions toward different portions of the public—. . . . In each case the definition is aligned in terms of what will make these different publics respect the police.[27]

48

Paul Rock (1970) isolated the 'maintenance of authority' over a geographical area and over a particular group of deviants as the overriding concern of police officers, which may even transcend the need to enforce the law wisely and in a judicious manner. He suggested that the criminal law may become transformed into an instrument which can be used to engineer the personal control of a policeman.[28]

Many other similar observations could be cited, but it will suffice just to include a quotation from Reiss, as what he says leads into the final point to be raised in this section, namely the distinction between, on the one hand, achieving control of an immediate situation, and on the other hand, how a policeman may then use this control once it has been achieved:

> When an officer is confronted by calls about family troubles, neighbourhood disputes, and business disturbances, as well as more general situations of public disorder, the success of his intervention will depend largely on his authority and skill in establishing order in the situation. . . . It is reasonable, then, that the most common complaint officers in our studies voice about citizens is their failure to show respect for authority. Perhaps the main reason police officers seek deference toward their authority is that it assures order and control in the situation they are expected to handle.[29]

Assuming, therefore, that police control and authority have been established in a particular situation, to what extent is there a secondary handling problem of 'what to do next'? Two common areas of police intervention will be used to examine this question, in an attempt to relate it to the original distinction between peace-keeping and law-enforcement; the examples are (i) police intervention in domestic disturbances, and (ii) the handling of drunks and skid-row alcoholics.

In one of the very few studies of police intervention in domestic disturbances, Parnas indicated the main reasons behind the usual non-arrest policy and outlined the main methods used in 'adjusting' the situation.[30] The most important reasons for non-arrest in these situations derived from the wishes and attitude of the victim-complainant, who frequently did not want the offender (usually the husband) arrested, but called the police for more short-term 'first-aid' measures, e.g. to scare the offender into behaving himself or get him

49

out of the house for a while, to take a victim to hospital, or use the future threat of arrest for her benefit; sometimes the non-arrest decision derived from the policeman's own interpretation of the situation, where the behaviour was seen as acceptable to the cultural norms of the parties involved, or where he saw that an arrest might cause greater harm to the family in the long-term, whether on grounds of their economic situation or their personal relationships. It was found that the most common measures adopted by the police in adjusting domestic disturbances without resorting to arrest, included mediation, referral to other social agencies, *threat* of arrest or other formal sanctions and temporary separation of the parties. The conclusions drawn by Parnas reintroduce the theme of the 'support' role of the police:

> Perhaps the most important result of this description is an awareness of the policeman's role as a support figure rather than merely as an instrument of control in the community. In exercising the support function—the use of alternatives other than arrest in *aid* of *both* disputants—it is uncertain whether this police response is a recognition of the underlying value of preserving the private, personal, intimate, or family integrity of the disputants, or whether their response results from an awareness of the practical difficulties inherent in either a full-enforcement or no-response approach to the domestic disturbance.[31]

As a final example, the way police handle drunks on skid-row is particularly instructive because it brings into sharp relief a situation where sometimes the police *enforce laws* in circumstances where the aims of such law enforcement could be seen as synonymous with those of *peace-keeping*. In fact, this is more or less the conclusion reached by Bittner in his perceptive analysis of the exercise of police discretion on skid-row.[32] Bittner argues that the roles of 'law officer' and 'peace officer' are enacted by the same person and are thus contiguous; police patrolmen do not act alternately as one and then the other, with certain actions determined by the intended objective of keeping the peace and others by the duty to enforce the law; instead his research shows that *'peace keeping occasionally acquires the external aspects of law enforcement'*. In other words, the police do not often enforce the law, for its own sake, but use it instrumentally to solve certain immediate practical problems of keeping the peace:
50

In keeping the peace on skid-row, patrolmen encounter certain matters they attend to by means of coercive action e.g. arrests. In doing this, they invoke legal norms that are available, and with some regard for substantive appropriateness. Hence, the problem patrolmen confront is not which drunks, beggars, or disturbers of the peace should be arrested and which can be let go as exceptions to the rule. Rather, the problem is whether, when someone 'needs' to be arrested, he should be charged with drunkenness, begging, or disturbing the peace.[33]

In fact, Bittner's analysis brings together many of the themes that have been examined in this section: it is misleading to talk about 'peace-keeping' and 'law-enforcement' as if these were distinct roles between which a choice has to be made by a police officer facing a particular situation of 'on-the-street' discretion; equally, it is an over-simplification to talk exclusively about the 'social control' function of the police, because so much of police activity is initiated by a cross-section of the population seeking various kinds of 'support'. The first immediate task of any police officer must be to gain control of the situation, and his success in achieving this varies not only according to who initiated police intervention but according to the degree of public support received, and the dynamics of the interaction between the police, the parties involved and the audience on the spot. Thus use of force and police reaction to any disrespect or challenge to their personal authority in the situation, should be seen not only as understandable in purely human terms but also as crucial instrumental elements in gaining control of the situation.

Once primary control has been achieved, other decisions have then to be made by the police officer as to what further action is necessary. Many of these decisions will reflect the 'social support' role in which the police and the public view much of police activity, and obvious constraints upon what this role involves derive from the views and attitudes of the victim-complainant, as well as the policeman's own interpretation of the demands of the situation, including what, if anything, may be achieved by the stages of the penal process subsequent to formal police arrest. Both the invocation and the non-invocation of certain laws will be influenced by 'instrumental' concerns on the part of the police, rather than by theoretical con-

51

siderations of police duties of 'law enforcement' or the appropriateness of discretion:

> In real police work the provisions contained in the law represent a resource that can be invoked to handle certain problems. Beyond that, the law contains certain guidelines about the boundaries of legality. Within these boundaries, however, there is located a vast array of activities that are in no important sense determined by considerations of legality. In fact, in cases in which invoking the law is not a foregone conclusion, as for example in many minor offences or in the apprehension of mentally ill persons, it is only speciously true to say that the law determined the act of apprehension, and much more correct to say that the law made the action possible. The effective reasons for the action are not located in the formulas of statutes but in considerations that are related to established practices of dealing informally with problems.[34]

'Moral character' and arrest discretion

By its very nature, most of what happens in police work 'on-the-street' is not easily accessible for study by the academic criminologist; police arrest discretion is of extremely 'low-visibility', except to the people directly involved in each incident. Most of the observational studies have concentrated on police encounters with juveniles in the United States, and there is a certain risk in generalizing from these studies to other age groups and other countries; however, an examination of the information currently available will at least provide a sounding-board for future comparisons.

An idea of the range and extent of police discretion *not* to arrest juveniles can be gained from statistics available in a few American studies. In the encounters analysed by Piliavin and Briar less than a quarter resulted in an arrest, with more than 6 out of every 10 juveniles being 'let off' with nothing more than an informal reprimand or admonishment;[35] in his comparative study of police handling of suspected juveniles, Wilson found that the proportion arrested ranged from 16 per cent of white juvenile suspects in Eastern City to 51 per cent of negro suspects in Western City;[36] and in their study of police activities in Boston, Chicago and Washington, in 1966, Black and

52

Reiss found that only 15 per cent of encounters with juvenile suspects resulted in arrest.[37] This section will concentrate particularly on those characteristics of *offenders* (or, more accurately, 'suspects') which influence the highly selective arrest process, as many of the situational and *offence* characteristics have been discussed in the previous sections of the chapter.

Piliavin and Briar emphasized the importance of what they called the 'moral character' of the juveniles in influencing the way police approached the difficult decisions in the exercising of their discretion to arrest, although fully aware that the shift from the offence to the offender increased the uncertainty and ambiguity for the police officers in the situation:

> Thus, for nearly all minor violators and for some serious delinquents, the assessment of character—the distinction between serious delinquents, 'good' boys, misguided youths, and so on—and the dispositions which followed from these assessments were based on youths' personal characteristics and not their offenses.[38]

There are several aspects of the character and behaviour of juveniles which clearly influence the outcome of their encounters with the police. In the first place, there is their outward show of respect to the individual police officer, of which the significance has already been indicated by the attempt in the previous section to show its relationship to police control of the situation. In the study by Piliavin and Briar, the patrolmen considered the 'demeanour' of the juvenile to be the major factor in 50–60 per cent of their dispositions, and a classification of actual dispositions according to whether or not a youth's demeanour was cooperative or otherwise, confirmed this situation (see Table 2.2).[39] Similarly, in a recently published study, Sullivan and Siegel (1972) used an information-board exercise (of the type developed by Wilkins) to analyse the factors that police would take into account in deciding how to handle a juvenile found drunk and disorderly on the street; it was found that three quarters of the police in the sample made their final decision after selecting the information item *'attitude of offender',* with the more experienced officers selecting this item much sooner than those with less than five years' experience of police patrol work.[40]

53

TABLE 2.2: *Severity of police disposition by youths' demeanour.*

Severity of police disposition	Youth's demeanour		
	Cooper- ative	Uncooper- ative	Total
Arrest (most severe)	2	14	16
Citation or official reprimand	4	5	9
Informal reprimand	15	1	16
Admonish and release (least severe)	24	1	25
Total	45	21	66

Source: I. Piliavin and S. Briar 'Police Encounters with Juveniles', *Amer. Jo. Soc.* Vol. **70** (1964) p. 206, Table 1.

In the second place, there is what could be described as the complex 'working philosophy' of the police which underlies practically all their crime detection and 'law enforcement' work. This philosophy is based not only on environmental characteristics thought to be associated with crime, but more especially on *personal* characteristics of individuals thought to be likely suspects. One of the environmental 'cues' which Bayley and Mendelsohn picked out as working to the general disadvantage of minority groups was that of *incongruity* between an individual and the surroundings in which the police may find him:

> The fact that policemen are alert for incongruity probably does militate against minority persons. Policemen do believe crime emanates from the disadvantaged more commonly than from members of the dominant or well-to-do community. Furthermore, due to the geography of American cities there is simply more opportunity, indeed necessity, for minority people and the poor to enter surroundings in which they appear incongruous.[41]

A similar search for information 'cues' contributes to the development of police stereotypes; they use what Quinney has called a *'probabilistic'* model of law enforcement, looking for personal characteristics that may be indicative of criminal behaviour, so that if

54

a suspect seems to live up to this police image or expectation his chances of being arrested are considerably increased.[42] For stereotypes to be of any practical use in 'on-the-street' encounters, they must be based on immediate visual cues, rather than on detailed knowledge of family background and social history; Piliavin's and Briar's list of such cues included the youth's age, group affiliations, race, grooming, dress and demeanour, so that older juveniles, members of known delinquent gangs, Negroes, youths with well-oiled hair, black jackets and soiled denims, and boys not showing the appropriate signs of respect in their interactions with officers, tended to receive the more severe dispositions.[43] This kind of stereotyping of suspects clearly leaves the police wide open to criticism, although realistic appraisal of the police task in crime detection shows that some techniques of 'narrowing the odds' must be adopted, with the resources at present available. The method of crime detection as portrayed in detective novels bears little, if any, relation to most actual police work today; instead of the crime itself pointing to a range of suspects, the police usually attempt to solve crimes by first checking on known criminals and previously located suspects, or, alternatively, by discovering certain individuals in 'suspicious' circumstances and then trying to link them with certain crimes that are known to have been committed.[44] Skolnick recognized that the tendency to stereotype is an integral part of every policeman's working world:

> They are called on in many aspects of their work to make 'hunch' judgments, based on loose correlations. For example, the concept of *modus operandi* is nothing more than a technique for drawing defeasible analogies between one criminal pattern and another. In effect, it is a stereotype, probably right more often than wrong, which may not be claiming much. Similarly, ethnic stereotypes, like the *modus operandi* of criminals, become part of the armory of investigation.[45]

The inextricable link between police methods of detection and the assessment of the 'moral character' of individuals and environments has been well summarized by Werthman and Piliavin:

> Policemen develop indicators of suspicion by a method of pragmatic induction. Past experience leads them to conclude that

55

more crimes are committed in the poorer sections of town than in the wealthier areas, that Negroes are more likely to cause public disturbances than whites, and that adolescents in certain areas are a greater source of trouble than other categories of the citizenry. On the basis of these conclusions, the police divide the population and physical territory under surveillance into a variety of categories, make some initial assumptions about the moral character of the people and places in these categories, and then focus attention on those categories of persons and places felt to have the shadiest moral characteristics.[46]

Before considering the crucial self-fulfilling nature of this process, a final aspect needs to be briefly mentioned: the essentially *judicial* nature of police decision-making, whereby their discretion is often exercised on the basis of criteria more relevant and appropriate to the later court disposition of the offender. Piliavin and Briar did not fail to realize that the tendency, in 'on-the-street' encounters, for the police to focus on the offender rather than the offence could easily develop into a brief but decisive pre-trial adjudication of the suspect's likely guilt and appropriate sentence.[47] Similarly, when Reiss was attempting to explain the low arrest rate of suspected juveniles, he suggested that the extra element required, over and above 'probable cause', was a *moral belief* on the part of the police officer that the law should be enforced and the offence sanctioned by the criminal justice system:

> The line officer usually reaches that decision by conducting an investigation to establish probable cause and by conducting a 'trial' to determine who is 'guilty'. His decision, therefore, is an important sense judicial. This judicial determination will be influenced, as it is in the courts, by the deference and demeanor of the suspect, argument as to mitigating circumstances ... [etc.]. All in all, an officer not only satisfies probable cause, but also concludes after his careful evaluation that *the suspect is guilty and an arrest is therefore just.*[48]

This further characterization of police discretion as having a definite *judicial* element makes it even more crucial for the self-fulfilling nature of the entire 'working philosophy' of the police to be recognized and attempts made to mitigate its most insidious and harmful consequences. On the working assumption that most police

56

stereotyping of areas and individuals, and their 'perceptual shorthand' in interpreting various information cues, is not entirely explained simply on the basis of personal prejudices, the alternative explanation locates the origin of the working philosophy in the collective experience of the police in crime detection; however, one of the basic fallacies in accepting this experience as a reliable guide for future practice, is that the majority of even those crimes which are known to the police are never in fact 'cleared-up'; so that even if it were true that, for example, all known burglaries or sexual offences *cleared-up* were committed by a distinct type of person, this might be a most inadequate guide to clearing up the majority of these crimes, where the characteristics of those responsible are mainly a matter for speculation. The existence of official statistics, purporting to show the contribution to the 'crime rate' of persons of a particular age, sex or race, can only confound the problem by giving spurious support to police stereotypes of the criminal, because (as we saw in the first chapter) official statistics are the direct product of a series of decisions taken by the public and the police themselves. In America, the most significant example of this phenomenon is that of Negro crime: the official statistics seem to show that Negroes make an above average contribution to the American crime-rate, and yet at the same time statistics of police discretion, such as those given by Wilson[49] and Black and Reiss,[50] show that in some American cities the proportion of Negro suspects who are arrested is two or three times greater than the proportion of White suspects receiving the same disposition, which not only accords with the police working stereotype, but helps to *create* the official statistics which contribute towards the stereotype. Hood and Sparks comment:

> It may be true that the police regard Negroes more often as potential recidivists, and there are statistics to show a higher Negro crime rate—but by enforcing the law in this way they are, of course, simply ensuring a self-fulfilling prophecy. The Negro is, in fact, in an analogous situation to any sub-group with both a high [official] crime rate and distinguishing physical or attitudinal characteristics.[51]

As Hood and Sparks go on to say, the cues and stereotypes used by the police in deciding to arrest *may* all be highly correlated with previous criminality and a poor prognosis, but 'previous criminality' is far from being an objective criterion which can be called in aid of police decision-making; and Box has criticized those criminologists who fall into the trap of accepting a previous criminal record as an objective assessment of a person's behaviour, when it is simply a collection of previous decisions by the police (and the community), heavily influenced by ascriptive factors such as social class and race.[52] The real need is for criminologists to put forward better prognostic criteria (if such exist) than those the police currently rely upon, in order to break free from the vicious circle of self-fulfilling prophecies, and to define criminality in other terms than by the tautological use of the records of official reaction to the selected activities of certain individuals.

'Styles' of policing: organization and community

Included in the list of factors influencing the *need* for police discretion, discussed in the first section of this chapter, were 'organizational demands' and 'societal pressures'; the work of James Q. Wilson, particularly *Varieties of Police Behaviour*,[53] represents one of the most comprehensive and detailed attempts to present a typology of police discretion, centred round the main variables of police *organization* and *community* characteristics. Discussion of Wilson's approach has been deliberately postponed until this point, so that an assessment can be made of how successfully his analysis is able to integrate the theoretical and empirical material, so far presented, on the operation of police 'on-the-street' discretion.

In his study of Western City and Eastern City, Wilson distinguished between *'professional'* and *'fraternal'* forces, reflecting two very different kinds of police 'ethos':

> Far more important, it seems to me, than any mechanical differences between the two departments are the organisational arrangements, community attachments, and institutionalised norms which govern the daily life of the police officer himself, all of which might be referred to collectively as the 'ethos' of the police force. It

is this ethos which, in my judgement, decisively influences the police in the two places. In Western City this is the ethos of a *professional* force; in Eastern City, the ethos of a *fraternal* force.[54]

Detailed statistics and observation showed how the two police departments interpreted and exercised their arrest discretion very differently, and Wilson plausibly suggested that organizational measures introduced by the professional force with respect to *non-discretionary* matters, such as accepting bribes, also had the consequence of affecting police behaviour in matters over which they *did* have discretion, such as the handling of juvenile suspects, in which the police of Western City arrested 47 per cent of all juveniles contacted, compared to only 30 per cent in Eastern City.[55] He also suggested (rather less plausibly) that the apparently discriminatory handling of Negro juveniles in Eastern City could be explained, not by racial prejudice, but by the fact that the fraternal ethos of the Eastern City police encouraged officers to concern themselves with the quality of family life in their community, which they perceived to be lower among the lower-class Negroes and therefore justified a greater degree of court referral.[56]

In *Varieties of Police Behaviour* Wilson reported a larger-scale study of police organization and discretion, carried out in eight separate American communities, during 1965–7. Although he accepted the validity of many of the constraints upon police discretion already mentioned, the main thesis of this study was that *'the principal limit on managing the discretionary powers of patrolmen arises, not from the particular personal qualities or technical skill of these officers, but from the organizational and legal definitions of the patrolmen's task.'*[57] He attempted to explain the differences in police discretionary behaviour from community to community, by the three main variables of (i) the nature and extent of social behaviour facing the police in any particular community, (ii) the role and attitudes of local police administrators, and (iii) the influence of local politics upon police policy; and he presented his now well-known typology of police 'styles', being a development of his earlier distinction between *professional* and *fraternal* forces.

The *'Watchman'* style operated in three working-class urban communities; officers were encouraged to use their discretion 'as if order

59

maintenance rather than law enforcement were their principal function ... and to use the law more as a means of maintaining order than of regulating conduct'—phrases very reminiscent of Bittner's analysis of police peace-keeping on skid-row. Informal police action was the norm, adopting a 'familial' or *'in loco parentis'* role towards juveniles; recruitment tended to be on a local basis, with relatively little specialization within the department, but with the 'personal' style stressed in all police activities.[58]

The *'Legalistic'* style operated largely in the two remaining working-class urban communities and also in one of the more prosperous suburban areas; this had much in common with the 'professional' ethos described in Western City. The police administration attempted to control the exercise of discretion as much as possible, and the patrolman was expected to take a strictly 'law enforcement' view of his role. Recruitment was on a wider geographical basis, with emphasis placed on specialization, record-keeping and technical efficiency. Wilson suggested that many of the typical characteristics of the style derived from historical origins in take-overs by new police chiefs of corrupt departments, and their consequent overriding desire to maintain control within the department.[59]

The *'Service'* style operated in the two remaining suburban areas, largely consisting of homogeneous middle-class communities. The police took seriously all requests either for law enforcement or for order maintenance, but did not necessarily respond by making an arrest or imposing some other formal sanction. They acted frequently, to 'show the flag', but not usually in a very formal way. The 'Service' style departments were very responsive to public opinion in the community, with its generally lower tolerance of disorder than other communities, and did all they could to foster police-community relations.[60]

This typology has many attractions, particularly in the way it seeks to integrate organizational and political constraints, while not ignoring the way police officers' own ideological orientations might be related to the differential recruitment policies and career prospects within the different styles of police departments. The preliminary findings of a comparative study of urban and rural police forces in Britain suggest some similarities with Wilson's American studies.[61] However, Wilson's own analysis of the variables influencing discretion suggests that the typology has only a limited usefulness by describing the broad outlines of different 'styles' of policing, for within each police department there is still a great need for more detailed observation and study of the nature of police behaviour in 'on-the-street' encounters. In particular, Wilson stressed the importance of whether police intervention was 'police-invoked' or 'citizen-invoked', so that with his other major variable being whether the situation could be described as 'law enforcement' or 'order maintenance', he described four main types of situation, viz. (i) *police-invoked law enforcement*, often 'crimes without victims' or traffic offences, where police discretion is controlled very much by the policy of the department of Chief Constable, (ii) *citizen-invoked law enforcement*, for example, the most common crimes against property, (iii) *police-invoked order maintenance*, also influenced very much by local policy, and (iv) *citizen-invoked order maintenance*, where there is most scope for the operation of individual police discretion.[62] Further refinement of some such situational typology would seem to hold out more hope for the development of an integrated 'theory' of police discretion in arrest decisions than an exclusive concentration on differences in police operating styles in different kinds of communities. Wilson's oversimplified dichotomy between 'law enforcement' and 'order maintenance' would need to be reconsidered, in the light of our earlier discussion, and some account taken of the important part played by 'stereotypes' in the everyday working philosophy of the police, in such a way that the focus of attention should never be allowed to stray too far from the imperatives of the immediate situation facing the police patrolman.

DISPOSITION DECISIONS AND POLICE CAUTIONING

Once a decision has been made to arrest a suspected offender or to bring him into police custody for further questioning, the second stage of police decision-making becomes a little more 'visible' and open to more systematic documentation than the earlier stages of police discretion. In America there have been several studies of the extent and nature of these police disposition decisions, especially in juvenile cases, and in Britain considerable interest has been focused in recent years on police cautioning policy, which is a disposition falling short of formal court prosecution. Some of this evidence will now be examined, in order to assess the extent and variations in the type of dispositions made by the police at this stage of the penal process, and to consider how the kind of factors which seem to influence police discretion 'in-the-station' compare with the factors which have been seen to influence their 'on-the-street' discretion.

Statistical background

Shannon examined the disposition decisions in 4,554 juvenile offences coming to the notice of Madison police between 1950–55; for the whole sample during this period, 1,818 cases (40 per cent) resulted in referral to the Probation Department or other similar agency.[63] Despite this being one of the earliest studies of its kind, it is one of the few to present data about practice in the same police department over a considerable period of time; Table 2.3 shows how there was a sudden increase in the rate of referral between 1951 and 1952, but that for the rest of the period the rate remained surprisingly constant.[64]

TABLE 2.3: *Delinquent and other acts resulting in police contact and referral: sample of city of Madison juveniles from files of crime prevention bureau, 1950–5.*

Year	No. of contacts	No. of referrals	Per cent of contacts referred	No. of contacts per referral
1950	373	55	14.7	6.8
1951	779	114	14.6	6.8
1952	753	357	47.4	2.1
1953	726	372	51.2	1.9
1954	961	452	47.0	2.1
1955	962	468	48.6	2.0
Total	4,554	1,818	39.9 (mean)	2.5 (mean)

Source: L. W. Shannon 'Types and Patterns of Delinquency Referral in a Middle-sized city', *Brit. Jo. Crim.* Vol. **4** (1963) Table 1 at p. 29.

In Goldman's important Pennsylvanian study of the referral rate of 1,083 arrested juveniles to juvenile court, only 387 (36 per cent) were referred to court by the police; in the four separate communities in Allegheny County studied by Goldman, the percentage of arrested juveniles who were referred varied from less than 9 per cent in Manor Heights to 71 per cent in Trade City, with more consistency in the way *serious* offences were handled than minor offences.[65]

Terry analysed disposition decisions with regard to 9,023 juvenile offences recorded in the police files of an industrial Midwestern city (pop. *c.* 100,000) between 1958–62.[66] From Table 2.4 it can be seen that in only 11 per cent of all cases was any formal action taken

TABLE 2.4: *Distribution of dispositions relating to 9,023 juvenile offences in a mid-western city, 1958–62.*

	No.	%
Police department		
Released	8,014	88.8
Referred to Social or Welfare Agency	180	2.0
Referred to County Probation Department	775	8.6
Referred to State Department of Public Welfare	54	0.6
Total	9,023	100.0
Probation department		
Released	229	29.5
Informal Supervision	243	31.4
Referred to Juvenile Court	246	31.7
Waiver to Criminal Court	54	7.4
Total	772	100.0
Juvenile court		
Formal Supervision	94	38.2
Institutionalized	152	61.8
Total	246	100.0

Source: R. M. Terry 'The Screening of Juvenile Offenders' *Jo. Crim. Law, Crimin and P.S.* Vol. **58** (1967) Table 1 at p. 177.

against the juveniles, and this table shows the 'sifting' process that operated for those cases which the police referred to the County Probation Department, to such an extent that only 300 (3 per cent) of the original 9,000 offences resulted in a Juvenile Court appearance.

As a final example from the United States, Weiner and Willie analysed the decisions made by juvenile officers in Washington D.C. and Syracuse N.Y.[67] In Washington, out of 6,099 youth contacts in 1963, 2,300 (38 per cent) were referred to Juvenile Court; and in Syracuse, out of 1,351 contacts in 1968, a total of 946 were referred to Family Court, where official action was taken against 557 (viz. 41 per cent of total contacts).

In Britain, as yet, there have been no comparable studies of the full range of police decision-making, at this stage of the process, but there have been some analyses of the rate and variation of police cautioning of suspected offenders, whereby an official warning is given by a senior police officer—an intermediate decision between complete release and formal court prosecution; thus, statistics of cautioning provide only a *minimum* indication of the extent to which individuals are not formally prosecuted by the police, as there clearly are large numbers of juveniles and adults who are released by the police without even the semi-formal disposition of being cautioned in this way.

McClintock and Avison (1968) carried out a detailed study of police cautioning of offenders admitting indictable offences, in England and Wales, during the period 1955–65; there was a steady annual increase from nearly 13,000 in 1955 to 28,000 in 1965 (with a continued rapid rise to over 55,000 in 1970), but, because the number of court convictions also increased at the same time, cautioned offenders always formed approximately 11 per cent of 'known offenders'.[68] They found considerable variations among police forces, so that less than 1 per cent of 'known offenders' were cautioned in the London Metropolitan District, but 20 per cent in a sample of small towns (less than 100,000 pop.); in fact, there was as much difference between forces in the *same* category as between the different categories, so that McClintock and Avison concluded:

> From a close study of the individual variations in cautioning rates between forces and within forces over a period of time, it can be stated that there is no agreed national policy on the extent to which

the police can legitimately exercise their discretion not to prosecute. The variations are too great to be explained in terms of differences in types of crime or sex and age of offenders in the different local areas.[69]

Other British studies have confirmed the variations found by McClintock and Avison, particularly in the handling of juvenile cases. In 1962–3, Patchett and McClean found that certain police forces in the north of England cautioned three or four times the proportion of known juvenile offenders as other forces in the same region; Barnsley and Derbyshire cautioned 60 per cent of known juvenile offenders under the age of 14 years, and at least a third of those aged between 14–17 years, compared with Doncaster and the West Riding who cautioned less than a fifth of those under 14, and only 11 per cent of those aged 14–17 years.[70] Somerville analysed the juvenile cautioning practice in 18 selected police forces in England, including those of cities, boroughs and counties: Table 2.5 shows the range of variations within each category of police force, indicating the highest and lowest

TABLE 2.5: *Police cautioning and court decisions in selected police forces in England and Wales.*

	Known offender rate	Appeared in court		Court discharge		Police caution	
		No.	%	No.	%	No.	%
City A	1,080	(929)	86	(260)	28	(151)	14
City B	864	(438)	51	(46)	11	(426)	49
Borough A	666	(629)	94	(203)	32	(37)	6
Borough B	273	(153)	56	(14)	9	(120)	44
County A	683	(636)	93	(178)	28	(47)	7
County B	785	(521)	66	(111)	21	(264)	34

Source: J. G. Somerville 'A Study of the Preventive Aspect of Police Work with Juveniles' *Crim. L. R.* (1969) Table 4 at p. 473.

cautioning forces in each category; the total variation ranged from City B, where only half 'known offenders' appeared in court, to Borough A, where 94 per cent appeared in court.[71]

Finally, Steer carried out one of the very few studies, either in Britain or America, of police cautioning decisions relating to *adult* male offenders who had committed indictable offences in 1965–7; his sample was taken from five different police forces, in cities of varying size, and the proportion of known adult offenders who were cautioned varied from less than 2 per cent to more than 7 per cent.[72]

This preliminary outline of the statistical background sets the scene for a closer examination of some of the characteristics associated with police disposition discretion, which might provide important clues to the rationale behind this stage of decision-making.

Age and socio-economic status

Most of the British studies of cautioning have no detailed information about the social backgrounds of the persons cautioned, but they do show a direct correlation with age and sex; McClintock and Avison showed that in 1965, of known offenders under 14, approximately one third of the boys were cautioned compared to nearly half of the girls, whereas, of those aged between 14–17 years, one sixth of the boys were cautioned compared to one quarter of the girls.[73] In Patchett and McClean's study, the majority of courts in their sample cautioned nearly twice the proportion of the under 14 age group as of those between 14–17 years; and of course, it is found that as the age of offenders increases so the proportion cautioned decreases.[74] Only Steer provided information about the social class of cautioned offenders, and he concluded that 'the social class distribution of cautioned offenders clearly approximates to the social class distribution of most offender populations, viz. the lower social classes are *over*-represented, the higher classes *under*-represented'.[75]

The American studies focus much more on the racial and socio-economic status of offenders given the different police dispositions. Goldman found that 34 per cent of White juveniles were referred to the juvenile court, whereas 65 per cent of Negroes arrested were similarly referred to court, but he explained this difference mainly on
66

the grounds of differential handling of *minor* offences, with much more 'equality' of handling in serious offences.[76] In a study of six inner-city areas in 1964, Ferdinand and Luchterhand found that 63 per cent of white juvenile offenders were referred to court, compared to 76 per cent of Negroes, and that this difference remained when offence, sex and age, were controlled; however, the factor which they suggested differentiated black from white juveniles was that the former had higher scores on a test of 'authority rejection':

> Since Authority Rejection is an attitude that is likely to be quite obvious to an arresting officer, it may well be that the Easton police take this factor into account when about to make a disposition. . . . From these findings it would appear that black youngsters who come to the attention of the police are given dispositions largely in terms of their superficial attitudes and demeanor towards the police, whereas white offenders are judged by different and probably more basic criteria.[77]

The main conclusions drawn by Weiner and Willie, on the influence of race and socio-economic status on the decisions taken by juvenile officers, were that these factors have much greater influence on the extent of initial police contacts than on the proportion of those contacted who are referred to court.[78] These findings were particularly strong in Washington D.C.; Table 2.6 shows that the police *contact* rate was

TABLE 2.6: *Rates of police contact and court referral of juveniles in different socio-economic areas of Washington, D.C., 1963.*

Socio-economic area	(a) Police rate contact	(b) Court rate referral	Ratio of (b) to (a)
I (High status)	14.8	4.8	0.32
II	48.8	16.3	0.33
III	70.5	25.8	0.37
IV	77.3	31.8	0.40
V (Low status)	139.7	49.2	0.35
Total city	71.0	26.8	0.37

Source: N. L. Weiner and C. V. Willie 'Decisions by Juvenile Officers' *Amer. Jo. Soc.* Vol. 77 (1971) Table 2 at p. 202.

almost ten times higher in the lowest socio-economic area than in the highest, but that the court referral rate was about one third of all contacts in every area—this, of course, may seem to answer one problem, by simply pushing it back to the earlier stage of the policy of deploying police manpower to different areas for patrol duties; similarly, the police contact rate with black juveniles in Washington was more than twice that of white, but the court referral rate was virtually identical.

Evidence of a relationship between police disposition decisions and these kind of characteristics, even where it is consistent, can only hint at possible causal connexions, and a better understanding is likely to come from a rather more subjective and interpretative examination of the circumstances and justifications surrounding the police decisions.

Offence and 'moral character'

The empirical studies confirm that many of the reasons and circumstances surrounding police decisions not to take formal court proceedings against offenders are similar to the reasons influencing police 'on-the-street' decisions not to arrest, but, by definition, they are applied to a slightly different, already 'sifted', group of individuals. For example, persons arrested for more *serious* offences are referred for official action more frequently than those involved in trivial offences. In cases where there is a 'participant victim' or the complainant does not wish to prosecute, the police often comply with the wishes of the complainant; thus, in Steer's study of the cautioning of adult offenders in five English police forces, in 28 per cent of all cases the principal reason for the police decision to caution (instead of prosecute) was a 'participant victim', and in a further 19 per cent of cases it was that the complainant declined to prosecute.[79] Hohenstein analysed a 10 per cent sample of juvenile offences coming to the notice of the Philadelphia Juvenile Division in 1960, and he concluded that the single most important factor determining police disposition was the attitude of the victim towards prosecution, so that in 96 per cent of the cases where the victim told the police they were against the prosecution of the offender, the offender was 'remedialed' informally.[80]

It is also clear from the evidence that the perceived or known 'moral character' of an offender has a definite influence upon the police deci-

68

sion whether or not to prosecute, yet the rationale behind this may be slightly different, at this stage of the process, than in the context of the initial 'on-the-street' encounter. In the earlier discussion it was suggested that the police were particularly concerned with the extent to which their authority might be challenged in the immediate face-to-face situation, and also that a stereotyped assessment of personal characteristics was an essential element of the working philosophy of crime detection; however, at the stage when the police have to make the more considered decision about prosecution, the attitudes and past behaviour of an individual may assume a rather different relevance—despite findings such as those by Ferdinand and Luchterhand (quoted above) concerning police reaction to the attitudes of Negro juveniles. The strict relevance of 'moral character' ought not to be so much with regard to the personal interaction between policeman and suspect, but to a concern with the *future* behaviour of an individual, for which past behaviour and present attitudes may be seen as a guide by the police; however, it is only too easy for a decision stemming mainly from the face-to-face interaction to be justified in terms of predicted future behaviour of an individual. In this respect Goldman's conclusions are probably quite realistic and nearer to the truth, when he included the following two factors in his list of reasons affecting police referral decisions:

E. *The necessity for maintaining respect for police authority in the community.* A juvenile who publicly causes damage to the dignity of the police, or who is defiant, refusing the help offered by the police, will be considered as needing court supervision, no matter how trivial the offense. . . .
J. *The attitude and personality of the boy.* An offender who is well mannered, neat in appearance, and 'listens' to the policeman will be considered a good risk for unofficial adjustment in the community. . . . Maliciousness in a child is considered by the police to indicate need for official court supervision.[81]

Similarly, in a study of disposition decisions in Detroit, 1952–61, Bordua found that the attitudes of first offenders towards officers were related to court referral: those who were assessed as 'honest' or 'responsive' were referred to court in 67 per cent and 70 per cent of cases, whereas those assessed as 'evasive' or 'antisocial' were referred

69

to court in 78 per cent and 80 per cent of cases, respectively—statistics which Bordua interpreted as 'a quite provisional clue that some of the 'on-the-street' factors may operate at the disposition stage'.[82] Nevertheless, in the same article, Bordua suggested that there were considerable differences between the orientation of patrol policemen and juvenile officers:

> The patrol police differ from juvenile officers in at least three main respects. They are more offense-oriented, especially toward offenses constituting forms of public disorder. They are more often charged with the job of maintaining pressure on suspected offenders in high crime areas under police doctrines of aggressive patrol. Most significantly, they must maintain respect for police authority even when dealing with gang boys whose morale may derive largely from successful baiting of the police. Juvenile officers tend to be offender-oriented and, indeed, perform a quasi-judicial role not unlike that of state's attorney.[83]

A related kind of justification for paying attention, at the disposition stage, to the character of the offender is in the association this might have with his home background, and the potential resources within the family for keeping a juvenile offender out of further trouble. Sellin and Wolfgang examined the criteria operating in the Philadelphia Juvenile Aid Division for disposition decisions:

> Two additional factors officially recognised as important in the arrest versus remedial decision are closely interrelated; the home condition, the attitude of the parents, and their resources and ability to help the child; and the availability of other community agencies which might be useful in helping the offender. . . . With apparent justification, these officers believe that uncooperative or hostile parents are likely to promote in the boy a rationalisation for his offense. Thus, making his future adjustment more difficult.[84]

'Legalistic' criteria and the courts

There seems to be general agreement among most commentators and students of police behaviour, that the prosecution decision is taken on rather more 'legalistic' grounds by the police than the arrest decision.

70

Whitaker has described this stage in the discretion of the English police as similar to the role of examining magistrate:

> Apart from the local police area's policy, each station officer, when he weighs evidence to decide if there is a *prima facie* case and whether or not to accept a charge, has a role not far different from that of the continental examining magistrate. Both stages of the discretion whether to prosecute happen to be innocent of any legal authority.[85]

In a general way, the term 'legalistic' may indicate the broad approach adopted by juvenile officers and senior police officers responsible for making the prosecution decision, but it has already been seen how in certain respects the discretion at this stage can be as 'particularistic' as at the arrest stage. Nevertheless it is true that there are certain 'technical' factors surrounding the prosecution process which affect the decision, including not only the willingness of the complainant to prosecute or give evidence against the offender, but also the more general question of whether there is in any event enough evidence to be likely to secure a conviction; in 23 per cent of Steer's cases, of adults cautioned for indictable offences, 'insufficient evidence' was the reason given for not prosecuting.[86]

It is also at this stage that the police are more immediately aware of the relationship between any decision they may take and the subsequent stage of court hearing. This relationship is complex and can work in various ways to influence police disposition decisions; for example, if the police are in agreement with the aims of the juvenile court system and have confidence in the way it operates in their area, they are likely to refer more juveniles to court; but, conversely, if they feel that the juvenile court operates too leniently *or* too severely, they might 'take the law into their own hands', so that justice, as they see it, may be done.[87] Wheeler's survey, of the attitudes and aims of different penal agents, indicated that the situation was not quite so straightforward as this, mainly because of the lack of communication between the different agencies concerned with the handling of juvenile offenders.[88] Although the police officers in the survey showed more 'punitive' attitudes toward juvenile offenders, they were *less* likely to feel that they should be referred to court than were the probation officers and the juvenile court judges. Two possible interpretations were suggested: (i) the police see the function of the court in a different light to the other agents, as a 'way station' into penal institutions, rather than as a place for deciding what is in the best interests of the child; (ii) each group is concerned to extend its *own control* over the fate of the juveniles, so that there was greater police control over those *not* referred to courts, whereas the other agents had very little control *unless* a juvenile was referred to court.[89] In this sort of situation, it is inevitable that conflict will be not far below the surface (see below).

Although reinforcing the complex nature of the relationship between police decisions and the courts, the evidence from the British studies of police cautioning seems to suggest a rather plausible interpretation of the situation. Most of these studies have shown that there is a general trend for courts in areas of low rates of police cautioning to give only nominal sentences (e.g. absolute or conditional discharge) to a larger proportion of persons appearing before them, than courts in areas where there is a high rate of police cautioning. The implication of this seems to be that there is a 'pool' of minor or special circumstance cases where no serious formal action is necessary, so that all that varies is the organizational question of whether the police handle them by official caution or the court, by a nominal sentence; clearly, a police caution or other action short of prosecution is likely to be much more economical than the formal process of court hearing.[90]

Community and organization

Finally, does the evidence about police disposition decisions and cautioning indicate any consistent relationship with the type of community or nature of police organization, similar to Wilson's typology of 'styles' of arrest discretion? The brief answer would seem to be 'unproven'.

Goldman suggested that both arrest and referral patterns are a function of the relations between the police and the community, so that where there is an impersonal relation between the police and the public, court referrals will be high and there will be little discrimination with respect to personal characteristics of the offender; but where there exists a personal face-to-face relation between the police and the

72

public, there will be more discrimination with respect to court referrals of arrested juveniles.[91] McEachern and Bauzer (1967) found that police discretion was influenced by the characteristics of individuals being handled, but also equally by characteristics of individual police officers and police departments, with the implication that these latter effects were idiosyncratic and unpredictable, rather than fitting into a neat framework, relating police organization to disposition decisions.[92] Bordua's Detroit study showed how practice can change dramatically in the same department over a period of time, and he concluded that progress in understanding police decision-making could best be furthered not by more microscopic studies of decisions within single departments but by attempts to study organizational variation directly, instancing Sterling's finding that the existence of a specialized juvenile bureau within a police department could be one important variable accounting for different practices.[93]

British evidence on variations in police cautioning is equally inconclusive; although McClintock and Avison's study of national variations seemed to show that cautioning was more frequent in police districts of smaller population, and higher police 'clear-up' rates, they admitted that there was almost as much variation between areas of the *same* size and characteristics, as between areas of *different* sizes; this seems to be generally supported by the studies of Patchett and McClean, and Somerville, where the variations in cautioning policy were as great between cities of the same type, as between cities and rural county areas.[94] It would seem necessary to agree with Bordua that before anything definite can be claimed about the relationship between police prosecution decisions and community or organizational factors, much greater attention needs to be paid in future research to the central issue of *variation,* both within departments over time and between departments.

POLICE AND THE CRIMINAL JUSTICE SYSTEM

This chapter opened by stating the crucial role played by the police in controlling the 'input' to the criminal justice system; if few other definite conclusions have emerged from the discussion of police discretion, it should at least be clear that the combined effects of this discre-

73

tion, first at the arrest stage and then at the prosecution stage, result in only a small minority of all 'offenders' handled by the police proceeding to the next stage of court hearing and judicial decision-making. Not only does this minority represent virtually the total input to the subsequent stages of the penal process, but in a very real sense it is a highly selected sample of all police contacts. Whatever the appropriateness or ultimate justification of the various criteria used by the police in exercising their discretion, the fact remains that the criteria by and large reflect strongly held views or traditions within the police service, and it is because of this that the police have a large psychological investment in the decisions that have been taken and in following the progress of cases through to the next stage of the penal process. The ways in which these cases are handled and, in particular, the attitude of the courts towards police practices and procedures of decision-making, probably go a long way towards explaining the low morale among the police and their sense of isolation from the rest of the criminal justice system. This concluding section will therefore summarize the main aspects of the underlying conflict between the police and the other parts of the system.

An important element in understanding the police role in the penal process is the lack of appropriate and realistic criteria for assessing the 'success' or achievements of most day-to-day police work. For a variety of theoretical and practical reasons, the total amount of 'crime' in a community cannot usefully be taken as a measure of police efficiency, and it has been seen, in the previous chapter, that the official 'clear-up' rate is equally inadequate to fulfil this function. In fact, it could be plausibly argued that one of the fundamental reasons for the traditional exercise of police discretion on such a wide scale, and with such low visibility, is precisely because it is one way of ensuring the achievement of many internal objectives of policing the community, particularly when the exercise of discretion receives official organizational support or traditional peer group sanction among the police.[95] Nevertheless, this process of internal self-justification of police work does not seem to provide an adequate or 'authoritative' enough confirmation of the value and correctness of police activity, with the result that the police look for confirmation to the courts which handle the cases referred to them as a result of police discretion:

74

The policeman's triumph comes when the court vindicates his judgement by a conviction. ... At any rate, a conviction reassures him of his own competence and at the same time of the worth of his job. ... It provides for him a reassurance as to the correctness of his judgements.[96]

Not unnaturally, the courts and the judges have very different views of their own role from that which the police see them as filling; they are probably reluctant to accept the necessity for such a wide exercise of discretion whereby the police drastically sift the cases to appear before them, and perhaps partly to compensate for this lack of control over their input, various procedural rules have been developed in most systems to govern police practices in methods of criminal investigation and obtaining evidence. The existence of such rules may simply mean that the police resort to rather more devious ways of achieving their desired objectives, as Newman has suggested:

To the extent that generalization is possible, it is apparent in current administration that there is wide disparity in attitudes of trial judges toward police practices; there is no effective communication between police and judges; and the judge's efforts at control are resisted by police, who do not rethink the propriety of the enforcement program but rather adopt alternative methods of achieving their objectives. ... This serves once again to illustrate the difficulty of effective control of one part of the criminal justice process by authority elsewhere. Just as trial judges avoid legislative sentencing mandates by systematically downgrading charges, so the police avoid trial court controls by arresting vice offenders for lesser crimes.[97]

In this situation, the police must have very ambivalent attitudes towards the courts; on the one hand, they see them laying down rules about the detailed conduct of police investigation practices and yet, on the other hand, they look to court decisions as the main external validation of all their preceding decisions and exercise of discretion.

Any selection process, like that inherent in the criminal justice system, creates various problems for each set of decision-makers, not only because of the basic lack of communication comparable to that in a game of 'consequences', in which each player works within his own private context, but also because the process of sifting offenders changes the composition of the group being processed at each stage.

75

Even if all the decision-makers were using the same criteria, there would still be inherent frustrations and dissatisfactions within the process, inasmuch as at each stage some are 'rejected' and others are 'accepted' for further process, out of a group who were *all* 'accepted' at the previous stage as being in need of further processing. Thus, when the police have carefully selected a minority of arrested offenders for formal court proceedings, they naturally feel that what happens to these people in court should be something more than a 'mere formality' or nominal sentence; judges, in their turn, having no clear knowledge of the number or type of cases handled informally by the police, usually operate on the assumption that the full range of sentences should be used for those convicted in court.[98] When, in addition to the cumulative sifting process, there are also different aims operating at each stage, the situation becomes even more complex and ripe for conflict, as Terry has described with regard to the handling of juvenile offenders:

> The variations that exist between agencies may be a function of the differences in orientation which characterise the agents of social control. If the police, probation officers, and juvenile court judges vary in terms of their conceptions of delinquency causation, delinquency prevention, and the rehabilitation of delinquents, we may expect corresponding variations in their reactions to delinquent behaviour. On the other hand, variations may be due in large part to the characteristics of the offenders who appear before each of the agencies. Thus, the populations that are screened at each of the stages vary in terms of a number of important respects and the criteria utilized in according sanctions may derive from this rather than from preconceived notions concerning what is in the child's best interests. Probably, these are mutually reinforcing dimensions of the same problem.[99]

An attempt to understand the police situation and some of the grounds for conflict within the criminal justice system does not, of course, explain that conflict away. Although, idealistically, it might be desirable to aim towards an integrated system with common objectives, yet a certain 'division of labour' and consequent friction between the parts seems almost inevitable. If the criminal justice system is to be viewed as a series of decisions, then these decisions must also be seen as taken by separate 'sub-systems', each with considerable discretion within their own sphere of activity as to how to handle or create their particular input and output. Reiss has recently developed this conceptual model of the penal process, indicating the conflict inherent in it:

> This kind of structure makes it very difficult to resolve conflicts concerning the actual exercise of discretion or the authority to exercise it. . . . Such conflicts are endemic to the system, since each sub-system is organised more around its central concerns than around those common to the legally constituted system of criminal justice. The police, for example, are more concerned with problems of enforcing the law than they are with those of abstract justice. . . .[100]

Our analysis would seem to give general support to Reiss' claim that the police 'sub-system' is organized around its own particular central concerns, based on a particular perception of their role as peacekeepers and enforcers of the law. A primary police concern in 'on-the-street' encounters is to gain initial control of the face-to-face situation, to enable decisions to be made about appropriate action whether of a supportive or more coercive nature; and in subsequent disposition decisions, the main concern of the police is to take that action which reflects their interpretation of the situation and will achieve their objectives in the most economical and efficient way possible.

NOTES

1. J. Goldstein 'Police Discretion Not to Invoke the Criminal Process: Low-visibility Decisions in the Administration of Justice' *Yale Law Journal* Vol. **69** (1960) p. 543; see also W. R. LaFave *Arrest: the Decision to Take a Suspect into Custody* Boston (1965) pp. 61–2.
2. I. Piliavin and S. Briar 'Police Encounters with Juveniles', *Amer. Jo. Soc.* Vol. **70** (1964) p. 206.
3. For an important discussion of the interrelationships between discretionary decisions in different parts of the criminal justice system see A. J. Reiss *The Police and the Public* New Haven (1971) pp. 114–20.
4. See, for example, Goldstein *op. cit.*; LaFave 'The Police and Nonenforcement of the Law', *Wisconsin Law Review* (1962) p. 104 and 179; LaFave, *Arrest* pp. 61–71, 103–37; S. Box *Deviance, Reality and Society* New York (1971) pp. 166–97; R. Quinney *The Social Reality of Crime* Boston (1970) pp. 104–5; President's Commission on Law Enforcement and Administration of Justice *The Challenge of Crime in a Free Society* Washington D.C.(1967) pp. 103–6; and *Task Force Report: The Police* Washington, D.C.(1967) pp. 13–41.
5. Quinney *op. cit.* p. 104.

6. A. Stinchcombe 'Institutions of Privacy in the Determination of Police Administrative Practice', *Amer. Jo. Soc.* Vol. **59** (1963) p. 150.
7. LaFave *Arrest* p. 69.
8. D. R. Cressey and E. Elgesem 'The Police and the Administration of Justice' in N. Christie (ed.) *Aspects of Social Control in Welfare States,* Scandinavian Studies in Criminology, Vol. 2 London (1968) p. 59; see also LaFave 'The Police and Nonenforcement' p. 179.
9. J. R. Lambert *Crime, Police and Race Relations* London (1970) p. 164.
10. See Goldstein *op. cit.,* and J. H. Skolnick *Justice Without Trial: Law Enforcement in Democractic Society* New York (1966) pp. 112–38.
11. B. Whitaker *The Police* Harmondsworth Penguin (1964) p. 30.
12. Whitaker *op. cit.* p. 177.
13. President's Commission on Law Enforcement *The Challenge of Crime* p. 104.
14. President's Commission on Law Enforcement *Task Force Report* pp. 19–20: Proper and consistent exercise of discretion in a large organisation, like a police department, will not result from the individual judgement of individual police officers in individual cases. Whatever the need for the exercise of judgement by an individual officer may be, certainly the development of overall law enforcement policies must be made at the departmental level and communicated to individual officers. This is necessary if the issues are to be adequately defined and adequately researched and if discretion is to be exercised consistently throughout the department [p. 19].
15. Box *op. cit.* p. 172.
16. Box *op. cit.* p. 183. For the most recent discussion of this issue see R. W. Balch 'The Police Personality: Fact or Fiction?' *Jo. Crim. Law, Crimin. and P.S.* Vol. **63** (1972) p. 106.
17. Quinney *op. cit.* p. 105.
18. See Reiss *op. cit.,* where Reiss talks about the different 'subsystems' of the criminal justice system, of which the first is the 'citizen subsystem' and the second is the 'law enforcement' or 'police subsystem'—'we have tried to show here that, in fact, citizens enter the criminal justice system not only as violators but, more importantly, as enforcers of the law. Their discretionary decisions to mobilize the police are a principal source of input into the system, and these decisions profoundly affect the discretion exercised by the police' (p. 114).
19. Reiss *op. cit.* p. 11.
20. See J. R. Hudson 'Police-citizen Encounters that Lead to Citizen Complaints' *Social Problems* Vol. **18** (1970) p. 179.
21. W. A. Westley *Violence and the Police* Cambridge, Mass. (1970) p. 19; see also E. H. Johnson 'Interrelatedness of Law Enforcement Programme: A Fundamental Dimension' *Jo. Crim. Law, Crimin. and P.S.* Vol. **60** (1969) p. 509: The number and character of police contacts with members of the public are skewed toward humanitarian and service functions. Rather than law enforcement *per se,* the policeman's activities are guided more by popular morality than by the letter of the law as indicated by the tendency to ignore some violations and to pursue others with special enthusiasm. Furthermore, law enforcement is granted a moral authority by the public beyond the policeman's legal authority by virtue of a general belief that he symbolises civic virtue' [p. 510].
22. E. Cumming, I. M. Cumming and L. Edell 'Policeman as Philosopher, Guide and Friend' *Social Problems* Vol. **12** (1965) p. 276.

23. In his early and formative discussion of the 'peace officer' and 'law officer' roles of the police, Michael Banton isolated the question of public support as a key factor in influencing police discretion: 'Policemen do not like taking aggressive action unless they believe they have public support, and they often refuse to enforce the law upon their fellow citizens if they believe it would be unfair to do so. Full enforcement would require policemen to be far more detached from society than is possible under the present system' (M. Banton *The Policeman in the Community* London [1964] p. 131). See the most interesting survey reported by M. Shaw and W. Williamson 'Public Attitudes to the Police' *The Criminologist* Vol. 7 No. 26 (Autumn 1972) p. 18.

24. Quinney *op. cit.* p. 116. For illustration of the problems of policing a racially mixed community in Britain, see J. R. Lambert *op. cit.*

25. LaFave *Arrest* pp. 112ff.

26. Skolnick *op. cit.* p. 111.

27. Westley pp. 126–39; see also E. A. Bittner, 'The Police on Skid-Row: A Study of Peace Keeping' *Amer. Soc. Rev.* Vol. 32 (1967) p. 699.

28. P. Rock 'The Police: A Case Study in Social Control' Part Two of an unpublished paper by D. M. Downes and Rock 'Social Reaction to Deviance and its Effects on Crime and Criminal Careers', presented at the Fourth National Conference on Research and Teaching in Criminology, Cambridge (July 1970); see also Hudson *op. cit.* p. 179: 'But in all instances where the citizen and the police come into contact, whether it is for law enforcement or maintenance of order, the policeman feels he must keep control of the situation. . . . No matter what the social status of the individual and no matter what the situational context in which the encounter takes place, the policeman's authority is the crux of police-citizen encounters' (p. 193).

29. Reiss *op. cit.* p. 47.

30. R. I. Parnas 'The Police Response to Domestic Disturbance' *Wisconsin Law Review* (1967) p. 914.

31. Parnas *op. cit.*

32. Bittner *op. cit.* p. 699; see also Bittner 'Police Discretion in Emergency Apprehension of Mentally Ill Persons' *Social Problems* Vol. 14 (1967) p. 278.

33. Bittner 'The Police on Skid-Row' p. 699; see also the comments in Lambert *op. cit.* p. 68:
    Most policemen do not interpret their role as requiring them to arrest every drunken person. If a man is going home quietly and on the pavement, an erratic course is tolerated. Policemen often express concern for the man's safety and will often say, somewhat apologetically, for no great merit attaches to bringing in a drunk, that he had to be brought in for his own safety—the threat of danger coming from motor traffic and from 'drunk-rollers'.

34. Bittner 'Police Discretion' p. 278.

35. I. Piliavin and S. Briar *op. cit.* Table 1, p. 206.

36. J. Q. Wilson 'The Police and the Delinquent in Two Cities', in S. Wheeler (ed.) *Controlling Delinquents* New York (1968) Tables 1 and 2, pp. 9–30.

37. D. J. Black and A. J. Reiss 'Police Control of Juveniles', *Amer. Soc. Rev.* Vol. 35 (1970) pp. 63ff, at p. 68.

38. Piliavin and Briar *op. cit.*

39. See also Cressey and Elgesem *op. cit.* pp. 53–72, in which a majority of the Uniformed Division, in an Oslo survey, agreed that it was right to report and punish minor offenders who took up an abusive attitude (Table 3, p. 65).

79

40. D. C. Sullivan and L. J. Siegel 'How Police Use Information to Make Decisions—An Application of Decision Games' *Crime and Delinquency* Vol. **18** (1972) p. 253.

41. D. H. Bayley and H. Mendelsohn *Minorities and the Police* New York (1969) p. 93. Since this was written, there has been the interesting discussion by H. Sacks 'Notes on Police Assessment of Moral Character' in D. Sudnow (ed.) *Studies in Social Interaction* New York (1972).

42. Quinney *op. cit.* pp. 127–8.

43. Piliavin and Briar *op. cit.*

44. C. Werthman and Piliavin 'Gang Members and the Police' in D. J. Bordua (ed.) *The Police: Six Sociological Essays* New York (1967) pp. 68–9.

45. Skolnick *op. cit.* p. 83.

46. Werthman and Piliavin *op. cit.* p. 75; see also A. V. Cicourel *The Social Organisation of Juvenile Justice* New York (1968) pp. 105ff.

47. Piliavin and Briar *op. cit.* p. 214; see also LaFave *Arrest* p. 493.

48. Reiss *op. cit.* p. 135.

49. Wilson *op. cit.* Tables 1 and 2.

50. Black and Reiss *op. cit.* at p. 68.

51. R. G. Hood and R. F. Sparks *Key Issues in Criminology* London (1970) p. 77.

52. Box *op. cit.* p. 197; Box, like many other writers cited in this section, owes a great deal to the formative work of Cicourel, especially Cicourel *op. cit.*

53. Wilson *Varieties of Police Behaviour* Cambridge, Mass. (1968).

54. Wilson 'The Police and the Delinquent, p. 21.

55. Wilson *ibid.* p. 22 and Table 2.

56. Wilson *ibid.* p. 26.

57. Wilson *Varieties of Police Behaviour,* p. 11.

58. Wilson *ibid.* pp. 140ff.

59. Wilson *ibid.* pp. 172ff:

> A legalistic department will issue traffic tickets at a high rate, detain and arrest a high proportion of juvenile offenders, act vigorously against illicit enterprises, and make a large number of misdemeanour arrests even when, as with petty larceny, the public order has not been breached. The police will act, on the whole, as if there were a single standard of community conduct—that which the law prescribes—rather than different standards for juveniles, Negroes, drunks and the like [p. 172].

60. Wilson *ibid.* pp. 200ff.

61. See M. E. Cain 'On the Beat: Interactions and Relations in Rural and Urban Police Forces', in S. Cohen (ed.) *Images of Deviance,* Harmondsworth, Penguin (1971); also Cain *Society and the Policeman's Role* London (1973).

62. Wilson *Varieties of Police Behaviour* pp. 84–139.

63. L. W. Shannon 'Types and Patterns of Delinquency Referral in a Middle-sized City', *Brit. Jo. Crim.,* Vol. **4** (1963) p. 24.

64. See also Bordua 'Recent Trends: Deviant Behaviour and Social Control' *The Annals of the American Academy of Political and Social Science* Vol. **57** (1967) p. 149, in which it is stated that court referral rate in Detroit increased from 44 per cent in 1951 to 80 per cent in 1964.

65. N. Goldman *The Differential Selection of Juvenile Offenders for Court Appearance* New York (1963).

66. R. M. Terry 'The Screening of Juvenile Offenders' *Jo. Crim. Law, Crimin. and P.S.* Vol. **58** (1967) p. 173; see also Terry 'Discrimination in the Handling of

Juvenile Offenders by Social Control Agencies', *Jo. Res. in Crime and Del.* Vol. **4** (1967) p. 218.

67. N. L. Weiner and C. V. Willie 'Decisions by Juvenile Officers', *Amer. Jo. Soc.* Vol. **77** (1971) p. 199.

68. F. H. McClintock and N. H. Avison *Crime in England and Wales* London (1968) pp. 155–62, 208–14; in this context 'known offenders' means all those who are either found guilty of or cautioned for indictable offences.

69. McClintock and Avison *op. cit.* p. 210.

70. K. W. Patchett and J. D. McClean 'Decision-making in Juvenile Cases' *Crim. L.R.* (1965) p. 699, see Table IV at p. 706.

71. J. G. Somerville 'A Study of the Preventive Aspect of Police Work with Juveniles' *Crim. L.R. (1969)* pp. 407, 472.

72. D. J. Steer *Police Cautions—A Study in the Exercise of Police Discretion* Oxford (1970) Table 5, p. 24.

73. McClintock and Avison *op. cit.* Table 6.5, p. 159.

74. For example, in 1970 in England and Wales 50 per cent of boys under 14 were cautioned, 24 per cent of those aged 14–17, 5 per cent of those aged 17–21, and just 3 per cent of male known offenders over the age of 21; see *Criminal Statistics, England and Wales, for 1970* (Cmnd. 4708), Table 11, p. xxiv of Introductory Note.

75. Steer *op. cit.* p. 43 and Table 8.

76. Goldman *op. cit.*

77. T. N. Ferdinand and E. G. Luchterhand 'Inner-city Youth, the Police, the Juvenile Court and Justice' *Social Problems* Vol. **17** (1970) p. 516–17; see also W. F. Hohenstein 'Factors influencing the Police Disposition of Juvenile Offenders' in T. Sellin and M. E. Wolfgang (eds) *Delinquency: Selected Studies* New York (1969).

78. Weiner and Willie *op. cit.*

79. Steer *op. cit.* pp. 27ff and Table 7, p. 26. A large proportion of 'participant victim' cases involved sexual offences with girls under the age of 16; the cases where the complainant declined to prosecute were often domestic incidents, e.g. 'husbands who had violently assaulted their wives, offenders who had stolen property belonging to another member of their own family, and similar offences involving neighbours and friends' (p. 27). For further illustrations see Lambert *op. cit.* pp. 56–7, and McClintock and Avison *Crimes of Violence* London (1963) pp. 87ff.

80. Hohenstein *op. cit.* p. 146.

81. Goldman *op. cit.*; see also T. Sellin and M. E. Wolfgang *The Measurement of Delinquency* New York (1964): 'The officer sometimes is guided by the behaviour, attitude, and appearance of the offender himself. . . . More important than clothes, however, is the presence or absence of cooperation and respect shown the investigator in the current contact and possibly in the past as well. It is important that the officer evaluate the sincerity of a cooperative attitude to determine whether it is feigned or whether the suspect is telling the truth' (p. 98).

82. Bordua 'Recent Trends' p. 149.

83. Bordua *op. cit.*

84. Sellin and Wolfgang *op. cit.* p. 98. Somewhat similar thinking seems to have underlied the Children and Young Persons Act, 1969, in England, with its provision for taking into account aspects of the home background in the decision to prosecute juveniles.

85. Whitaker, *op. cit.* p. 30; see also Terry 'Screening of Juvenile Offenders' p. 173: 'The police appear to utilise basically legalistic criteria in making disposition decisions. . . . In other words, the police appear to interpret the 'best interests of the child' in terms of criteria also used when dealing with adult offenders' (p. 179); and Box *op. cit.* pp. 190–7.
86. Steer *op. cit.* Table 27, p. 26 and pp. 34ff.
87. See Ferdinand and Luchterhand *op. cit.*: '. . . the fact that the police are reluctant to send a boy to the Juvenile Court may mean that they are giving the youngster the full benefit of the doubt, especially when he is likely to receive a severe disposition in the Juvenile Court. Hence, those teenagers who are dealt with most severely by the court seem to be handled most cautiously by the police' (p. 521); see the comments on police cautioning in M. Grünhut, *Juvenile Offenders Before the Courts* Oxford (1956) p. 65, and the summary in Hood and Sparks *op. cit.* p. 74.
88. S. Wheeler *et al.* 'Agents of Delinquency Control: A Comparative Analysis', in Wheeler (ed.) *op. cit.* pp. 31–60.
89. Wheeler *et al. op. cit.* p. 48.
90. See Steer *op. cit.*: 'The practice of cautioning may also be defended on the grounds of plain commonsense, there are cases in which a clear warning to the offender is the only action which needs to be taken. Besides, the primary duty of the police is to prevent crime, and prosecution is only one of the means to this end. If the aim can be achieved without a prosecution, and without the cost and suffering this may involve, then such a system can only be welcomed' (p. 57).
91. Goldman *op. cit.*; from his empirical data, Goldman showed that the main differences between the communities he studied were in *minor* offences—which probably fits our earlier interpretation of a 'pool' of offenders available either for police handling *or* nominal sentences by the court.
92. A. W. McEachern and R. Bauzer 'Factors Related to Disposition in Juvenile Police Contacts', in M. W. Klein (ed.) *Juvenile Gangs in Context* Englewood Cliffs, Prentice-Hall (1967) p. 152.
93. Bordua *op. cit.* citing J. W. Sterling 'The Juvenile Offender From Community to Court: Two Stages of Decision', paper read before the Illinois Academy of Criminology (November 1962).
94. K. W. Patchett and J. D. McClean *op. cit.* p. 699; Somerville *op. cit.* pp. 407, 472; see also L. Sebba 'Decision-making in Juvenile Cases—A Comment' *Crim. L.R.* [1967] p. 347, where it was found that many of McClintock's and Avison's findings of association were not supported by a closer analysis of Patchett's and McClean's data.
95. See Reiss and Bordua 'Environment and Organisation: A Perspective on the Police' in Bordua (ed.) *The Police* pp. 25ff.
96. Westley *op. cit.* p. 81:
   The policeman, being essentially a man of action, must have the confidence to make quick, sure judgments. Frequently, he is in situations where he must judge the guilt or innocence of a particular person. To make such a judgment, he has to be certain of himself. Once he has made such a judgment, he finds it difficult to admit that he is wrong, for this would indicate uncertainty. This fear of uncertainty thus forces him to stick to his initial judgments, in the face of contrary evidence and in spite of the decisions of the court. . . . The policeman, needing the security of past judgments for future judgments, tends to rationalise away the decisions of the court [pp. 81–2].

See also Johnson *op. cit.* esp. p. 513.

97. D. J. Newman *Conviction: the Determination of Guilt or Innocence Without Trial* Boston (1966) p. 196; see also his earlier comments on the role of the trial court as 'overseer' of the entire criminal justice system: '. . . the issue is whether the actual administrative system is composed of a number of linked but relatively independent agencies, notably the police, the prosecutor, the court, and correctional services, each with its own sphere of activities and influence and more or less equal powers in decision making, or whether among them the trial court occupies a supervisory and controlling position' (p. 175).

98. See Wheeler *et al. op. cit.* p. 50; a rather unsatisfactory solution would be for each stage to be much more tactical and strategic in its decision-making, by 'over-selection'—in the knowledge that the next stage in the process would operate its own selection–rejection procedure *whatever* kind of input it received.

99. Terry 'Screening of Juvenile Offenders' p. 180.

100. Reiss *op. cit.* p. 117.

3 PRE-TRIAL DECISION-MAKING

In England, when the police have arrested a suspect and decided to charge him with an indictable offence, he appears initially before a magistrates' court. This first appearance in court might seem to mark a distinct new judicial stage in the penal process, but it will be seen, particularly in the pre-trial stage, that although many important decisions are located in the judicial context of a court room, they are influenced by many 'extra-judicial' factors which give the lie to the idea that the court appearance can be viewed as distinctly separate from the police decisions which have preceded it. The two main pre-trial processes to be discussed in this chapter, the decision as to whether or not to grant bail to remanded persons and the defendant's choice of plea, illustrate the close relationship between the police and the courts and many of the problems surrounding these issues are a direct consequence of the conflict of interests underlying this relationship, which has already been mentioned in the previous chapter. Similarly, just as the exercise of police discretion to arrest suspected offenders has been described as being of 'low-visibility', so this same description could be applied to much of the pre-trial decision-making; paradoxically, however, this 'low-visibility' is sometimes as much a problem for the magistrates directly involved as for the public at large. An equally paradoxical feature is that although it is at these judicial stages of the penal process that great weight is traditionally attached to the principle of the 'presumption of innocence', yet it will be seen that once a person has appeared in court facing a criminal charge many of the subsequent decisions taken by the various parties concerned (e.g. police, magistrates, defendants) often seem to be influenced rather by a principle of 'assumption of guilt', and a failure to recognize this renders the pre-trial process much less comprehensible.[1]

84

THE GRANTING OF BAIL

Examining, as this book attempts to do, the 'career' of an offender through the different stages of the penal process, the pre-trial bail decision might appear at first sight to be rather peripheral to that main progress, but in fact many claims have been made that a refusal of bail at this stage may have direct consequences on a defendant's subsequent likelihood of conviction and the nature of his sentence; in addition, of course, the immediate consequence of a refusal of bail is a period of imprisonment before trial, which is of vital significance in personal and social terms, and needs serious justification irrespective of any other impact it might have for the defendant's later progress through the stages of the penal process.[2] Official sources fail to provide adequate statistics and information for a proper understanding of the essential elements in the pre-trial processes surrounding the decision to remand in custody or grant bail to defendants awaiting trial; English statistics are in this respect no worse than most and in the provision of certain items of relevant information are considerably better than many comparable countries, but nevertheless much of the statistical background for the discussion derives from special research studies rather than routinely collected and officially published statistics.

Official statistics for England and Wales, in 1970, show that 350,705 persons appeared in magistrates' courts facing one or more police charges for indictable offences; almost 90 per cent of the persons dealt with during the year were tried summarily by the magistrates' courts, so that a total of 42,852 persons were committed for trial to higher courts; on committal for trial, magistrates had the choice of remanding in custody or granting bail to defendants, and more than 70 per cent were granted bail, leaving just 12,569 (29 per cent) who were remanded in custody awaiting trial at higher courts.[3] These judicial statistics provide no information about the number of persons refused bail by the magistrates in the course of summary trial or in proceedings leading up to committal for trial at higher courts. However, the annual *Report on the Work of the Prison Department for 1970* shows that a total of 43,042 persons were received as 'untried prisoners' during the year, providing the only general indication available of the numbers *refused bail* by magistrates in summary cases and in the early stages of subsequent committals, allowing only speculation on the numbers *granted bail* in these circumstances.[4] Thus these official statistics show that in 1970 there were over 30,000 receptions into prison of persons who were refused bail in the course of summary trial in magistrates' courts or before being committed for trial, with an additional 12,000 receptions of persons refused bail after having been committed for trial to a higher court; in the case of the latter group, this was slightly under 30 per cent of all persons committed for trial, but in the case of the former we do not know what percentage of all persons remanded in summary proceedings were granted bail by the magistrates.

An important gap in our knowledge, therefore, relates to information about the number of indictable offenders whose cases are not disposed of at their first court appearance, but where there are one or more adjournments before trial (during which any person facing an indictable charge must either be remanded in custody or granted bail). Research in selected magistrates' courts in northern and eastern England, 1963–5, showed that approximately 36 per cent of persons appearing in court charged with indictable offences were remanded, instead of having their cases disposed of at their first appearance in court, although there were considerable variations in different types of offence such that threequarters of defendants charged with theft were dealt with immediately without any remand, compared to less than half of those charged with 'breaking and entering'.[5] In this particular sample, 60 per cent of persons remanded during proceedings in magistrates' courts were always remanded in custody, with 30 per cent always granted bail. A more recent national study by the Cobden Trust showed that, in 1970–1, approximately two thirds of persons remanded by magistrates were granted bail, and this proportion would seem to match the very rough estimate that can be made from a combination of official statistics.[6]

Inasmuch as the majority of adjournments are needed to enable the police to complete their inquiries into the case or to prepare for committal proceedings, with only a minority requested by the defendant to obtain legal aid or time to prepare his defence, many decisions about bail or custody before trial could be avoided by the greater use of summonses by the police instead of arrests. There has been very little study of the use of the summons as an alternative method of

86

proceeding against indictable offenders, despite the pioneering development of Summons Projects in America by the Vera Institute of Justice.[7] In Friedland's study of 6,000 offences heard in Toronto Magistrates' Courts, 1961–2, it was found that in more than 92 per cent of indictable *and non-indictable* cases the accused was arrested, rather than summonsed, and he compared this situation with that obtaining in England where less than three quarters of *indictable* offenders are arrested.[8] It is clear that there are considerable differences in police practices with regard to arrest and summons, not only comparing one country with another, but even comparing different areas within the same country, which stem from different organizational and administrative practices as well as reflecting relevant differences in the 'criminal' population being handled. For example, the author's research in English urban and rural courts, 1963–5, showed that only 21 per cent of adult offenders in the urban court were summonsed to appear in court, compared to 36 per cent in the one rural court for which this information was available, reflecting much more the organization and number of court sittings in the two areas studied than the relative characteristics of the persons proceeded against.[9] Such findings suggest that the summons could probably be used more frequently by many urban police forces, without any necessary increase in risk to the public or great inconvenience to the judicial system.

The fact that a defendant has appeared in court in response to a summons means that, even if an adjournment is necessary, the court has some firm evidence about the likelihood of his appearing for a subsequent hearing without the need for a remand in custody, so that it is not surprising that bail is more often granted in these circumstances. Similarly, this points to the probably even greater significance of police decisions as to whether to keep arrested persons in police custody overnight, or until court appearance, or whether to release on police bail or 'delayed charge'. Once again there is an almost complete lack of information about police decisions of this kind, but the obvious relationship between police bail and court bail must be noted, giving even more scope for variations due to police practices as well as court organization.[10] In an English urban court, 80 per cent of persons remanded appeared in court, having spent the previous night in police cells, compared to only 40 per cent of cases at the rural courts; similarly, just as the next section will show a statistical association between court bail and the chances of acquittal and non-custodial sentences, so there is a clear association between police bail and a defendant being granted bail by the magistrates at his first court appearance: of the persons who appeared in police custody, 83 per cent of those in the urban court and 90 per cent of those in the rural courts were remanded in custody, whereas, of the persons who had been released on bail by the police, only 18 per cent were refused bail by the courts.[11]

Bail and the judicial process

One of the main targets for attacks on the bail system by criminologists, especially in America, has been the evidence that defendants who are refused bail are much more likely to be convicted than are persons granted bail, and much more likely to receive custodial sentences. This evidence needs careful scrutiny, for if these claims are substantiated then the bail decision plays a central rather than merely peripheral role in the progress of a defendant through the penal process. Assuming the accuracy of the statistical association between bail and conviction/sentence, the crucial question is whether this is in any sense a *causal* association, or whether the same factors independently influence both the bail decision and the subsequent ones. Unfortunately the available evidence does not allow firm conclusions either way, despite some suggestive indications from various research studies.

In America in the 1950s the University of Pennsylvania Law School carried out two important studies of the operation of the bail system, which seemed to provide strong evidence that defendants who were granted bail were more likely to be acquitted than those remanded in custody before trial, but a closer examination of these studies shows that the authors were usually much more cautious in interpreting their data than were many subsequent commentators. In the first study, of 946 cases remanded before trial in Philadelphia during October–November, 1953, Foote and his colleagues found that 48 per cent of bailed defendants were not convicted compared to 18 per cent of defendants remanded in custody; however, one reason for this

88

difference was that in a greater proportion of bail cases the prosecution withdrew the charges before trial ('nol prosse'), so that when these 'nol prosse' cases were discounted only 25 per cent of bail cases going to trial were acquitted, compared to 16.5 per cent of cases remanded in custody.[12] A second study, of 3,223 felony cases in New York in 1956, found that 20 per cent of the defendants in custody were acquitted at their trial, compared to 31 per cent of those on bail, but the authors were cautious in the conclusions which they drew from these statistics:

> The figures tend to support the propositions advanced earlier that jail in itself is likely to produce a guilty plea and that incarceration impairs a defendant's ability to defend himself. But the differences are not large and could be due in some measure to the fact that magistrates often set higher bail and thus keep the defendant in jail, in cases where they realize that the weight of evidence is against him.[13]

This New York study was careful to restrict analysis of acquittal/conviction rates to those cases where there was a plea of not guilty, as only 10 per cent of persons remanded in custody pleaded not guilty, compared to 25 per cent of bailed defendants.[14] Friedland's study of 6,000 cases in Toronto magistrates' courts in 1961–2, is perhaps the most detailed study of this aspect of the problem. He analysed the acquittal rate in indictable cases where there was a plea of not guilty, and found that 55 per cent of those on bail were acquitted, compared to 43 per cent of those in custody; this difference remained, even when he took into account other relevant factors differentiating between bail and custody cases.[15]

The two English studies which have provided some information on this question broadly support the evidence from America and Canada, although they were on a much smaller scale. Davies' Liverpool study of 418 men, remanded on charges of 'breaking and entering', found that in a partially-matched subsample of 191 defendants 12 per cent of those remanded in custody before trial pleaded not guilty, compared to 31 per cent of those released on bail, and that only 14 per cent of those in custody were acquitted at their trial, compared to 47 per cent of those on bail.[16] Bottomley's study in a north of England city, in 1964, found that 39 per cent of those committed in custody for trial to a higher court pleaded not guilty, compared to 64 per cent of those committed on bail, although the eventual acquittal rate was 46 per cent of those in custody and only 43 per cent of those on bail; the importance of taking the plea into account is shown by the fact that if the simple acquittal rate of those committed for trial by the urban court had been used, it would have showed that 18 per cent of those committed for trial in custody were acquitted, compared to 27 per cent of those on bail.[17]

On the basis of this evidence, there seems little room for serious doubt that more persons who are refused bail by magistrates plead guilty at their trial, and, without needing to impute any kind of improper coercion upon defendants to make such a choice of plea, it is easy to understand how defendants in custody might reach their decision, on purely personal terms preferring their trial to be over as quickly as possible, and perhaps even with the knowledge that almost half the 'untried prisoners' in English and Welsh prisons are not subsequently given a custodial sentence by the courts![18] Nevertheless, the general problem of guilty pleas, dealt with more fully in the next section, and the possible extent to which defendants' pleas may not exactly reflect the 'truth' of the situation, but result from various pragmatic considerations, is clearly one which needs closer examination in relation to the pre-trial bail/custody decision, which itself adds an extra (and possibly crucial) dimension to the situation. Similarly, although the crude conviction rates should not be taken as an accurate guide, yet the evidence points to the fact that, when account has been taken of the different proportions of remanded offenders pleading not guilty and of those cases withdrawn before trial, there is still a difference of some 9–12 per cent between the proportion of defendants on bail who are acquitted and that of those in custody before trial. Clearly some of this difference may well be due to the fact that defendants on bail are in a much better position to consult with solicitors and prepare their own defence, but part of the explanation is also likely to be due to the fact that the initial decision by magistrates to grant bail is sometimes influenced by their assessment of the strength of the case against the accused and the likelihood of his guilt (see below).

Moving from the question of pleas and acquittal to a consideration of the sentences passed on remanded offenders, the evidence for an association between the granting of bail and receiving a non-custodial sentence seems even stronger. Thus, in America, the Philadelphia study found that 22 per cent of those convicted after being on bail received a prison sentence, compared to 59 per cent of those who had been in custody before trial;[19] and in the New York study it was found that 45 per cent of those convicted after being on bail were imprisoned, compared to 84 per cent of those appearing for trial in custody.[20] In Toronto, Friedland found that only 15 per cent of indictable offenders on bail were sentenced to imprisonment, compared to 61 per cent of those in custody before trial.[21] Finally, in England, the Home Office Research Unit study in 1956 showed that 40 per cent of persons committed for trial on bail to higher courts were given custodial sentences, compared to 78 per cent of those committed for trial in custody; and, in summary cases, 14 per cent of those remanded on bail were given custodial sentences compared to 39 per cent of those in custody.[22] Davies found that, in his matched subsample, 69 per cent of those remanded in custody were sentenced to imprisonment, compared to 51 per cent of those on bail; and in Bottomley's urban and rural study, of those committed for trial to higher courts, 23 per cent of those on bail were given a custodial sentence, compared to 48 per cent of those in custody, and, in cases tried summarily, 11 per cent on bail were sentenced to imprisonment compared to 87 per cent of those remanded in custody.[23]

These statistics consistently show great differences between the sentences passed on defendants who have been in custody before trial, compared with those passed on defendants who have been released on bail; the differences are greater than those found in the previous analysis of choice of plea and acquittal rates and yet, on the face of it, there would seem to be more valid 'common-sense' explanations of the relationship between bail and the chances of acquittal, than between bail and the chances of a non-custodial sentence, if convicted. An obvious explanation of the statistical *associations* that have been found would seem to be simply that many of the factors associated with the chances of receiving custodial sentences are in practice found more frequently among those defendants refused bail by magistrates, but we still await a definitive study to confirm or reject this 'explanation', in view of the fact that different researchers have reached somewhat different conclusions on this matter. For example, the most detailed examination so far of the relationship between pre-trial detention and

91

sentence was the analysis of 732 felony cases in New York City carried out by Rankin during 1961–2; in this sample, 64 per cent of the offenders in custody before trial were sentenced to imprisonment compared to only 17 per cent of those who had been remanded on bail.[24] A complex analysis of the data was carried out, controlling many different factors likely to be related to custodial sentences, but none of the factors, individually or in combination, was found to account for the large proportion of custody cases sentenced to imprisonment; for example, controlling the effect of previous criminal record, Rankin found that 59 per cent of first offenders who were in custody were sentenced to imprisonment, compared to only 10 per cent of the first offenders who were on bail, and, conversely, 81 per cent of those with previous records who were in custody were sentenced to imprisonment, compared to 36 per cent of those who were on bail.[25] Bottomley's analysis of his sample, according to similar factors, revealed a rather different finding with regard to the influence of previous criminal record on the bail decision and the eventual sentences passed on remanded offenders: the effect of controlling the influence of the previous criminal record was to reduce considerably the gap between the proportions on bail and in custody who received custodial sentences and in one instance (although involving small numbers) to reverse the association, so that only 25 per cent of persons committed for trial in custody with *no previous convictions* were sentenced to imprisonment, compared to 47 per cent of persons committed on bail, with no previous convictions.[26]

Until a more definitive study is carried out, judgement about the possible reasons for the refusal of bail having a direct impact upon the chances of a convicted offender receiving a custodial sentence must be based on a balanced assessment of the available statistics set against the reasons which have been put forward to provide a possible *causal* link. The main suggestions from researchers in the United States have been (a) the detrimental effect that a loss of employment (during a remand in custody) might have on an accused's chance of being put on probation, and (b) the likely prejudice created by the defendant's apearance in court in the custody of police or prison officers.[27] These suggestions do not seem particularly convincing, at least in an English context, and it seems much more likely that when magistrates decide to grant or refuse bail to particular defendants they take into consideration very similar factors to those which will be taken into account in the sentencing decision, thus 'explaining' any statistical association which may be found in subsequent analyses. This guarded scepticism about some of the statistical studies carried out in America is not intended to detract from the impressive achievements of the bail reform movement in the United States during the 1960s, which derived much impetus from these same studies, but it is believed that much needed reform can equally derive from a consideration of the personal and social harm caused by unnecessary remanding in custody before trial, as from an apparently more objective statistical approach to this particular problem.

Criteria for bail decisions

Incidental reference has already been made to the fact that statistics for annual prison receptions in England and Wales show that almost half of all 'untried prisoners' are not given any form of custodial sentence by the trial court; for example in 1970, almost 19,000 of these prisoners (41 per cent) were given non-custodial sentences after being remanded in custody before trial, with a further 2,000 (5 per cent) acquitted.[28] These statistics seem to raise disturbing questions about the validity of the criteria being used by the courts to remand in custody such a large proportion of persons who are not thought to need a custodial sentence on conviction; on the other hand, many critics are concerned to point out that the pre-trial bail/custody decision is in no way comparable to the later sentencing decision, so that by following the logic of their argument it would be possible to explain such prison statistics—despite the fact that this type of argument has almost exclusively been used by critics claiming that *too many* persons are refused bail, rather than in defence of the existing situation. Most people would probably wish to maintain an uneasy compromise position on this issue, emphasizing that the criteria for the bail decision should be entirely separate from those for sentencing, but that the operation of these criteria should rarely (if ever) result in a defendant being kept in custody for whom a later sentencing court would not consider a custodial sentence necessary or appropriate. Before attempting to assess the relative merits of these viewpoints, it is important to consider the findings of empirical studies of magistrates' bail decisions.

Despite a truly impressive collection of statistical information about large numbers of bail decisions, neither the American nor Canadian studies provide the kind of first-hand empirical data from observation in court which is necessary even to begin to understand some of the reasons underlying magistrates' decisions to refuse bail to defendants before trial; this is one of the rare occasions in the study of the penal process where it is necessary to rely on the findings of two or three English studies. These English studies approached the task of discovering magistrates' reasons for their decisions in a rather indirect manner, by concentrating on analyses of police objections to bail stated in open court, instead of attempting a more direct study of the magistrates' reasoning processes; various factors contributed towards the choice of method, but the research workers were influenced by the apparently high degree of 'congruence' that was consistently found between police recommendations on bail and magistrates' final decisions.[29] The relevant findings of two of these studies will be summarized: firstly, the author's own study of selected urban and rural courts in England, 1965–6,[30] and, secondly, the more recent national study carried out by the Cobden Trust, in 1970–1, which was able to examine the situation following the coming into force of ss. 18–23 of the Criminal Justice Act, 1967, intended to restrict the circumstances in which magistrates could refuse bail to defendants facing summary trial for certain indictable offences.[31]

Police objections to bail in the urban and rural courts, observed by the author, could be divided into the following six main categories, with examples of the kind of reasons included in each category:

1. *Impeding police inquiries:* e.g. further charges to be made, defendant found in possession of stolen property, other suspects to be traced.
2. *Defendant's criminal record and likely repetition of offence.*
3. *Non-appearance at trial:* e.g. no fixed abode, unemployed, no family ties, 'on-the-run' from the police.
4. *Likelihood of guilt:* e.g. admits the offence, arrested 'red-handed'.
5. *Seriousness of the offence.*
6. *Threats to witnesses.*

94

Table 3.1 shows the frequency with which the different categories were put forward by the police. In more than two thirds of all cases (three quarters of the urban cases) the police opposed bail on the grounds that if the defendant was released he might impede their further inquiries; in more than half of the cases the police indicated that the accused had a previous criminal record and might commit further offences, if released on bail; in more than four out of ten of all cases (almost two thirds of the rural cases), bail was opposed on the grounds that the defendant might abscond before trial; other important reasons included the *prima facie* likelihood of the defendant's guilt (31 per cent) and the seriousness of the offence (24 per cent).

TABLE 3.1: *Police objections to bail: proportion of cases in which different reasons were put forward; English urban and rural courts, 1965–6.*

Category of reason	Total % (n = 67)	Urban courts, 1965 % (n = 50)	Rural courts, 1966 % (n = 17)
1. Police inquiries	67	76	41
2. Criminal record	55	54	59
3. Non-appearance at trial	42	34	65
4. Likelihood of guilt	31	38	12
5. Seriousness of offence	24	26	18
6. Threats to witnesses	12	16	—

The research carried out by the Cobden Trust in 1970–1, involved a national survey of 1,000 remand cases from six large cities in England; no rural areas or small communities were included in this particular survey, and, in fact, more than half of the cases in this analysis of police opposition to bail were drawn from magistrates' courts in London. Table 3.2 shows the reasons for police objections to bail, many of which relate specifically to the discretionary categories set down in s. 18(5) of the Criminal Justice Act, 1967.

Traditionally, in both England and America, the main (if not exclusive) legal justification for keeping an untried defendant in

95

TABLE 3.2: *Reasons for police objections to bail: Cobden Trust Survey, 1970–1.*

Reasons	No. of times mentioned (total no. of cases = 247)
Previous convictions	95
No fixed abode	77
Offence punishable by more than 6 months' prison, and accused previously sentenced to prison or borstal	64
Further inquiries to be made	64
Likely to commit another offence, unless remanded in custody	38
Offences involving violence, firearms, indecency etc.	27
Previously failed to comply with conditions of bail	23
Might abscond	23
May interfere with witnesses	17
Offence allegedly committed on bail	14
Remand in custody for medical report	12
Unemployed	9
To establish identity or address	9
Normally resident outside Britain	9
Necessary for own protection	8
Cannot find surety	7
Other reasons	6

Source: M. King *Bail or Custody* London (1971), Figure 5, p. 19.

custody has been the likelihood of his absconding and so not appearing to face his trial.[32] Nevertheless, observation in English courts shows that several other reasons are put forward by the police opposing bail *more frequently* than the claim that a particular defendant might abscond before trial. It would seem an artificial distortion of the situation to argue, as some lawyers have done, that most of the reasons for the refusal of bail are *indirectly* related to appearance at trial; this leads to greater obfuscation of the issues involved. In the author's experience, which is supported by the statistical evidence of these studies, a major concern of the police in the pre-trial handling of arrested suspects centres round their perception of the broader police tasks of crime detection and crime prevention; according to this perception, when a person has been arrested on suspicion of having committed an offence, the police feel that it is their job to keep him in custody before trial if this helps to protect the community from the risk of further crimes, and enables the police to complete their inquiries as quickly and efficiently as possible; they would also probably argue that a man's criminal record, particularly if he has served a previous custodial sentence, is a good guide to his propensities in this direction, and that the nature and seriousness of the alleged crime is an important element in weighing the various considerations in the balance. Such a portrayal of police attitudes and involvement in the bail decision naturally raises many controversial issues, such as the validity of 'preventive detention' before trial, but many of the common police objections to bail seem to square better with some such picture than with the usual arguments focusing on the risk of non-appearance at trial.[33] Despite the fact that the legislators of the Criminal Justice Act, 1967, failed to make any general statement of principle, it is difficult to see how some of the Act's criteria can be understood except as signifying support for the need to decide the question of bail by having due regard for the degree of risk to the community if the person is released on bail, e.g. 'where ... it appears to the court that he has been previously sentenced to imprisonment or borstal training' (s. 18(5)a), 'where the act ... consisted of an assault on or threat of violence to another person ... or of indecent conduct with or towards a person under the age of sixteen years' (s. 18(5) f), 'where it appears to the court that unless he is remanded or committed in custody he is likely to commit an offence' (s. 18(5) g). These kinds of considerations are very different from simply being concerned to ensure the defendant's appearance at his trial, but they are very similar to typical considerations at the time of *sentencing* a convicted offender, and thereby derive more from an implicit 'assumption of the guilt' of the accused than the traditionally expected 'presumption of innocence' before trial.

Just as certain elements of the bail decision have been found to confirm the earlier criticism that sentencing criteria seem to influence the issue of *pre-trial* custody, being mediated through police attitudes and legislative provisions, so it is clear that the application of the traditional criteria of non-appearance at trial might result in many people being remanded in custody to ensure their trial, who might not be subsequently given a custodial sentence. Whatever philosophy of punishment, treatment or deterrence, is held by a society, it is perfectly

97

possible for pre-trial custody to be defended on the grounds that it is important for 'justice' to be handed out to those convicted offenders, who might need the 'treatment' of a probation order, or the 'punishment' of a large fine, or some form of non-custodial 'exemplary' sanction, without drawing up an oversimplified equation in which only post-trial custody 'deserves' pre-trial custody.

Having said this, however, it is difficult to avoid the provisional conclusion that a defendant's chance of being granted bail by magistrates seems to be much more affected by the nature and seriousness of his crime, the nature and extent of police inquiries surrounding the crime, and his own previous criminal record, than by the question of whether or not he will appear to stand his trial at the adjourned hearing. Investigations have consistently found that persons refused bail have many more features in their criminal and social background which put them at a cumulative disadvantage, compared to persons who are granted bail, e.g. with respect to criminal record, previous sentences, employment, family situation, etc.;[34] it is this complex combination of personal and social characteristics which ultimately renders it an almost impossible task to disentangle definite causal links, not only between bail and sentencing decisions, but at practically every stage of the penal process.

Information in decision-making

The 'quality' of decision-making in most social contexts is directly related to the amount of *relevant* information which is available to the decision-makers at the time when they are making or about to make their decisions; in the particular context of decisions in the penal process there are relatively few occasions when really adequate and relevant information is available to those who have to make vital decisions which affect the personal and social lives of many members of society. Fortunately there seems to be a growing awareness of this deficiency in the more 'formal' stages of decision-making in the penal process, such as sentencing and parole decisions, but there is a relative neglect of the perhaps greater inadequacies of information at the pre-trial stage.

The amount and nature of the information about a defendant and his alleged offence, which is available to magistrates deciding whether or not to grant bail before trial, has been studied in English courts by Bottomley, King (for the Cobden Trust) and Zander. Bottomley found that the main factors influencing the provision of information in bail decisions were whether or not the police opposed bail, and, if they did, whether or not the defendant asked for bail. In the urban and rural courts studied, there was a group of 77 remand cases (45 per cent of the total observed) in which there were no police objections to bail: in 32 of these cases, no information at all was provided for the magistrates, and in the remaining 45 cases there was usually only the details of arrest or a brief statement about the alleged offence from the Prosecuting Solicitor or Police Inspector. Only 12 of the 77 cases included any details about the defendant's 'community ties',* and in the majority of these it was usually just a single item of information about his job or family; thus it would appear that when the police did not object to bail, the magistrates accepted on trust the defendant's reliability as assessed by the police.

A second group of cases in these courts, where there was a serious lack of information, was that of those where the defendant was remanded in custody after having made no application for bail: there were 44 cases in this group (25 per cent of the total), in a third of which no information at all was provided to the court; in the remaining two thirds of this group, details of arrest were given in 16 cases and a brief item about some aspect of the defendant's family or employment in 12 cases, constituting just a quarter of a group whom the magistrates proceeded to remand in custody.

The remaining cases were those where the defendant (with or without legal representation) applied for bail in the face of police objections; this was the only circumstance in which anything approaching adequate information was available to the magistrates, but always inherent in such situations was the 'adversary' element, typical of so much of the English judicial system. In 22 of these cases, the defendant was without legal representation, but some information was

* This is a phrase, used mainly in the American literature on bail, which refers to several aspects of a person's social circumstances (e.g. employment, residence, family) and which forms the basis of the evaluation developed in The Manhattan Bail Project, described below.

available in all but one case; nevertheless, in three quarters of the remaining cases all the information was presented to the court *by the prosecution*, most often by a C.I.D. officer being called to the witness box to testify on oath. Despite the inevitable 'bias' of the procedure, information about the defendant's community ties was available in as many as half these cases. The final group was the 26 cases in which the defendant was represented by a solicitor, who applied for bail on his behalf; only in these cases was comprehensive information available, and more balanced by the fact that much of it was presented by the defence rather than by the prosecution. Particularly significant was the fact that in *all* these cases there was some information about the defendant's community ties, virtually all of which was provided by the defendant's solicitor. For the purposes of comparison and easy reference, Table 3.3 presents details of the extent and nature of the information provided for the magistrates, in the three types of cases in which the police opposed bail, viz. (i) no application for bail by the defendant, (ii) defendant applied for bail, without legal representation, (iii) solicitor applied for bail, on behalf of the defendant.

TABLE 3.3: *Information provided for magistrates, in remand cases with police objections to bail, according to different circumstances.*

Nature of information	No application for bail by defendant		Defendant applied for bail. without legal representation		Solicitor applied for bail, on behalf of the defendant	
	%	No.	%	No.	%	No.
No information	34	(15)	5	(1)	—	—
Details of arrest and/or offence	59	(26)	86	(19)	100	(26)
Admits offence	18	(8)	18	(4)	19	(5)
Criminal record	9	(4)	59	(13)	73	(19)
Police inquiries	—	—	68	(15)	58	(15)
Serious offence	—	—	18	(4)	39	(10)
Threats to witnesses	—	—	5	(1)	31	(8)
Community ties	27	(12)	50	(11)	100	(26)
Sureties available	—	—	—	—	62	(16)
Denies offence	—	—	—	—	23	(6)
Total No. of cases		(44)		(22)		(26)

In the national survey carried out by the Cobden Trust, in 1970–1, an 'information points score' was calculated for each case: all information given to the court was recorded under six headings—(i) Job, (ii) Family, (iii) Home, (iv) Prior. convictions, (v) Medical history, (vi) Other. Items under each heading were coded according to a three-point scale, viz. no information—0 points; very little information—1 point; some information—2 points, so that the maximum score possible for any case was 12 points. In this way, numerous comparisons could be made between the amounts of information available in different kinds of cases and circumstances.[35] In well over half the 1,000 bail decisions in the survey, *no* information at all was available to the court; and confirmation was provided for Bottomley's findings, in that '... 138 defendants were remanded in custody without any details about them being given to the court, except the offence with which they were charged'.[36] In general, rather more information was available in those cases where bail was refused, but as has already been noted, most of this information would come from the police, with the purpose of objecting to the granting of bail. When the cases were analysed according to the 'community ties' points score, from the first three categories only, viz. job, home and family, no information of this kind was available in two thirds of all cases, and in only 6 per cent of cases did the 'community ties' score exceed three points. The authors concluded that by far the most influential factor in determining the amount of information available was whether or not the police had opposed bail:

Almost twice as much information was given when the police raised objections to bail compared to those cases where they did not oppose bail or expressed no view either way.... This result is hardly surprising since the adversary nature of applications for bail means that in the majority of cases where there is no contest between the prosecution and the defence, no information is given. What is surprising is the fact that even where the police did oppose bail, there was no information at all available in 22 per cent of the 247 cases and no information about community ties in 34 per cent. Thus, in these cases the magistrates must have based their bail/custody decisions solely upon the nature of the offence and police objections on such grounds as 'further inquiries' or 'might interfere with witnesses'.[37]

101

Although the Cobden Trust's analysis found no apparent difference in the amount of information available to the court, according to whether or not the defendant was legally represented, this somewhat unexpected finding was almost certainly due to their failure to consider the effect of legal representation *only* in those cases where the police opposed bail, rather than in all cases. Zander carried out a closer analysis of the data from the 17 London magistrates' courts included in the survey, and although he did not isolate the cases of police opposition to bail in this way, he found that the information provided in the legally represented cases was more often of a 'positive' or 'very positive' kind than that provided in cases where the defendant was unrepresented.[38]

These studies of the provision of information in the bail decision-making process raise several important questions. Is there a *need* for more information in all cases, even where the police do not oppose bail or the defendant makes no application for bail? Where more information is required, from what *source* should it come? What kind of information is likely to be most *relevant*? Answers to these three basic questions are progressively more difficult, providing increasing scope for disagreement, both on practical matters and matters of principle; the brief discussion which follows is clearly, therefore, very much a personal view.

The first question, whether magistrates need more information in those cases where either (a) the police have no objections to bail, or (b) the defendant makes no application for bail, raises the important issue of the meaning of magistrates' 'discretion' in bail decisions and their degree of control and initiative in the decision-making process. In the related context of sentencing discretion Hogarth has pointed out that a court's discretion can only be exercised with proper responsibility when adequate information is available:

> Real discretion can only be exercised in full awareness of pertinent information. Decision-making in ignorance of pertinent information is not the exercise of discretion, it is pure speculation.[39]

Statistics show that, where the police do not object to bail, magistrates grant bail in all but 1 or 2 per cent of these cases; as research also shows that very little (if any) information is presented to the court, in

102

support of the police recommendation, it can only be concluded that in these circumstances the magistrates seem quite prepared to accept the police assessment of the defendant. It may well be that the magistrates have found, from past experience, that the judgement of the police can be trusted in this matter, but in open court it looks very much like an evasion of their prime responsibility to exercise their discretion in an independent manner. Perhaps, however, provided that the decision is in *favour* of the defendant's interests it should not be a cause of great concern in practice, despite the important principle at stake; but, on the other hand, when a defendant makes no application for bail in the face of police objections, and the magistrates remand him in custody with very little more information about his background than in the previous group of cases, more serious questions need to be asked about the propriety and justice involved.

Whatever the reasons behind the failure of a large proportion of defendants to ask for bail, whether stemming from a realistic appraisal of their chances of being successful in such an application, or whether from a genuine confusion about court procedure and the exercise of their rights to bail,[40] it seems absolutely imperative for magistrates to take the initiative, not only in satisfying themselves that the defendant knows exactly what is happening in court and of his right to bail, but also, whether or not the defendant chooses to exercise his right to ask for bail, to satisfy themselves that the defendant's background and alleged offence are such as to make bail inappropriate. This principle was emphasized recently by the Howard League for Penal Reform in its proposals to the Home Office Working Party on Bail in Magistrates' Courts, in which it recommended that 'the onus of applying for bail should not be upon the defendant, but that the court should normally grant it, unless there are exceptional circumstances'.[41]

If it is accepted, in principle, that more information ought to be provided for the assistance of magistrates in making their decisions about bail and remands in custody, the next practical question is from what *source* should such information come. In the light of the fact that the provision of information at the moment directly reflects the 'adversary' element of English court proceedings, with the vast majority of it coming from the police or prosecuting solicitor (except in the minority of cases where a defendant is legally represented), many critics feel

103

that the potential bias ought to be overcome by some arrangement whereby an 'independent' agent collects and presents standardized information to the court on all remand cases. In America, the Manhattan Bail Project pioneered a similar scheme for bail decisions, in which all defendants were interviewed by law students before appearing in court, who subsequently presented a summary of the relevant information to the court, including the defendant's previous criminal record, family ties, employment, residence in area etc.[42] It is unlikely that law students could provide a viable basis for any permanent scheme in most English courts, but in the hundred or more jurisdictions in the United States that have developed bail projects modelled on the Manhattan scheme, the collection and presentation of information to the court has been shared between probation officers, law students, volunteers and police authorities. In England the most practical suggestion, which would not compromise the principle of an 'independent' source by requiring the police to provide regular information in every case on an official court 'pro forma' sheet, would involve either court staff with legal training from the Clerk to the Justices' office or a 'duty solicitor', whose introduction (following the example of Scotland) has been recently proposed by a report from *Justice,* mainly to increase legal representation of defendants in magistrates' courts.[43] It is hoped that the Home Office Working Party on Bail might make some proposal for the introduction of a pilot scheme to test the feasibility of these alternative arrangements.

The final most basic and controversial question is what kind of information is likely to be most *relevant* in the context of the typical criteria used in bail decisions. The information about 'community ties' used in the Manhattan Bail Project has been criticized in England for its omission of items probably more relevant in many cases.[44] Our earlier discussion of the criteria used in English courts reached the tentative conclusion that the principle of 'preventive detention' seemed to underlie many bail decisions, relying on such factors as the nature and seriousness of the offence, the defendant's criminal record, and the police inquiries surrounding the alleged offence; conversely, the issue of non-appearance at trial (for which 'community ties' information would be relevant) was probably less often the overriding criterion. Clearly, an authoritative ruling would have to be made about the validity of the various principles underlying bail decisions, before it

104

was possible to decide what items of information would be relevant and necessary for the courts. A simple reiteration of the exclusive principle of the risk of non-appearance at trial might seem to solve the problem of what kind of information needs to be presented to the court, but unless this principle represents a realistic reflection of judicial and magisterial opinion (not to mention the wider views of the community) it would merely perpetuate the confusion that at present exists, invalidating much information that would be provided, and almost certainly resulting in little change in the unsatisfactory relationship between the police and the courts in bail decisions.[45]

THE DECISION TO PLEAD GUILTY

Perhaps the most important decision in the penal process is that which results in the *conviction* of persons who have been charged with criminal offences; this is the culmination and focus of the earlier processes of law enforcement and social action against suspected offenders, as once a person has been convicted, he becomes subject to the official and unofficial sanctions of society, as reflected by the sentencing authority of the courts and the social stigma attached to the label of 'criminal'. In view of the obvious importance of this stage in the process, it is easy to understand public interest in the 'trial' process, reflected and encouraged by the treatment given in the mass media to this aspect of crime, both of a fictional and non-fictional kind. The popular image tends to emphasize the power and vagaries of judges and juries, in deciding the fate of persons facing criminal charges, thereby seeming to locate the crucial decision firmly in their hands. In practice, however, the 'decision' which results in a criminal conviction is neither so simple nor quite so arbitrary (at least not in the same way) as the popular image would have us believe; the vast majority of convictions are not the result of any form of trial in open court, but are the result of *pleas of guilty* by defendants, and therefore it is the manner in which these guilty pleas are 'decided' upon by the defendant in the pre-trial stages that ought to be seen as the single most important aspect of decision-making in the penal process, although typically one of the most under-researched and complex of all.

In England, there have been no national surveys of the proportion of defendants who plead guilty in cases tried by magistrates' courts. Informed estimates and small research studies indicate that the proportion of guilty pleas is probably anywhere from three quarters to well over 90 per cent. There is rather more information available about the proportion of indictable offenders who plead guilty at *higher courts* in England and Wales, but even this is not found in any officially published statistics on a regular basis, but rather derives from special studies of different aspects of procedure in the higher courts. In the course of its study of the time spent awaiting trial, the Home Office Research Unit found that 75 per cent of all persons committed for trial in 1956 pleaded guilty, with considerable variations not only between different offences, but also between courts in different areas of the country; thus, in the London area, the proportions pleading guilty at the Central Criminal Court and the London and Middlesex Sessions were 48 and 62 per cent, respectively, well below the national average; and whereas more than 96 per cent of the persons charged with burglary pleaded guilty, less than half those charged with felonious and malicious wounding did so, and only 25 per cent of those facing charges of indecent assault against girls under the age of 16.[46] Ten years later the Association of Chief Police Officers of England and Wales, concerned about the outcome of jury trials, carried out a detailed analysis of all persons committed for trial to higher courts in England and Wales, during 1965, by individual police forces and according to five main offence groups: of the 21,645 persons committed for trial in that year, 64 per cent (13,880) pleaded guilty, varying from less than 50 per cent in the London M.P.D. and around 60 per cent in Liverpool and Leeds, to 73 and 86 per cent in Birmingham and Coventry, respectively; in the different offence groups the variation was from 45 per cent of offenders facing charges of theft to 80 per cent of those charged with breaking and entering offences.[47]

In the United States, where there is not quite the same division between lower and higher courts, most of the available statistics show that approximately 90 per cent of all defendants plead guilty before trial. In Newman's important early interview study of 97 men convicted of felonies in a mid-west county, he found that 94 per cent had pleaded guilty at their trial;[48] similarly, Blumberg found that over a

15-year period, 1950–64, the proportion of defendants pleading guilty in Metropolitan Court remained constantly over 90 per cent, varying from 91 per cent to 95 per cent.[49] Table 3.4 shows the guilty plea statistics collected for the President's Commission, in which the average proportion of guilty pleas in those states where information was available was 87 per cent.

TABLE 3.4: *Guilty plea 'convictions' in trial courts of general jurisdiction, in states for which such information was available.*

State (statistics are for 1964, unless otherwise stated)	Total convictions	Guilty pleas	
		No.	% of total
California (1965)	30,840	22,817	74.0
Connecticut	1,596	1,494	93.9
District of Columbia	1,115	817	73.3
Hawaii	393	360	91.5
Illinois	5,591	4,768	85.2
Kansas	3,025	2,727	90.2
Massachusetts (1963)	7,790	6,642	85.2
Minnesota (1965)	1,567	1,437	91.7
New York	17,249	16,464	95.5
Pennsylvania (1960)	25,632	17,108	66.8
U.S. District Courts	29,170	26,273	90.2
Average (exc. Pennsylvania)			87.0

Source: President's Commission on Law Enforcement and Administration of Justice *Task Force Report: The Courts* Washington, D.C. (1967) p. 9.

Available statistics, therefore, clearly support the view that the emphasis in the study of the 'conviction' process should be as much, if not more, on the pre-trial decision to plead guilty as on the more traditional area of open court trial, by judge and/or jury. The main issues which seem to emerge from studies of guilty pleas are those focused on the relationship between guilty pleas and the needs and pressures inherent in the judicial process, and in the second place, the role of 'plea-bargaining' in relation to the perceived interests of the individual defendant.

107

The starting point, in any discussion of the relationship between guilty pleas and the judicial process, must be recognition of the fact that without such pleas the machinery of justice would quickly find itself unable to cope with its assigned task of processing persons facing criminal charges, so that there are inherent pressures upon all sections of judicial administration and organization to maintain the high level of guilty pleas. The unpredictable outcome of contested trials, before judges and especially juries, not only influences the defendants' choice of plea, but also clearly exerts pressures on the prosecution to settle a case, without the 'risk' of taking it to a jury.[50] In one of the very few empirical studies, shedding some light on aspects of 'plea-bargaining' in England, McCabe and Purves recently summarized these influences upon the prosecution:

> There are very real and practical reasons for the prosecution's desire to seek an acceptable negotiated disposal of a case, and the 90 cases provided clear examples of these reasons. The advantages attendant upon the rapid disposal of cases in the administration of justice are as apparent in England as in America. . . . It is not surprising that the prosecution is in many cases willing to exchange the uncertainties of a contested trial for the assurance of a guilty plea to a lesser charge. . . . Furthermore, the prosecution will generally be especially ready to reach a negotiated disposal of a case where the outcome consequent upon conviction on the more serious charge, or in some cases on all the charges, even if successfully achieved after a fight, would in effect be the same.[51]

It is largely the existence of this complex pattern of needs and pressures on *all* participants in the pre-trial process, viz. defendant, prosecutor, judicial administrator, etc., that has resulted in the development of what the Americans have termed 'plea-bargaining' and 'negotiated justice'. Unfortunately, these concepts have a rather different significance and relevance for the American system of justice than for the English, because of the different structures and judicial traditions obtaining in the two countries, but nevertheless useful lessons can be learned about the English situation from an examination which is necessarily based largely on the American literature.

108

From this point of view, it is important in the initial stages to try to keep as separate as possible the empirical data provided by American criminologists and particular ideological 'models' of the criminal justice system, in support of which this data is often put forward; not only may the interpretations of the link between the two sometimes be questionable, but for comparative purposes neither data nor interpretational 'models' ought to be rejected out of hand simply because of a perceived degree of 'irrelevance' of the one or the other to the English situation.[52]

In America, and to a lesser extent in England, 'plea-bargaining' is directly associated with various kinds of *charge manipulation* and similar procedural devices; thus, in Newman's study, the 'bargains', in return for which the majority of his sample decided to plead guilty, were of four main kinds: (i) *reduced sentence,* e.g. probation instead of imprisonment (45 per cent of sample); (ii) *concurrent sentences/charges* (22 per cent); (iii) *reduced charges* (20 per cent); (iv) *dropped charges* (13 per cent).[53] The common link between all these kinds of bargain is that they are all aimed at and, if successful, result in a reduced sentence for the defendant who pleads guilty on their terms.[54] The important interrelationship, between charge reduction and guilty pleas, is well illustrated by Table 3.5, presenting data from Blumberg's study of felony cases in Kings County, New York (1960–2), and providing dramatic illustration of the 'needs' of the system for guilty pleas and other sifting mechanisms before cases arrive at the final stage of contested trial.

The central role of the decision as to how to plead is shown by the way in which many elements of the process derive from the same basic principles as those affecting the initial police discretion to prosecute and, at the same time, anticipate the principles of individualized justice which are fundamental to the later sentencing decision. Newman has expressed this succinctly:

> The guilty plea process, much more than the trial, encapsulates the steps immediately preceding and following conviction. Both the charging decision and sentencing merge into the conviction decision, particularly in the negotiated plea, so that concerns at this stage are not uniquely those of adjudication, of final guilt or innocence, but are intertwined with the prosecutor's discretion and the sentencing discretion of the trial judge.[55]

109

For this reason, the practice of charge reduction must be understood not only by reference to its pragmatic and 'tactical' elements but also by reference to more fundamental issues of individualized justice and prosecution policy.

TABLE 3.5: *Disposition of adult felony arrests, Kings County, New York: 1960–2.*

Stage of proceeding	No. of cases	Per cent of total	Per cent remaining
1. Preliminary arraignment in a lower criminal court	32.000	100	100
2. Discharged, dismissed on technical or procedural grounds at preliminary arraignment	2.000	6.2	93.8
3. Dismissed on merits (case not proven) at preliminary arraignment	6.000	18.6	75.2
4. Reduced to misdemeanour charge at preliminary arraignment	12.000	37.6	37.6
5. Held for grand jury	12.000	37.6	37.6
6. Dismissed by grand jury	1.000	3.1	34.5
7. Charge reduced by grand jury to a misdemeanour	1.000	3.1	31.4
8. Indicted by grand jury	10.000	31.4	31.4
9. Indictments dismissed for procedural reasons as defective	320	1.0	30.4
10. Indictments dismissed on facts and law of case	640	2.0	28.4
11. Adjudged youthful offender	860	2.6	25.8
12. Pleas before trial to a felony	3.200	10.0	15.8
13. Pleas before trial to a misdemeanour	4.280	13.4	2.4
14. Convicted, after trial, of a felony	350	1.2	1.3
15. Convicted, after trial, of a misdemeanour	50	0.3	1.0
16. Acquitted	300	1.0	0.0

Source: A. S. Blumberg *Criminal Justice* Chicago (1967) Table 4 p. 54.

The pragmatic and tactical elements surrounding the manipulation of charges can be seen in various ways: in the initial stages of charging an arrested offender, the police or prosecution often prefer to make the most serious charge warranted by the *prima facie* facts, to give themselves more 'room for manoeuvre' if this should be necessary subsequently;[56] the decision to reduce the charge may be made because the prosecution realizes that the evidence is probably not sufficient to guarantee a conviction in a contested trial; or, in other cases, charge reduction may be necessitated by the unwillingness of victims or witnesses to testify.[57] In fact, the 'negotiated justice' which results from plea-bargaining can be a much more realistic and 'fair' outcome than might be thought conceivable in a system, such as the English, so often characterized by artificiality and legal gamesmanship. McCabe and Purves expressed this very well, in drawing conclusions from their Oxford study:

> A review of the 90 cases in the present study leaves a firm impression ... that changes of plea are the result of a realistic and practical approach adopted by police, defence and prosecution lawyers, judges and, often, the defendants themselves. ... They are generally disposed of after informal negotiations between lawyers of both sides acting not so as to impress and confound a jury by rhetoric, innuendo, suggestion, intimidation and manipulation of the rules of evidence and procedure, but in order to reach as expeditious and as economical an agreement as possible after an abandonment of pretence, a concentration on practical calculation and an open confrontation with hard facts and real probabilities.[58]

A major difficulty, however, is that this *favourable* evaluation of 'negotiated justice' is almost as subjective as, for example, Blumberg's highly *critical* characterization of the same process (in America), as lacking essential elements of 'due process', and reflecting the 'closed community' features of the judicial bureaucracy.[59] Paradoxically, the only way to test the validity of either interpretation would be to 'open up' the pre-trial negotiations to greater public scrutiny and formalization, in such a way that Blumberg's interpretation would be invalidated *by definition*, and at the same time the nature of any future such negotiations would inevitably be changed beyond recognition,

111

thus making it impossible to prove or disprove the validity of inter-pretations of *previous* practices.

Moving from the pragmatic elements to the 'policy' aspects of charging suspects with particular offences, we find much the same concern for 'individualized' justice as is to be found in studying the exercise of police discretion, and in the more formal sentencing decisions of magistrates and judges. In Newman's major study of the pre-trial 'conviction' process, he indicated five main factors influencing charge reduction, and relating to the characteristics of the offender or the circumstances of the offence: (i) age or inexperience of the offender, (ii) 'respectability' of defendant, (iii) disreputable status of victim, (iv) low mentality of defendant, (v) conduct regarded as sub-culturally 'normal'.[60] The President's Commission on Law Enforce-ment and Administration of Justice, Task Force Report on The Courts, supported the flexibility and individualization imparted to the penal process by the pre-trial negotiations in such an enthusiastic fashion that all the usual pejorative connotations of 'plea-bargaining' seemed far from their thoughts:

> The flexibility and informality of these discretionary procedures make them more readily adaptable to efforts to individualize the treatment of offenders than the relatively rigid procedures that now typify trial, conviction and sentence. . . . Moreover, by placing less emphasis on the issue of culpability, discretionary procedures may enable the prosecutor to give greater attention to what disposition is most likely to fit the needs of those whose cases he considers. The pressures on the prosecutor to insist on a disposition that fits the popular conception of punishment are less before conviction, when the defendant has not officially and publicly been found guilty.[61]

The converse aspect of the charge reduction process is that, just as charges may be reduced or dropped because of the prosecution's desire to 'individualize' the effects of the law enforcement process against certain offenders, so may the prosecution decide to press cer-tain charges through to the contested trial stage for reasons of 'policy'. Thus Sudnow showed how, on the one hand, the prosecutor is con-cerned wherever possible to obtain a guilty plea, so long as the defen-dant 'receives his due' in terms of the anticipated sentence, but, on the

112

other hand, in cases which arouse public attention and raise important policy issues it is felt more appropriate to bring the defendants to trial in open court:

> The privacy of the P.D.–D.A. conviction machinery through the use of the guilty plea can no longer be preserved. Only 'normal defendants' are accorded this privacy. The pressure for a public hearing, in the sense of 'bringing the public in to see and monitor the character of the proceedings', must be allowed to culminate in a full blown jury trial.[62]

In England, McCabe and Purves (1972) have shown how the complexity of the police function, and the need they feel to implement social and peace-keeping policies, results in them pursuing certain 'policy prosecutions' for other aims than the prospect of conviction; examples included 'deterrent' prosecutions of shoplifters and motoring offenders, or behaviour particularly prevalent in a locality.[63] Clearly such prosecutions are unlikely to result in any form of acceptable pre-trial negotiated solution, although in the Oxford survey many featured in the group of cases which resulted in 'directed acquittals' by the judge.

Inasmuch as one of the main aims of plea-bargaining from the defendant's point of view, is to obtain a reduced sentence, it is important to recognize the crucial role played in the plea-bargaining process by the sentencing structure which obtains in particular jurisdictions. This is perhaps the most significant factor which distinguishes the situation in England from that in America,[64] and even in America there are important differences between states. In England, only one offence, that of murder, carries a mandatory sentence (viz. life imprisonment), so that the judiciary have a degree of discretion and flexibility in sentencing which makes any bargaining between the prosecution and the defence, about sentence, an entirely unpredictable and largely redundant procedure, compared to the situation in America where many offences carry mandatory sentences. Newman found there were significant differences in this respect among the states he studied: the larger proportion of 'on-the-nose' pleas (i.e. guilty pleas to the charges as they stood) in Wisconsin, was explicable by the fact that Wisconsin law allowed great discretion to the court to fix the sentence for almost all offences, whereas in Michigan and Kansas the greater number of negotiated pleas of guilty to reduced charges was explicable by the fact that their legislatures set fixed sentences for most offences. In the light of these differences in the sentencing structure of different states, he concluded that the significance of charge reduction *per se* needed careful examination in its total context:

> The negotiated plea and the on-the-nose plea cannot be so neatly separated. They are both variations of a single process, occurring because sentencing provisions for similar conduct differ from one state to another and because trial judges, desiring equity in sentencing, will achieve it by manipulating conviction labels if this is the only way it can be done.[65]

The same cautionary warning needs to be given to those tempted to draw comparisons too readily between America and England, in the matter of plea-bargaining and the nature and purposes of 'negotiated justice'; not only is the sentencing structure of the two countries very different, but, related to this, the traditional role of the judge in pre-trial negotiations is very different. In America, because a large proportion of plea-bargains are based on the promise of particular *sentencing recommendations* to be made by the prosecutor, it is clear that the judge may easily become involved in the negotiating process, in order to increase the likelihood of particular recommendations being accepted, as was admitted by the President's Commission, whose main report stated that 'in some cases there is a tacit or explicit agreement by the judge to bargain, and in extreme cases the judge may participate in its negotiation'.[66]

In England, on the other hand, not only is there apparently less 'need' for plea-bargaining (in the American sense), for some of the reasons that have already been mentioned, but any part that the judge might have played in pre-trial negotiation has been officially curtailed by principles laid down by the Court of Appeal in *R.* v. *Turner*.[67] In this case, the general principle allowing freedom of access between counsel and judge was reiterated, although both counsel for the defence and for the prosecution must be present at any such discussion with the judge; more importantly, the judge should never indicate the sentence he has in mind to impose, according to whether the accused pleads guilty or not guilty. The judge in England, as in America,

114

has a responsibility to satisfy himself as to the appropriateness of any guilty plea from a defendant, and his is the ultimate decision as to whether to accept reduced charges; the main principle that should operate in these circumstances is that, for the charge to be accepted by the judge, it should bear a very close relationship indeed to the actual behaviour of the accused, rather than merely being a 'tactical' device to ensure the smooth running of the judicial machinery.[68]

From the discussion so far, it should be clear that guilty pleas are extremely functional for the working of any criminal justice system; but, for a fully rounded picture of the process which culminates in such a large number of defendants pleading guilty—often to very serious criminal charges—it is also necessary to consider the process from the point of view of the individual defendants themselves, to see to what extent they appear to control or 'yield' to the processes of negotiated justice before trial.

'Bargain justice' and the individual

A few surveys of defendants have been reported, in which attempts have been made to discover their main reasons for pleading guilty and their attitudes towards the pre-trial negotiation process. The main findings of these surveys will be summarized, as they provide a basis for discussing the individual defendant's perspective on 'negotiated justice'.

In his early survey of 97 men convicted of felonies in an American mid-west county, Newman found that 94 per cent had pleaded guilty, although as many as 38 per cent had originally entered a plea of not guilty.[69] Amongst those who had pleaded guilty, almost two thirds (64 per cent) received a *less severe* sentence than they had expected, with less than a quarter (23 per cent) receiving a more severe one than expected; 47 per cent were not legally represented, and the main reasons why they said they had not bothered seeking legal advice were because they had made a deal for reduced/dropped charges or a lighter/concurrent sentence (54 per cent), or because they were 'obviously guilty' and hoped for leniency from the court (20 per cent).[70] Newman drew attention to the fact that the majority of those who had bargained for a guilty plea were experienced recidivists:

115

The recidivists were both conviction wise and conviction suscepti-
ble in the dual sense that they knew of the possibility of bargaining
a guilty plea for a light sentence and at the same time were
vulnerable, because of their records, to threats of the prosecutor to
'throw the book' at them unless they confessed. Over half (54.3 per
cent) of the men claimed they had bargained for their sentences and
84 per cent of these men had been convicted previously.

The experience of such men enabled them to 'recognize a good
bargain when they saw one', as they kept themselves well informed of
the usual rate of sentence for their offences, and at the same time they
felt that a guilty plea might antagonize judge and jury, particularly
when their previous records were disclosed.

Blumberg analysed the attitudes and responses of more than 700
defendants, who had pleaded guilty, over a three-year period 1962–4,
in a large metropolitan court (see Table 3.6). More than half this sample (51 per cent) claimed 'innocence' in some way and with varying

TABLE 3.6: *Defendants' responses as to guilt or innocence after pleading,
Metropolitan Court, 1962–4.*

Nature of response		No. of defendants	%
Innocent (Manipulated)	'The lawyer or judge, police or D.A. "conned" me'	86	11.9
Innocent (Pragmatic)	'Wanted to get it over with', or 'You can't beat the system', or 'They have you over a barrel when you have a record'	147	20.3
Innocent (Advice of counsel)	'Followed my lawyer's advice'	92	12.7
Innocent (Defiant)	'Framed'—betrayed by complainant, police, squealers, lawyer, friends, wife, girl-friend	33	4.6
Innocent (Adverse social data)	Blames probation officer or psychiatrist for 'bad report' in cases where there was pre-pleading investiga-tion	15	2.1
Guilty	'But I should have gotten a better deal.' Blames lawyer, judge, D.A., police	74	10.2
Guilty	Won't say anything further	21	2.9
Fatalistic (Doesn't press his 'innocence', won't admit guilt)	'I did it for convenience'. 'My lawyer told me it was the only thing I could do'. 'I did it because it was the best way out'	248	34.2
(No response)		(8)	(1.1)
Total		724	100.0

Source: A. S. Blumberg *Criminal Justice* Chicago (1967) Table 5, p. 90.

116

degrees of credibility; the most common attitude among the 'innocents' was the pragmatic approach of defendants claiming that e.g. 'I wanted to get it over with', or 'you can't beat the system'. However, by far the largest single group in the sample, more than one third of those pleading guilty, were those who adopted a 'fatalistic' approach, neither protesting innocence nor admitting guilt. An interesting finding by Blumberg was that more than half the group (57 per cent) claimed that their own defence lawyer was the biggest influence upon their decision to plead guilty, in contrast to a popular assumption that most guilty pleas are the result of pressure to confess from the police or prosecutor.[71]

In England, there have been two recent studies which shed some light on the attitudes and motives of those who plead guilty, although both were part of research studies which cannot be regarded as necessarily representative of all defendants appearing in English courts. Susanne Dell carried out a sample survey of 638 women received into Holloway Prison during 1967; 76 per cent of those tried in magistrates' courts had pleaded guilty, compared to 46 per cent of those tried in higher courts.[72] Apart from the fact that only 13 per cent of those pleading guilty at magistrates courts had legal advice (compared to 45 per cent of those pleading *not guilty* in these courts, and four fifths of *all* persons at higher courts), the main finding of this Holloway survey was the large number of women who pleaded guilty at magistrates' courts but who denied on interview that they had committed an offence; the fact that this 'denial of guilt' was very rare at the higher courts seems to confirm the vital importance of legal representation in this respect. There were 128 women who denied their guilt, either absolutely or on essential elements of their legal or moral 'guilt'; more than 60 per cent were not legally represented at any stage. Dell made a closer study of a sub-group of 56 women who pleaded guilty at magistrates' courts and yet, when interviewed, denied all guilt whatsoever; she called this group 'inconsistent pleaders'. Seventeen of the group (31 per cent) said they pleaded guilty in response to police advice or pressure; 8 (14 per cent) said there was no point in contesting the case, when it was only 'my word against the police'; 5 (9 per cent) said they wanted to avoid remands, and a further 5 said they thought that a plea of not guilty would result in a harsher sentence.[73] Fourteen of the 'inconsistent pleaders' were first offenders, and as many as 9 of these (64 per cent) gave police advice or pressure as their reason for pleading guilty; it is worth quoting Dell's comments on the nature and extent of this 'police advice':

> Some of them said that the police had threatened that they would be 'sent down' if they pleaded not guilty. . . . Several girls said they had been advised to plead guilty in a kindly, even fatherly spirit, the policemen telling them that this was the simplest way to get the case over, and to avoid the risk of publicity, or remands in custody. It was easy to see how those without experience of police stations or courts might gratefully accept such advice and it was significant that while only 9 per cent of inconsistent recidivists gave police advice as their reason for pleading guilty, 64 per cent of the inconsistent first offenders said they had done so in response to police persuasion.[74]

As in most of these studies, the decision to plead guilty was often seen by the defendant as the most 'expedient' course of action, with many of the women believing such a plea to be a 'lesser evil' than the others she feels threatened by, and in this context the importance of having legal advice before pleading emerged again and again as paramount.

In their Oxford study, McCabe and Purves selected a sample of 475 defendants who had originally indicated their intention to plead not guilty and go for trial before a jury; however, a total of 170 (36 per cent) never reached the final stage of jury trial.[75] One hundred and twelve defendants subsequently changed their plea to one of guilty, and 58 were acquitted on the direction of the judge; of the 112 'last-minute pleaders', 48 (43 per cent) pleaded guilty to the whole indictment as it stood, and 64 (57 per cent) to lesser charges. This by-product of a study of contested trials provided some interesting insight into the process of pleading guilty, confirming that most parties to the process, including the defendant, adopted a very practical approach:

> The bargain which was struck appeared either realistic or practical having regard to the nature and quality of the evidence, the triviality of the crime, the task of proving it before a jury, the tenor of the social enquiry report, and the consequences of sentencing procedures. In all of these cases the bargain was approved by the judge himself in full appreciation of the available evidence and

118

generally with the significant comment that the arrangement 'would represent the likely outcome of the matter' had the defendant contested the case.[76]

The researchers concluded that in the majority of the 90 cases, where there were pleas of guilty, the defendant himself was able to calculate the issues involved with almost as much precision as his lawyers; 79 per cent of these 'last-minute pleaders' had previous convictions and thus their previous knowledge of the police and courts would enable them to assess the strength of their bargaining position and the likely outcome of a contested or uncontested case.

To what extent are the implicit or explicit expectations of defendants who plead guilty, as revealed by these American and English studies, fulfilled in practice as regards the practical consequences of a plea of guilty? Certainly, an early plea of guilty to an indictable charge is likely to shorten the time spent being remanded while awaiting trial; to this extent, there would seem to be an immediate advantage for a defendant who pleads guilty, whether or not following any police advice to this effect. There seems to be somewhat inconclusive evidence about whether there are generally more guilty pleas in those types of cases which have a low acquittal rate; Kalven and Zeisel presented data which they felt supported the claim that 'the defendant's decision to plead guilty is to some extent affected by the odds of being acquitted in case he chooses to go to trial'[77] (see Table 3.7). However, the Home Office Research Unit's data for 1956 showed no such consistent relationship between guilty pleas and acquittal rate, either according to courts or according to offences; for example, the London courts with lower than average proportions of guilty pleas also had lower than average acquittal rates.[78] The national survey carried out by the Association of Chief Police Officers of England and Wales in 1965, did not find as much variation in the acquittal rates of the different offence groups as in the proportions of persons pleading guilty, but, at the opposite end of the scale, 'larcenies' had the lowest proportion of guilty pleas (45 per cent) and the highest proportion of acquittals (47 per cent), whereas 'breaking and entering' offences had the highest proportion of guilty pleas (80 per cent) and the lowest proportion of acquittals (30 per cent), giving some degree of support to Kalven and Zeisel's hypothesis.[79]

119

TABLE 3.7: *Guilty pleas and acquittal ratio for major crimes: U.S. Bureau of the Census, judicial criminal statistics, 1945.*

Crime	Proportion of guilty pleas		Trial acquittal ratio	
	%	Rank	%	Rank
Murder	34	1	31	7
Manslaughter	52	2	46	14
Aggravated assault	56	3=	37	12
Commercial vice	56	3=	27	4=
Rape	62	5=	34	10
Robbery	62	5=	31	7
Stolen property	63	7	31	7
Carrying weapons	71	8	38	13
Other sex offences	73	9	36	11
Drug law violations	74	10	27	4=
Embezzlement, fraud	80	11=	51	15
Larceny	80	11=	33	9
Burglary	82	13	22	2
Auto theft	89	14	23	3
Forgery	90	15	14	1

Source: H. Kalven and H. Zeisel *The American Jury* Boston (1966) Table 2, p. 20.

The main expectation held out to defendants who plead guilty is that, whether or not an explicit 'bargain' has been made to this effect, they are likely to receive a more lenient sentence by pleading guilty than by contesting the case. It has been seen that in Newman's sample almost two thirds had their expectations more than fulfilled in this respect, with less than a quarter receiving a somewhat heavier sentence than they had expected. A survey of federal district judges in America, carried out by the *Yale Law Journal* showed that two thirds of the 140 judges who completed the questionnaire (out of 240 mailed), considered that a defendant's plea was a relevant factor in sentencing, of whom as many as 87 per cent indicated their belief that a defendant pleading guilty would receive a more lenient sentence than one pleading not guilty, with estimates of the likely reduction in a fine or prison term varying from 10 per cent to 95 per cent.[80] The authors

120

also pointed out the dual advantage likely to be gained by a defendant who not only pleaded guilty but also had initial charges reduced or dropped by the prosecution (without the knowledge of the sentencing judge) as part of the plea-bargain.

In England, a closer re-examination of some statistics provided in the Home Office Research Unit's study shows that although there was no consistent relationship between the proportions pleading guilty and those acquitted after a plea of not guilty, yet there was a significant relationship between the proportions *detained* following a plea of guilty and those detained following conviction on a plea of not guilty, such that in practically every offence higher proportions were detained following *not guilty pleas* than pleas of guilty (Table 3.8).

TABLE 3.8: *Proportions detained following guilty pleas and convictions on not guilty pleas at higher courts in England, 1956, by offence.*

		Proportions detained following:	
Offence	Guilty pleas as % of total cases	(a) Guilty pleas %	(b) Found guilty on not guilty pleas %
Burglary	96	50	—
Housebreaking	88	60	84
Felonious wounding	46	78	100
Malicious wounding	49	44	52
Indecency between males	85	19	50
Indecent assault:			
(a) female over 16	77	23	100
(b) female under 16	25	11	22
Unlawful intercourse:			
(a) female under 13	90	100	100
(b) female aged 13–16:			
accused over 24	93	59	—
accused under 24	67	14	0

Source: derived from E. Gibson *Time Spent Awaiting Trial* London (1960) Table in Appendix C. p. 44.

121

The position in English law, concerning the effect of a defendant's plea on his sentence, has been examined by D. A. Thomas.[81] A guilty plea can properly be regarded as a mitigating factor, signifying remorse on the part of the defendant;[82] but it is improper for anything to be added to a man's sentence, because he has chosen to plead not guilty, so that the Court of Appeal has reduced the sentences in several cases where it appeared that the trial judge had given a more severe sentence because the defendant had contested a case.[83] The official position can be illustrated from the case of *Howard Temple and Jeeves* (1.12.66, 2674/66), where it was stated:

> It is of course wrong that anything should be added to a sentence by virtue of the fact that an accused person has pleaded not guilty. Credit can be given when a person does plead guilty to the fact that that person is facing up to realities and shows some sign of repentence and that may justify a reduction from what would otherwise have been the sentence.

The distinction, which is drawn between a guilty plea being a 'mitigating' factor and a not guilty plea not properly permitting any 'addition' to a sentence, may satisfy the niceties of legal and judicial minds but, in reality, the effects upon the convicted defendant cannot be denied; in other words, it is quite proper in certain circumstances for the sentence following a guilty plea to be less than that following a not guilty plea. It is understandable therefore, that a defendant's belief in this will often be a major influence in his decision to plead guilty, with a good chance that his confidence in his expectations will be well placed, having nothing to lose but much to gain.

Perhaps the most disturbing aspect of the entire process of plea-bargaining and 'negotiated justice', especially from the individual defendant's point of view, is the evidence that recidivists seem to be at a considerable advantage in the pre-trial process, with their experience of the workings of the judicial system enabling them to obtain the best possible outcome for themselves. The vast majority of defendants involved in specific plea-bargaining have previous criminal records, whereas more defendants with clean records may be 'persuaded' to put in 'on-the-nose' pleas, or run the uncertain risks of jury trial, without the subsequent advantage, if convicted, of having pleaded guilty (as a sign of remorse?). Newman has always been aware of this paradox: 'The way bargaining now works, the more experienced criminals can manipulate legal processes to obtain light sentences and better official records while the less experienced occasional offenders receive more harsh treatment.'[84] The very real risk of the innocent and the less criminally sophisticated coming off worse in the secret negotiations before trial confirms Blumberg's criticisms of the hidden quality of the justice of the 'closed door community':

> Secrecy creates possibilities and opportunities fraught with the danger of venal and dishonest release of defendants on the pretext of 'bargaining'. And there is the distinct possibility that dangerous individuals may receive inadequate punishment because of the bargaining system. Conversely, the gullible, unsophisticated defendant, who may be innocent, can be victimised through the manipulation of organisational pressures.[85]

However, at the end of their study of defendants who pleaded guilty, McCabe and Purves concluded that the possibility of an *innocent* defendant being induced by external pressures to plead guilty was no greater than the possibility of his being found guilty before a jury. They felt that the practice of plea-bargaining, at least as it exists in England, provides the defendant with the opportunity to confess 'under conditions of tactical advantage calculated to secure the best possible terms'.[86] Whatever personal conclusions may be drawn from these rather different opinions about the risk of 'innocent' persons pleading guilty, it is imperative to minimize whatever risk exists, either by opening up pre-trial negotiations to greater official scrutiny and control, or by extending the provision of legal aid and advice to all defendants at the very earliest stage in the process, before their first appearance in court when crucial decisions are taken both about plea and the granting of bail.

In this chapter, the examination of two major aspects of the pre-trial process has confirmed the important links that exist between different stages of the penal process; there have been the suggestions that a refusal of bail can seriously affect a person's subsequent chances of acquittal and type of sentence, and a strong relationship has been found between the factors influencing the exercise of police discretion in arrest/disposition decisions and those influencing the course of plea-bargaining before trial. It has been seen that, because of their decisions to plead guilty, the vast majority of persons facing criminal charges never reach the final stage of *trial* by jury; and even that small minority who do not 'negotiate' justice before trial have a further, final chance of 'by-passing the jury', by means of a directed acquittal from the trial judge. Although this 'open court' stage strictly falls outside the scope of this chapter, yet brief reference can be made to these judicial acquittals, simply to reinforce the picture already built up of each stage of the penal process reflecting upon the preceding stages and influencing those that follow. Newman showed how judicial acquittals could be used as an informal means of controlling police practices and prosecution policy, although the success of such a controlling mechanism depends on a number of factors, ranging from the consistency of particular judges' decisions to the channels of communication within police departments.[87] He also suggested that judges may acquit 'guilty' defendants for a number of reasons related to individualized justice, in the same way as similar factors can influence the manipulation or reduction of charges by the prosecution: for example, the judge may feel that other methods of 'treatment' are better than any the formal system is likely to be able to provide, or he may wish to prevent excessive hardship falling on a 'deserving' defendant by virtue of a criminal conviction.[88] In fact, his concluding comments on judicial acquittals are equally relevant and applicable to the subject of the next chapter, the sentencing process, as to this:

This final decision by the court has important consequences, not only for the defendants involved but for the entire administrative system including both preadjudication enforcement agencies and postconviction treatment agencies. It is in effect a review of the desirability of prosecution, rather than a review of the sufficiency of evidence.

NOTES

1. In his important discussion of the criminal process, Herbert Packer related the concepts of 'presumption of guilt' and 'presumption of innocence' to his two postulated models of the criminal process, viz. Crime Control Model, and Due Process Model; cf. H. L. Packer 'Two Models of the Criminal Process' *U. Pa. L.*

Rev. Vol. **113** (1964) p. 1: 'The key to the operation of the [Crime Control] model as to those who are not screened out is what I shall call a presumption of innocence. . . . Once a determination has been made that there is enough evidence of guilt so that he should be held for further action rather than released from the process, then all subsequent activity directed towards him is based on the view that he is probably guilty' (*op. cit.* p. 11); see also Packer *The Limits of the Criminal Sanction* Stanford (1969).

2. Much of this section derives from the author's own research into the operation of the bail system in England, of which further details can be found in A. K. Bottomley 'Custodial Remands: A Study of Policy and Practice in Magistrates' Courts', Ph.D. thesis, Cambridge University Library (1969), and Bottomley *Prison Before Trial* London (1970).

3. *Criminal Statistics, England and Wales, for 1970* Cmnd. 4708, London (1971) Table 1(a); for an analysis of statistical trends in previous years see Bottomley *Prison Before Trial,* ch. 1.

4. *Report on the Work of the Prison Department for 1970: Statistical Tables* Cmnd. 4806 London (1971) p. 2.

5. Bottomley *Prison Before Trial* Table 4 p. 23. An earlier Home Office Research Unit study estimated that about 31 per cent of persons being tried summarily for indictable offences in 1958 were remanded; see E. Gibson *Time Spent Awaiting Trial* London (1960) p. 23.

6. Bottomley *Prison Before Trial* p. 28; M. King *Bail or Custody* London (1971) pp. 15–16.

7. See, for example *Bail and Summons: 1965* Washington, D.C.(1965).

8. M. L. Friedland *Detention Before Trial* Toronto (1965) p. 12. In England and Wales, in 1970, 74 per cent of persons proceeded against in magistrates' courts for indictable offences were arrested, and 26 per cent were summonsed to appear, *Criminal Statistics, England and Wales, for 1970* Table 1(a).

9. Bottomley *Prison Before Trial* pp. 25–6.

10. For some perceptive comments on the interrelationships between police decisions on bail and the courts, see W. R. LaFavre *Arrest: the Decision to Take a Suspect into Custody* Boston (1965) pp. 166, 202ff.

11. Bottomley *Prison Before Trial* p. 26; for further details see Bottomley 'Custodial Remands' pp. 51–4.

12. C. Foote *et al.* 'Compelling Appearance in Court: Administration of Bail in Philadelphia' *U. Pa. L. Rev.* Vol. **102** (1954) p. 1031 and Table 1 at 1052.

13. J. W. Roberts and J. S. Palermo 'A Study of the Administration of Bail in New York' *U. Pa. L. Rev.* Vol. **106** (1958) pp. 685, at 727 and Table 16.

14. Roberts and Palermo *op. cit.* p. 726 and Table 15.

15. Friendland *op. cit.* pp. 112ff.

16. C. Davies 'Pre-trial Imprisonment: A Liverpool Study' *Brit. Jo. Crim.* Vol. **11** (1971) p. 32.

17. Bottomley *Prison Before Trial* p. 33. The Home Office's estimates for the proportion of persons committed for trial in England and Wales during 1957 who pleaded not guilty were 29 per cent of those on bail, of whom 46 per cent were acquitted, and 19 per cent of those in custody, of whom just 21 per cent were acquitted; see Gibson *op. cit.* p. 13 and Table 11.

18. *Report on the Work of the Prison Department for 1970* Table C1; of the untried prisoners received in 1970, 45 per cent were not returned to custody after conviction, including 5 per cent who were acquitted.

19. Foote *et al.* pp. 1031ff, at 1053.
20. J. W. Roberts and J. S. Palermo *op. cit.* p. 727.
21. Friedland *op. cit.* Table XIII.A p. 120.
22. Gibson *op. cit.* Table 8, p. 11 and Table 28, p. 28.
23. Bottomley *Prison Before Trial* Table 6 p. 37.
24. A. Rankin 'The Effect of Pre-trial Detention' *N. Y. U. L. Rev.* Vol. **39** (1964) p. 641.
25. Rankin *op. cit.* Table 3 at p. 647.
26. Bottomley *Prison Before Trial* Table 6 p. 37.
27. See Foote *et al. op. cit.* p. 1053; see also the comments by Patricia Wald in her introduction to Anne Rankin's New York study, 'Pre-trial Detention and Ultimate Freedom: A Statistical Study' *N. Y. U. L. Rev.* Vol. **39** (1964) pp. 631 at p. 635.
28. *Report on the Work of the Prison Department for 1970* Table C1.
29. See, for example, the Home Office Research Unit's study in which magistrates granted bail to only 8 per cent of the defendants for whom the police opposed bail, compared to 95 per cent of those where there was no police opposition; Gibson *op. cit.* Table 33, p. 31; also the author's own study, in which only 6 per cent of all observed decisions were not in accordance with police recommendations, Bottomley *Prison Before Trial* Table 7, p. 44, and p. 46. Most recently, Michael Zander has shown that in London courts stipendiary magistrates are almost twice as likely to overrule police objections to bail as are lay magistrates: Zander 'A Study of Bail/Custody Decisions in London Magistrates' Courts' *Crim. L. R.*, [1971] pp. 196–7.
30. Bottomley *Prison Before Trial.*
31. King *op. cit.*
32. For an analysis of the legal and historical background to the granting of bail in England, see Bottomley 'The Granting of Bail: Principles and Practice' *Modern Law Review* Vol. **31** (1968) p. 40.
33. See also Packer's elaboration of his 'Crime Control Model' of the criminal justice system, in H. L. Packer 'Two Models' p. 1.
34. For example Bottomley *Prison Before Trial*, ch. 6, pp. 74ff; and Gibson *op. cit.* pp. 32–4.
35. The scoring system and full data are presented in detail in King *op cit.* pp. 35–45.
36. King *op. cit.* p. 37.
37. King *op. cit.* p. 41.
38. Zander *op. cit.* Table 15, p. 206.
39. J. Hogarth 'Towards the Improvement of Sentencing in Canada' *Can. Jo. Corr.* Vol. **9** (1967) pp. 122ff., at p. 134.
40. See Susanne Dell's study of women in Holloway prison:
    When the unrepresented defendant first appears in court, she is in several ways at a disadvantage. The proceedings may be bewildering and unintelligible to her to an extent which the court can hardly appreciate. One remanded girl, when asked by the interviewer whether she had asked for bail in court, replied 'What is bail? Is it the same as legal aid?' Many others, even by the time they were interviewed, were confused about the correct meaning of terms like 're-mand' and 'bail'. . . . Many remanded women said they had left the court room without realising what the magistrates had decided; and it was the police who had to explain to them that they could not go home. . . . If a woman who has been remanded in custody is not aware of the fact before she leaves the court room, she cannot ask for bail. Nor can she ask for bail if she does not unders-

tand the meaning of the term [S. Dell *Silent in Court* London (1971) pp. 17–18].

41. Howard League for Penal Reform *Granting Bail in Magistrates' Courts: Proposals for Reform* London (1972) p. 6.

42. For further details of the Manhattan Bail Project see M. Zander 'Bail: A Reappraisal. Part III' *Crim. L. R.* [1967] pp. 128ff., 135ff.; and for a statistical assessment of its effect see C. E. Ares *et al.* 'The Manhattan Bail Project: An Interim Report on the Use of Pre-trial Release', *N. Y. U. L. Rev.* Vol. **38** (1963) p. 67.

43. Report by *Justice*, 'The Unrepresented Defendant in Magistrates' Courts' London (1971) pp. 23–32.

44. For example, Zander *op. cit.* pp. 139–41; Bottomley *Prison Before Trial* pp. 95–6.

45. In America the President's Commission recognized the problem of 'preventive detention' before trial, without making any specific recommendation on this aspect; cf. *Task Force Report: The Courts*, Washington D.C.(1967) pp. 39ff.:
    Concern that persons released pending trial may commit crimes while on bail is not unfounded. A study by the District of Columbia Crime Commission found that 7.5 per cent of all persons released while awaiting trial on felony charges were arrested and held for grand jury action for other offences allegedly committed prior to trial. . . . There would be obvious advantages if a system could be devised which would enable the issue of a defendant's dangerousness to be confronted candidly by a judge. But a number of interrelated obstacles stand in the way of such a system. First, methods and data for predicting dangerousness have not been adequately developed . . . the degree of confidence in the accuracy of the decision must be far greater because there has been no finding that the defendant has committed a criminal act. . . . A second major obstacle is that imprisonment of an individual based on a prediction of future crimes raises constitutional questions that have not been passed on by the Supreme Court [pp. 39–40].

46. Gibson *op. cit.* Tables 6 and 7, pp. 9–10, and Appendix C, pp. 44–5.

47. Association of Chief Police Officers of England and Wales, 'Trial by Jury' *New Law Journal* Vol. **116** (1966) p. 928.

48. D. J. Newman 'Pleading Guilty for Considerations: A Study of Bargain Justice', *Jo. Crim. Law, Crimin. and P.S.* Vol. **46** (1956) p. 780.

49. A. S. Blumberg *Criminal Justice* Chicago (1967) Table 1, p. 29.

50. See the comments in H. Kalven and H. Zeisel *The American Jury* Boston (1966):
    We saw at every stage of this informal process of pre-trial dispositions that decisions are in part informed by expectations of what the jury will do. Thus, the jury is not controlling merely the immediate case before it, but the host of cases not before it which are destined to be disposed of by the pre-trial process. The jury thus controls not only the formal resolution of controversies in the criminal case, but also the informal resolution of cases that never reach the trial stage. In a sense the jury, like the visible cap of an iceberg, exposes but a fraction of its true volume [pp. 31–2].

51. S. McCabe and R. Purves *By-passing the Jury* Oxford (1972) pp. 19–21; see also A. W. Alschuler 'The Prosecutor's Role in Plea Bargaining' *Univ. Chic. Law Rev.* Vol. **36** (1968) pp. 50ff., at 52–3.

52. For an example of the undesirable confusion in which reference to empirical studies is followed by interpretational claims of a subjective and value-laden kind, see S. L. Hills *Crime, Power and Morality* Scranton (1971) p. 39:

127

On the basis of several empirical studies, it would appear that the presumption of innocence, the right to trial by jury, and the procedural safeguards of due process of law are commonly compromised and subordinated to the bureaucratic organizational goals of efficiency, productivity, and career enhancement. Furthermore, the relative invisibility, secrecy, and immunity from public scrutiny of these legal and extra-legal operations by this close-knit network of judges, prosecutors, lawyers, and officials result in a largely 'closed court community'.

See also Blumberg *op. cit.* p. 70.

53. Newman *op. cit.* Table 5.
54. See A. Davis 'Sentences for Sale: A New Look at Plea Bargaining in England and America' *Crime. L. R.* (1971) p. 150 and p. 218:

> The defendant may get a promise of a sentence recommendation, or a reduction of the charges against him, or a dismissal of some charges; but the linking factor between these elements is that their effect—or supposed effect—from the defendant's point of view, is on the sentence which will be passed on him as a result of his plea of guilty. The reduction or dismissal of charges as part of a plea agreement is merely a less direct way of affecting sentence than having the prosecution make recommendations on the subject to the court (as it can in most of the United States' jurisdictions) [p. 151].

55. Newman *Conviction: the Determination of Guilt or Innocence Without Trial* Boston (1966) p. 232.
56. See President's Commission on Law Enforcement *The Challenge of Crime in a Free Society* Washington, D.C.– (1967) p. 135: 'A distorting aspect of charge decisions is that the prosecutor, because of lack of information and contact with defence counsel before charge may be under pressure to make the most serious possible charge. This leaves him freedom to reduce the charge later, if the facts are not as damning as they might be, and places him in an advantageous position for negotiating with defense counsel on a plea of guilty.'
57. See R. M. Quinney *The Social Reality of Crime* Boston (1970) p. 148.
58. McCabe and Purves *op. cit.* pp. 26–7.
59. See Blumberg *op. cit.* p. 70: 'One of the major requisites of due process is a "public trial", but justice by negotiation avoids public scrutiny. . . . The court, unlike most other formal organisations functions as a genuinely "closed community", in that it successfully conceals the true nature of its routine operations from the view of outsiders—and sometimes even from some of the participants themselves. It socialises its members and participants towards compliance with specific objectives which are not part of the official goals of justice and due process.'
60. Newman *op. cit.* pp. 114–25.
61. President's Commission on Law Enforcement *Task Force Report* p. 4; but see also the cautionary comments in Alschuler *op. cit.* p. 50:

> The utility of discretion must be balanced against the utility of pre-ordained rules, which can limit the importance of subjective judgments, promote equality, control corruption, and provide a basis for planning, both before and after controversies arise. . . . The important point is simply that under the guilty plea system, an objective evaluation of treatment goals never occurs. Plea bargaining at its best merges the task of administration, adjudication, and sentencing into a single conglomerate judgment. And at its usual worst, plea negotiation depends on the personal interests of prosecutors, judges and defense attorneys as well [pp. 71 and 111–12].

62. D. Sudnow 'Normal Crimes: Sociological Features of the Penal Code in a Public Defender Office' *Social Problems* Vol. 12 (1965) p. 255.
63. McCabe and Purves *The Jury at Work* Oxford (1972) pp. 12ff.
64. For a good comparison of the English and American plea-bargaining situations, see A. Davis *op. cit.*
65. Newman *op. cit.* p. 55.
66. President's Commission on Law Enforcement *The Challenge of Crime* p. 135; thus, in Michigan, Newman found that the judge was often directly involved in the decision to reduce the charge; this was usually carried out in open court, with the judge sometimes actually initiating the reduction, see Newman *op. cit.* p. 92.
67. [1970] 2 *W.L.R.* 1093, see the discussion of this case in R. M. Jackson *Enforcing the Law* 2nd edn Harmondsworth, Penguin (1971) pp. 168ff.; also P. Thomas 'Plea Bargaining and the Turner Case' *Crim. L. R.* [1970] pp. 559; and Davis *op. cit.*
68. See *R. v. Soames* (1948) 32 *Cr. App. R.* 135, discussed in Davis *op. cit.* pp. 221ff.
69. D. J. Newman 'Pleading Guilty' p. 780.
70. Newman *ibid.* Tables 2 and 3.
71. Blumberg *op. cit.* pp. 62–3.
72. Dell *op. cit.* London (1971) p. 27.
73. Dell *ibid.* pp. 30–1.
74. Dell *ibid.* p. 33.
75. McCabe and Purves *By-passing the Jury.*
76. McCabe and Purves *ibid.* pp. 28–9.
77. Kalven and Zeisel *op. cit.* Table 2, p. 20.
78. Gibson *op. cit.* pp. 9–10 and Appendix C, p. 44.
79. Association of Chief Police Officers of England and Wales 'Trial by Jury' *New Law Journal* Vol. 116 (1966) pp. 928–9.
80. 'The Influence of the Defendant's Plea on Judicial Determination of Sentence' *Yale Law Journal* Vol. 66 (1956) pp. 204ff., at 206–7.
81. D. A. Thomas *Principles of Sentencing* London (1970) p. 53 and pp. 195–6.
82. See *Davis* (19.11.64) 1527/64 *Crim. L. R. [1965]; 251 Gray* (21.3.67) 3983/66; and *Harper* [1967] 3 *All E.R.* 617, 52 *Cr. App. R.* 21.
83. See *Flynn* (12.6.67) 682/67 *Crim. L. R.* [1967] p. 489.
84. Newman *op. cit.*
85. Blumberg *op. cit.* p. 179.
86. McCabe and Purves *By-passing the Jury* pp. 23–4: 'It is hardly the case that the defendant is denied his right to make the prosecution discharge its burden of proof; it is much more the case that he exploits the obstacles inherent in the discharge of this burden as a powerful bargaining point.'
87. Newman *Conviction: the Determination of Guilt* pp. 195–6.
88. D. J. Newman *ibid.* pp. 134ff.; see Quinney *op. cit.* pp. 148–9.

4 THE SENTENCING PROCESS

The sentencing decisions taken by magistrates and judges occupy a central place in the penal process, not only in the obvious chronological sense, but more significantly because of their direct and indirect influences upon the police and pretrial stages which precede them, and upon the subsequent implementation of the penal measures imposed upon convicted offenders. In England, as in most other jurisdictions to varying degrees, magistrates and judges possess wide discretionary powers in the choice of sentence, and consequently the sentencing process shares an important element of discretion comparable to that which has already been seen in the examination of police behaviour and judicial decision-making at the pre-trial stage. However, in contrast to these earlier stages, the discretion which is exercised by the courts in sentencing offenders is much more 'visible' and open to public scrutiny; unfortunately, because of the traditional independence of the judiciary and their theoretical freedom from external social and political pressures, this visibility more often results in public outcries against particular sentences rather than in a more constructive two-way process of communication between the courts and the general public.

A variety of historical, political and cultural factors have influenced the nature and extent of judicial discretion in sentencing in different countries, but its contemporary significance seems to be directly related to the relatively recent development of the concept of 'individualized justice' as an ideal towards which it is felt that all enlightened criminal justice systems ought to be striving. A system which is not so concerned with individualization in sentencing may have its own problems and conflicts over the exercise of discretion, according to some alternative retributive, social defence or 'tariff' framework, but disagreements seem more likely to arise over the exer-

130

cise of judicial discretion in situations where great importance is attached to considering the interests of individual offenders.[1] It is in such a context that the sentencing process will be discussed in this chapter, focusing on the evidence for sentencing 'disparities' and examining the factors which have been suggested as possible explanations for such disparities that have been found.

Before embarking on this examination, some preliminary observations must be made about the concept of disparity itself, and about some of the underlying assumptions of 'justice' and 'equality' in relation to sentencing decisions. The following quotation, from R. O. Dawson's study of sentencing in the important research series sponsored by the American Bar Foundation, gives some idea of the range of issues raised by the concept of sentencing disparity:

> Sentencing disparity presents serious problems. It manifests the failure of the system to achieve the goal of equal justice under law. . . . Perhaps most important, the existence of sentence disparity casts grave doubt upon the extent to which the goal of individualised correctional treatment can be achieved in practice because of inadequate knowledge about human behaviour, a lack of consensus about the goals of the criminal justice process, a failure of the trial judiciary to develop a method of minimising their different views about sentencing, and a willingness often to give administrative convenience a higher priority than the proper disposition of the individual offender.[2]

It is immediately obvious that there are insuperable difficulties in interpreting the phrase 'equal justice under the law', where there is an admitted lack of agreement about the overall goals of the criminal justice system, for as long as sentences reflect different goals they cannot easily be compared one with another according to some supposedly overriding criterion of 'equality'; it is more a question of the injustice of sentences being passed with *different objectives* in mind than sentences being *unequal* according to the same criterion, and to that extent unjust. In his pioneering study of sentencing in English magistrates' courts (1962), Roger Hood preferred to talk in terms of 'equality of consideration';[3] in many ways, however, the use of this more practical, applied definition of equality seems to avoid facing the implications of the belief that 'justice' means that like cases should be

131

dealt with alike. It is only by starting from some such fundamental definition that we can begin to disentangle the meaning of 'justice' and 'alike' in this context, as Aubert perceptively realized:

> The problem of justice involves still another principle that like cases shall be handled alike. Paradoxically enough, to invoke this principle is to contend that each case shall be treated according to its peculiarities, if we interpret 'likeness' to mean something more than that two cases shall be judged exactly alike if they fulfil exactly the same clear and simple conditions which are to be read from the law. There is hardly any doubt that most of people's ideas and beliefs about justice, unclear and ambiguous as they are, are based on something more than a mechanical-juridical 'likeness'.[4]

Aubert's emphasis on the meaning of 'likeness' brings us back full circle to the point made earlier, that the problem of sentencing disparity is closely related to the post-Classical emphasis on individualized justice, which has regard to the needs of the individual offender, in contrast to the 'mechanical-juridical' emphasis on the nature of the offence which was characteristic of criminal codes of the Classical School; thus, the characteristics of an offence or an offender which are relevant in any comparison of 'like with like' differ according to the aims of a particular criminal justice system. To the extent, therefore, that there exists a lack of consensus about the aims of the penal process in any society, to that extent it is inevitable that there will be disparity in sentencing decisions, not only because different factors are relevant to different aims but also because there is likely to be very real disagreement about what factors are rightly considered relevant for the *same* aim. In a report prepared for the President's Commission, *Task Force Report: the Courts,* it was admitted that 'within certain limits a lack of uniformity in sentences is justifiable', as the main reason for giving judges discretion in sentencing was to permit variations based on *relevant differences* in offenders.[5] The authors of this part of the *Task Force Report* wished to reserve the more pejorative term 'disparity' for cases where unequal sentences were imposed for the same offence, or offences of comparable seriousness, *without any reasonable basis.* Presumably, however, what seems 'reasonable' to one man or one community may not seem so to another!

132

After a survey of the evidence for disparities, the discussion of the sentencing process in the rest of this chapter will focus around three related aspects of the problem: (i) the role of individual personality characteristics and attitudes of judges; (ii) the relationship between sentencing disparities and the social/community context in which these decisions are taken; and (iii) the use made of information during the sentencing process.[6] In the light of the various definitions and views about sentencing disparities which have been touched upon in this introductory section, an underlying question to keep in mind during the discussion is the extent to which any or all of these factors enable conclusions to be reached not only about the 'causes' of disparities in sentencing but also about the desirability or possible justifications for any disparities that may be found.

EVIDENCE OF DISPARITIES

Statistical surveys showing the apparent extent of sentencing disparities have been conducted in Britain mainly during the last twenty years, but in the United States the earliest studies date from the first decades of this century. There are various possible ways of selecting and presenting this material, for example, according to the methods of comparison used, the type of cases included or the country where the research was carried out. For present purposes it was decided to concentrate upon a selection of the most important and accessible research studies, and to discuss, first of all, the small group of British studies of sentencing; and, secondly, to consider some of the studies from other countries which provide significant data for assessing the nature and extent of sentencing disparities. At the same time, throughout the discussion, attention will be paid to various methodological aspects of the studies being examined.

British studies

The first systematic studies of sentencing in Britain were carried out in the 1950s, and concentrated on juvenile court practices. Grünhut described the national pattern of sentences passed upon juvenile

133

offenders found guilty of indictable offences between 1948–50, in the 134 police districts of England and Wales. He calculated the percentages of juveniles given different sentences in the various police districts, and although he found considerable local variations from the national mean he concluded that four fifths of all juveniles lived in areas where the sentencing practices of the courts did not seem to differ very much from the average for the country as a whole.[7] He was not able to examine the characteristics of the different offenders and offences included in this national sample, in order to relate the 'input' to the sentences passed, but he did make a more detailed study of five selected areas, viz. Oxford City, Oxford County, Newcastle, Swansea and the West Riding of Yorkshire. In this part of the study he discovered certain relationships between differences in the types of juveniles appearing in the courts and the sentencing patterns of these courts, but his cautious conclusions were that 'within the range of this limited experience, the evidence shows certain common lines of present-day treatment policy, but also certain local differences in the sense that similar measures are sometimes applied to different cases, or different measures to similar cases'.[8]

Mannheim and his colleagues studied a sample of 400 cases from eight juvenile courts in London, of boys aged between 14–16 years, convicted of larceny.[9] The main purpose of the study was 'to assess the uniformity or otherwise of court decisions made by certain courts in a particular area', but the authors had no illusions about the difficulties of operationalizing the concepts of 'uniformity' and 'relevant differences', even with this fairly narrowly defined group of cases:

> It was difficult to recognise cases in which the circumstances of the offence and the offender were so similar that we might have expected all courts to prescribe a similar form of treatment. In essence the task was to establish the uniformity or non-uniformity of those factors which were significant to the study.... The fundamental problem remained—what constituted a classification of essentially significant factors.[10]

It was also realized that any search for 'significant factors', as possible explanations of apparent disparities, would have to take into account not only the subjective perceptions of the magistrates as to what was significant but also the extent and nature of the courts' sources of information—for, if the magistrates were completely unaware of a particular factor in a juvenile's background or his offence, it clearly could not be put forward as a contributory factor to a particular sentencing decision. A wide range of sentencing patterns was found in these eight London juvenile courts: the proportion of boys given absolute or conditional discharges varied from 18 per cent to 48 per cent; the proportion put on probation varied even more, from 18 per cent to 66 per cent. An analysis of the social-class composition of the six areas serving the courts provided no clue for explaining the apparent differences in patterns of sentencing; and, in fact, despite detailed statistical comparisons no consistent associations were found between a variety of sociological factors and the sentencing practices of the different courts, so that the authors were forced to the conclusion that 'the subjective or intuitive assessment of individual cases does in the main, prevail'.[11]

To complete our consideration of studies of sentencing practices in English *juvenile* courts, the most recent study, by Patchett and McClean (1965), will be taken slightly out of order. Patchett and McClean examined the sentencing practices of the juvenile courts in eight neighbouring areas in the north of England, during 1962–3 (viz. five towns: Derby, Barnsley, Doncaster, Rotherham and Sheffield; and the three adjacent county districts of Derbyshire, Nottinghamshire and the West Riding).[12] Once again, they found wide variations in sentencing practice within the region; but as they did not carry out any direct examination of the characteristics of the juveniles appearing at the different courts, they simply had to assume similarity of 'input':

There is no reason to suppose that the offenders, or their offences, vary appreciably in any way between one part of the region and another. The differences between urban and rural areas, which might be expected to be significant, were less marked than those between two similar towns such as Barnsley and Doncaster.[13]

Although such an 'assumption of similarity' is no adequate substitute for systematic investigation of the juveniles being sentenced, it was certainly true that some of the most striking differences were between similar towns; for example, in the 14–17 year old age group, Barnsley

135

courts fined 65 per cent compared to only 30 per cent fined by Rotherham courts, and when, in addition, comparisons were made over a period of time, equally dramatic differences in sentencing practices were found (see Table 4.1). These changes in the *same* courts, within a period of less than ten years, were thought to be due mainly to 'internal' changes in the approach adopted by certain juvenile court benches, not usually as a result of a deliberate policy decision but probably due to fortuitous factors such as the appointment of a new chairman, with particularly strong views, to the juvenile bench.

TABLE 4.1: *Percentages of boys under the age of 14 years given different sentences: Barnsley and Rotherham, 1954–5 and 1962–3.*

Court		Probation %	Fines %	Total no. of sentences passed
Barnsley:	1954–5	28	30	(100)
	1962–3	13	73	(147)
Rotherham:	1954–5	16	62	(68)
	1962–3	23	33	(151)

Source: K. W. Patchett and J. D. McClean 'Decision-making in Juvenile Cases' *Crim. L. R. (1965)* pp. 699ff. from Table III, at p. 703.

One of the most important studies of sentencing in English magistrates' courts was that carried out by Roger Hood, and published in 1962.[14] This study focused on the sentencing of adult males (aged 21 years or over) convicted of indictable property offences in magistrates' courts during 1951–4. For the country as a whole, the proportion of this group who were sentenced to imprisonment varied from 3 per cent to as high as 55 per cent, with a mean of 21 per cent. Hood selected a sample of twelve courts, from towns in different parts of the country, spanning the full range of sentencing practice for this type of offender; he set up the null hypothesis that 'differences in sentencing are not associated with variations in the types of offenders and offences confronting the magistrates in different areas'. Detailed analysis did reveal some differences in the distribution
136

of certain characteristics of offenders between different courts, but such variations as were found bore no consistent relation to the imprisonment rate, so that the author felt able to conclude:

> In general, conditions confronting all the courts are similar and variations in the characteristics of the offenders are not related to the variations in the imprisonment rate. . . . The differences in the imprisonment rates appear to have no general relationship to the variations between courts in the proportions of men who have certain personal characteristics.[15]

Not only did Hood find that *differences* in imprisonment rates could not be explained by different offenders appearing at each court, but he confirmed that *similar* imprisonment rates did reflect an 'equality of consideration' in the factors which these courts took into account in reaching their decisions. It will be seen (below) that various social and community characteristics were suggested as important variables, in trying to explain the considerable disparities which were the starting point for this research, but the general validity of Hood's conclusions still stands:

> The research has shown that some courts are using prison sentences far more frequently than are others and that this cannot be fully explained by the fact that they have a larger proportion of men appearing before them who are more likely to be imprisoned by any court. . . . Equality of treatment may be desirable from the point of view of reclaiming offenders, but it is also a problem in moral and legal philosophy. It is evident that some offenders' chances of being imprisoned are far higher in certain parts of the country than in others. . . . It has yet to be proved that differences in local attitudes are so large and potent that they necessitate wide disparities in sentencing policies.[16]

As a result of the findings of this early research study of sentencing in magistrates' courts, Hood was invited to carry out a further study of the sentencing of motoring offenders, of which the final report has recently been published.[17] There were various reasons for the choice of motoring offenders as the subject for this second study, but, from the point of view of finding and explaining wide disparities in sentencing

137

decisions, motoring offenders did not provide the same range of disparities as the earlier, more general study. Although, for the convicted motorist himself, the size of a fine or the length of a period of disqualification from driving may be of crucial importance, yet they have not the same degree of significance as the difference between a fine and a term of imprisonment and, in the event, did not really match the depth of analysis involved in the research, in which magistrates were interviewed at length, given personality questionnaires and took part in various sentencing exercises. Nevertheless, disparities were found, particularly in the more serious offences, such as driving while disqualified, drunken and dangerous driving; conversely, least variation occurred where the offence was of a more minor or 'technical' nature. Significantly, therefore, it was just those motoring offences (and offenders) which shared some of the characteristics of more 'traditional' crimes (and criminals) that resulted in greatest disparity, thereby providing at least indirect confirmation of the general claim that sentencing disparity is likely to be quite widespread in the area of traditional crimes.[18]

Studies from other countries

Two interesting early studies of sentencing in the United States of America, by Everson (1920) and Gaudet (1933–), shared certain methodological characteristics: they both examined the sentencing patterns of *individual* judges and magistrates, and, within their samples, they assumed a similarity of cases heard by the different judges, due to the equalizing effects of the rota system of judicial sittings. Everson examined the sentencing practices of 42 judges, sitting in rotation in 60 different criminal courts in New York, during 1914–16. The sentences imposed upon convicted offenders were analysed separately for each judge, and for a number of different types of offence; for example, in 1916 a total of 17,075 persons appeared on charges of public intoxication: the acquittal rate varied from 2 per cent to 79 per cent, and the sentencing disparities of the different judges included differences of from 7 per cent to 83 per cent in the proportion given suspended sentences, of from 7 per cent to 100 per cent in the proportion fined, and of from 3 per cent to 40 per cent in the proportion committed to the workhouse.[19] Typical examples of the way different magistrates handled all their cases in a single year were Judge McQuade, who sentenced 4,835 cases in 1916, so that 84 per cent were fined, 7 per cent received suspended sentences, and a further 7 per cent were committed to the workhouse; on the other hand, Magistrate Folwell sentenced his total of 4,253 cases so that only 34 per cent were fined, 59 per cent received suspended sentences, and just 2 per cent were committed to the workhouse.[20] Perhaps not surprisingly, Everson entitled his article 'The Human Element in Justice', and put forward the following explanation for the sentencing disparities which he had revealed:

> In the figures given above we have shown to what a remarkable degree the individuality of the magistrates is mirrored in their disposition of cases. Justice is a very personal thing reflecting the temperament, the personality, the education, environment and personal traits of the magistrate. . . . These studies of the work of the magistrates' records in the New York courts are startling because they show us so clearly to how great an extent justice resolves itself into the personality of the judge. However good or however inadequate the laws may be, their enforcement depends upon the magistrates' attitude toward them and toward those guilty of breaking them.[21]

Gaudet studied a sample of 7,638 cases from the court records of one county in New Jersey, constituting all the sentences passed by six different judges, over a ten-year period, in all the major categories of crime.[22] Like Everson before him, he assumed that, over such a long period of time, the rota system would equalize the types of cases handled by each judge; additional calculations of the percentages of recidivists and non-recidivists appearing before each judge, and the percentages of persons in each of four broad categories of crime, seemed to confirm the correctness of this assumption. Table 4.2 shows the various types of sentence given by each judge: it can be seen that Judges A and F appeared more lenient than their fellow judges, and this tendency was still found when property crimes (with and without violence) were analysed separately; the patterns for sentencing sex offenders were slightly different, but the author did not attach much significance to this, mainly because of the small numbers involved.

139

TABLE 4.2: *Percentages of various types of sentence given by six judges over a ten-year period, in a New Jersey County Court.*

	Prison %	Suspended sentence %	Probation %	Fine %	Total no. of cases
Judge A	37	30	30	2	(1,263)
Judge B	57	20	20	3	(1,446)
Judge C	53	25	20	2	(1,888)
Judge D	51	16	31	2	(635)
Judge E	46	25	27	2	(453)
Judge F	33	35	29	3	(1,953)

Source: F. J. Gaudet 'The Sentencing Behavior of the Judge'. in V. C. Branham and S. B. Kutash (eds) *Encyclopaedia of Criminology* New York (1949) Table 1. p. 453.

Investigations into other possible disparities between the six judges showed that the lengths of the probation sentences given by each judge were remarkably alike but that the median length of the prison sentences varied from 6 months (Judges D and F) to 12 months (Judge A), with no apparent relation between the *frequency* with which a judge gave prison sentences and the *length* of those sentences.[23] Partly, perhaps, because of his method of selecting his sample according to the case-loads of individual judges, Gaudet's conclusions were also in terms of individual personality factors and the 'personal equation'—'one is forced to conclude that the differences among these judges in their sentencing behaviour can best be accounted for by the use of the general term "personality"'.[24]

Among more recent American studies of sentencing, reference will only be made at this stage to the Philadelphia study carried out by Edward Green. Green studied 1,437 cases in the Philadelphia Court of Quarter Sessions, 1956–7, involving a total of 21 different judges; only a small part of the research project was directed to the question of disparities between the individual judges, as Green was mainly concerned with a broader investigation into the influence upon sentencing decisions of three types of factor, which he categorized as follows: (i) *legal factors* e.g. type of crime, number of charges, previous convictions, pre-sentence recommendations; (ii) *legally irrelevant factors*, e.g. sex, age, race, place of birth; (iii) *factors in the criminal prosecution*, e.g. roles of judge and prosecutor, plea, legal representation. As

140

the main part of the research investigation revealed that the 'legal factors' had the greatest effect on the type of sentence received, Green utilized them for the development of prediction tables, so that he could compare the sentencing patterns of the different judges for convicted offenders in the same prediction score categories.[25] Nevertheless, even with the help of this sophisticated 'matching' technique, there were still considerable differences between the sentences of the different judges which Green admitted, somewhat reluctantly, 'were great enough to meet the criterion of inconsistency'; in fact his figures show that, in cases of the least seriousness, the proportion imprisoned varied from 18 per cent to 70 per cent; in cases of medium gravity, the proportion imprisoned varied from 64 per cent to 100 per cent; and, even in the most serious group of cases, there were four judges who only imprisoned between 50–80 per cent, compared to eight of their colleagues who imprisoned all their cases in this highest score category.[26] Despite Green's ingenious attempts to group the 'out-of-line' judges in such a way that he claimed to show *internal consistencies*, it seems impossible to deny that glaring inconsistencies remained in the way the judges sentenced cases, even after important characteristics of the offences and the offenders had been carefully matched. The author's own summary of his findings almost, but not quite, admits as much:

> In cases of minor gravity, the sentences of 6 of the judges are so rigorous as to be out of line with the sentences of the other 12. In the most serious cases, 4 of the judges tend to be much more lenient than the others. The greatest disparity in sentencing occurs in the cases of intermediate gravity. Here the differences in sentencing are so great that the judges can be assimilated to no fewer than three groups—numbering 3, 8 and 7—within which there are no significant differences in sentences. We conclude that when cases are patently either mild or grave, the standards for sentencing are clearly structured and generally shared by the judges, as the cases move from the extremes of gravity or mildness toward intermediacy, judicial standards tend to become less stable and sentencing increasingly reflects the individuality of the judge.[27]

Outside the United States, Shoham studied the sentencing policy and practice of three district courts in Israel, during 1956.[28] A comparison of the relative frequency of the various sentences used by the

141

eight main judges showed variations in the use of imprisonment from 24 per cent to 53 per cent, and from 38 per cent to 73 per cent in the proportion of suspended sentences which were passed. When he compared the relative severity of the sentences passed by each judge, Shoham found differences in the 'severity median' for all offences, ranging from 30 per cent (Judge D) to 71 per cent (Judge N); however, the range of severity for offences against the person was even greater, from 10 per cent to 90 per cent, with Judge N being the most lenient, although he was most *severe* overall; conversely, in offences against property, Judge D was the most severe, despite being most *lenient* overall.

Finally, in this introductory survey, reference must be made to the statistical starting-point of John Hogarth's extremely comprehensive and sophisticated study of sentencing in Ontario.[30] To a large degree, Hogarth took for granted the existence of apparent sentencing disparity, so that he spent little time in documenting its extent, but concentrated on unravelling the complex web of factors which influenced the sentencing decisions of Canadian magistrates. However, Table 4.3 shows the variations in sentencing practice between courts in 37 judicial districts in Ontario, during 1964; the figures denote the use of particular forms of sentence as percentages of the total number of offenders sentenced for indictable offences in each judicial district. The author comments that these differences appear too large to be explained solely in terms of differences in the types of cases appearing

TABLE 4.3: *Variations in the sentencing practice of magistrates in 37 judicial districts of Ontario, 1964.*

Type of sentence	Highest %	Lowest %	Mean %
Suspended sentence, with probation	43	0	24
Suspended sentence, without probation	34	0	7
Fine	39	2	24
Gaol	60	4	24
Reformatory	37	1	12
Penitentiary	23	0	6

Source: J. Hogarth *Sentencing as a Human Process* Toronto (1971) Table 2. p. 11.

before courts in different areas, and therefore it was this 'apparent in-consistency' which became the first feature of sentencing in Ontario that the study attempted to explain.

THE HUMAN ELEMENT IN JUDGES' DECISIONS

It has already been seen that many of the statistical surveys of sentencing disparities in Britain and overseas suggested tentative explanations in terms of the influence of 'personality factors' or the 'human element' upon judges' decisions; this was true not only of the early American studies carried out by Everson and Gaudet, but also of the study of sentencing in London juvenile courts carried out by Mannheim; even Green had to admit to the importance of what he called 'the individuality of the judge'. To some students of the sentencing process, the introduction of concepts such as these into the analysis of the problem implies a retreat from systematic and objective investigation into the realms of subjectivity and irrationality; they seem to equate 'personality factors' with pure arbitrariness, inevitably resulting in injustice. Even Gaudet, who stressed the importance of knowing how large a part the 'human equation' played in the sentence which a man might receive from a judge, believed that 'if this *personality of the judge element* is present to a marked degree, we may assume that there are inequalities and even injustices in the administration of the criminal law'.[31] However, we would want to argue along with Hood and Sparks, that an acceptance of the importance of the human element in sentencing does not *necessarily* imply an acceptance of the corollary that most sentencing is therefore arbitrary and irrational;[32] this section will examine the various factors and influences which different researchers have included under this general heading, assessing their validity as explanations of observed disparities, and the extent to which they appear compatible with consistency and 'rationality' in sentencing.

One of the most common personal characteristics of judges and magistrates, which has been suggested as a likely influence upon their decisions, is that of their social class background. Virtually all studies show that judges and magistrates come from predominantly middle-class or professional backgrounds, and often hold relatively conser-

143

vative political views. Their general socio-economic status contrasts sharply with that of the vast majority of convicted offenders appearing before them for sentence.

The report of the *Royal Commission on Justices of the Peace, 1946–8,* analysed the occupational classification of the 13,000 male justices of the peace serving in England and Wales; only 15 per cent were wage earners (or had been before retirement), with more than half recruited from the professional or managerial classes.[33] Table 4.4 shows the occupational background of the 538 magistrates in Hood's recent survey, 1966–7, compared to that of the general population: three quarters were from professional or managerial backgrounds, compared to less than 4 per cent in the general population.

TABLE 4.4: *Occupational background of a sample of English magistrates, 1966–7, compared to the general population.*

Occupational class	% (n = 538)	% in general population (1961 Census)
1. Higher professional	21.7	⎫ 3.9
2. Managerial and other professionals	55.2	⎬
3. Clerical	9.7	14.4
4. Skilled manual	12.1	49.8
5. Semi-skilled	—	19.9
6. Unskilled	—	8.6

Source: R. G. Hood *Sentencing the Motoring Offender* London (1972) Table 1 p. 51.

In the United States of America, Nagel carried out a questionnaire survey of 313 state and federal court judges, who had occupied the judicial bench in 1955. This survey provided information about various aspects of the political and social backgrounds of the 119 respondents, and was particularly concerned to assess the degree of 'liberalism' of the judges, by which Nagel meant 'a viewpoint associated with the interests of the lower or less privileged economic or social groups in a society and, to a lesser extent, with acceptance of

144

long-run social change'.[34] He portrayed the typical criminal case as representing a conflict of social groups, in that the defendant generally tended to be a member of the lower-middle or working class, and the prosecutor a member of the upper-middle or upper class, enforcing laws promulgated by upper-middle and upper class legislators and judges. More than 80 per cent of the responding judges said their fathers had been professional men, businessmen or farm owners, which the author believed largely explained their extremely high 'conservatism' and correspondingly low 'liberalism' scores, especially as their average age was 63 years.[35] It was also found that these 'off-the-bench' judicial attitudes did correlate significantly with the judicial decisions taken 'on-the-bench', so that Nagel felt able to conclude:

> Because criminal cases frequently involve value-oriented controversies, and because different background and attitudinal positions tend to correspond to different value orientations, there will probably always be some correlation between judicial characteristics and judicial decision-making in criminal cases.[36]

Finally, Hogarth examined the social background of Ontario magistrates, and compared the occupation of their fathers with that of the general working population (Table 4.5). Once again there was found to be a gross over-representation of the professional and business classes, and although the proportion of magistrates coming

TABLE 4.5: *Occupation of Ontario magistrates' fathers, compared to total male labour force.*

Occupational category	Magistrates' fathers % (n = 70)	Total labour force (1931) %
Professional	26.9	3.7
Business	26.8	6.9
Skilled or semi-skilled wage earner	22.5	23.3
Clerical	11.3	10.5
Farmer	5.6	19.7
Unskilled wage earner	1.4	35.9

Source: J. Hogarth *Sentencing as a Human Process* Toronto (1971) Table 5 p. 53.

from families of skilled or semi-skilled wage earners (23 per cent) was almost identical to that of the general population, only 7 per cent of the magistrates' fathers were farmers or unskilled wage earners, compared to 56 per cent of the total labour force.[37] In a later part of the analysis, in which he tested the relationship between certain social background characteristics and the magistrates' penal attitudes, Hogarth found that magistrates from professional family backgrounds tended to be more 'reformative' in their beliefs, whereas the minority from working-class backgrounds tended to be more 'punitive'.[38]

In any attempt to relate social background factors to judicial decision-making, it is not enough simply to collect systematic information about magistrates' backgrounds in a purely descriptive way, but, as Grossman has stated, it is also necessary to measure the degree to which any particular characteristic is regularly associated with a particular type of sentencing decision, and, finally, to attempt to assess the extent to which any significant relationships might be said to account for sentencing disparities.[39] Unfortunately, with regard to the influence of social class, most analyses have not progressed far beyond the first, primarily descriptive stage, with the later causal relationships usually taken for granted. Nevertheless, a few researchers have gone a little further into the question of possible bias, resulting from the social class and occupational background of most magistrates and judges.

In Roger Hood's attempt to explain the apparent sentencing disparities of twelve selected magistrates' courts in England, 1951–4, it was suggested that 'the social composition of the bench may be an additional factor in affecting the prison rate', particularly as the majority of persons appearing before all courts were from working-class backgrounds. The benches of magistrates, which passed sentences of imprisonment most frequently, tended to include more members from the professions and management, and although it proved difficult to consider the effects of the social background of magistrates independently of the type of community in which they served, Hood concluded that predominantly middle- or upper-class benches *may* be more severe than benches with magistrates from working-class backgrounds, given certain local community conditions, and without wishing to make any sweeping generalization about middle-class magistrates always being more severe than working-class magistrates.[40]

146

In Aubert's small but interesting study of the decisions of Norwegian Military Courts, 1949–52, in cases involving conscientious objectors, he found that differences in the conviction/acquittal rate of the courts in different geographical areas could not be due to different degrees of 'criminality' of the offenders facing charges, but rather suggested that the judges' personal attitudes could have an effect on their decisions.[41] When he analysed the decisions according to the occupation of the conscientious objectors he found that, of the 42 unskilled workers in the court records, only 14 were acquitted, but in all other occupational categories the proportion was much more favourable, resulting in 34 acquittals in 52 cases. Various explanations were suggested for these findings:

Possibly the difference between unskilled workers and others indicates that the probability for acquittal is reduced as the accused's socio-economic status decreases. Whether this can be explained by a higher rate of lawbreakers among low-status defendants, whether these objectors have more difficulty in managing an effective defense, or whether some of the judges discriminate according to status, it is not possible to say.[42]

In America, Nagel carried out a broad investigation into the extent and nature of disparities at different stages in the penal process, with particular reference to the defendant's socio-economic and racial status.[43] Large samples were drawn from federal and state cases during 1962–3, but the data and conclusions to be cited here refer to subsamples of 2,000 grand larceny and 1,000 felony assault cases; throughout this part of the investigation, the defendant's offence and previous criminal record were held constant for purposes of comparison. From the start, Nagel recognized that disparities, related to the economic status of defendants, could often be due to the existence or quality of the legal representation received, but he felt that the appearance that an indigent defendant presented to a middle-class judge or probation officer might bring out some of their class-biased attitudes! Table 4.6 shows the apparent disparities in sentencing and probation recommendations according to the class and race of the defendants with previous criminal record controlled. On the basis of such statistics, he considered indigents and Negroes to be 'disadvantaged groups', as far as the American criminal justice system was con-

TABLE 4.6: *Class and racial disparities in criminal procedure: American federal and state cases, 1962–3.*

Disposition	Some prior record					No prior record				
	Class		Race			Class		Race		
	Indigent %	Non-indigent %	Negro %	White %	Total sample	Indigent %	Non-indigent %	Negro %	White %	Total sample
% *not* recommended for probation (n =)	74	52	72	54	(61) (270)	27	16	22	18	(19) (90)
% sentenced to imprisonment (n =)	62 (148)	52 (232)	66 (138)	50 (232)	(55) (380)	23 (44)	15 (151)	20 (46)	14 (143)	(17) (195)

Source: S. S. Nagel 'Disparities in Criminal Procedure', *U.C.L.A. Rev.* Vol. **14** (1967) p. 1272: Table 7. p. 1304.

cerned, but he made the very significant point that disparities of this kind in the penal process could not be considered independently of the organization of society as a whole:

> As a basic and general matter, however, it should be pointed out that there would probably be no criminal procedure disparities between the groups compared if the opposed groups did not exist or *if the groups were not given differential treatment in society in general*.... [emphasis added.] Therefore the problem of criminal procedure disparities is inherently tied to attempts to remove distinctions that are considered undesirable ... to decrease the indigent and the uneducated and to eliminate general racial discrimination.[44]

In other American studies that have examined apparent disparities in sentencing, according to the race of the convicted offender, the conclusions reached have usually been one of two kinds: on the one hand, judicial *prejudice* has been claimed to be responsible for the disparities, related to cultural and subcultural aspects of Negro crime; on the other hand, justifications have been put forward in terms of the *differential criminality* of racial groups in a society. For example, Sellin's early comparison of the length of prison sentences passed upon Whites and Negroes in 1931, found that there was very little difference in the length of fixed sentences of imprisonment, but that, with regard to *indeterminate* sentences, Negroes received longer maximum terms than Whites in all offences except homicide. Sellin suggested that the difference between the findings of the two types of sentence was due to the fact that most of the fixed sentences were passed in the Southern states, whereas the majority of indeterminate sentences were passed in the Northern and Pacific Coast states; in other words, there appeared to be greater prejudice toward the Negro in the North than in the South, which Sellin attributed to the fact that in the Southern states a certain paternalism, deriving from the slave period, still persisted whereas in the North the Negro was regarded as a competitor in industry and an 'outsider'.[45]

In 1961, Bullock reported the findings of a study of 3,644 White and Negro inmates of the Texas State Prison, Huntsville, during 1958, convicted of burglary, rape and murder.[46] Despite controlling various non-racial factors, such as type of offence, criminal record, plea and

149

region, he found that disparities still existed in the length of prison terms passed upon the Whites and Negroes in the sample: in cases of murder, Negroes were given shorter sentences than Whites, whereas in cases of burglary Negroes were given longer sentences than Whites convicted of the same offence. Bullock suggested that these judicial decisions reflected the 'indulgent' and 'non-indulgent' patterns that characterized local attitudes towards property and interracial morals; because murder and rape were predominantly *intra*-racial crimes, in which most of the victims of Negro offenders were themselves likely to be Negroes, the local norms tolerated a less vigorous pattern of law enforcement; but because burglary was largely an *inter*-racial offence, the local community was less tolerant of behaviour which threatened its own property:

> Assuming indulgent and non-indulgent patterns in which negro offenders are apparently under-penalized for one type of offense and over-penalized for another, racial discrimination appears to be motivated more by the desire to protect the order of the white community than to effect the reformation of the offender. If the study has any theoretical suggestion at all, it is this: those who enforce the law conform to the norms of their local society concerning racial prejudice, thus denying equality before the law. That criminal statistics reflect social customs, values, and prejudices appears to be further validated.[47]

This important theme of the relationship between judicial attitudes and the society or local community of which they are an important part will be returned to in the next section.

Finally, in this brief discussion of the racial factor in sentencing, there is Edward Green's study, in which an attempt was made to justify disparities by reference to the *differential criminality* of the different racial groups. In his main analysis of 1,437 cases heard in the Philadelphia Court of Quarter Sessions, during 1956–7, he included 'race' in the category of 'legally irrelevant factors'; his general conclusion was that none of these factors had any independent influence upon sentencing decisions, but that any apparent relationship was due to differences in patterns of criminal behaviour associated with the 'biosocial variables' rather than to hidden prejudice.[48] He suggested that White and Negro offenders differed considerably in their 'age-
150

cycles' of crime, so that the younger Negroes committed a much greater proportion of crimes of violence than White youths of the same age; when the effect of these different patterns of crime according to age were controlled, the differences in the sentences became negligible.

In a later article, Green examined in more detail a subsample of 400 inter- and intra-racial crimes of robbery and burglary from the Philadelphia court; he found little evidence for differential handling of the two categories of Negro and White interracial offences, and dismissed the slightly less severe sentences accorded to Negro *intra*-racial offenders as 'not in the writer's estimation of any consequence'.[49] With remarkable faith, he believed that judges were 'least likely to bow to local custom or prejudice where it opposes the American creed' (?), while admitting that there might be some judges less committed to this ideal, or communities where it was still unattainable. Green felt that any widespread racial prejudice that might exist in the American criminal justice system was more likely to occur in the less public phases of the administration of justice rather than in the more visible courtroom interaction. In his concluding comments, he repeated his firm belief in the *differential criminality* of the two major racial groups, but succeeded in combining (and to some extent confusing) it with a form of the *cultural* argument, by explaining the patterns of Negro criminal behaviour in terms of *cultural* factors:

> Variation in sentencing according to the race of the offender and the victim does exist, but it is a function of intrinsic differences between the races in patterns of criminal behaviour. The Negro pattern is a product of the isolative social and historic forces that have molded the larger Negro subculture. The wide social distance between the races has pointed implications for the situation context, the behaviour system and, accordingly, the legal character of interracial crime in contrast with intraracial crime. ... The fault then lies not with the subversion of the judicial system by undemocratic racial attitudes, but with the wall of segregation limiting the Negro's access to culturally patterned norms of deviant behaviour as well as conventional behaviour.[50]

It has been seen that the social class background of magistrates and the issue of racial prejudice have been two major focuses of attention in studies of judicial decision-making; but there is obviously no limit to the number of different background characteristics and attitudes which could be included for study under such broad headings as 'personality' or the 'human element' in sentencing. Additional factors which various researchers have found to be associated with sentencing decisions have included age, political sympathies, experience on the bench, judicial reference groups and 'role patterns'. It is extremely rare to come across pieces of research which do not manage to relate one or other of such factors towards at least a partial explanation of sentencing disparity, although Roger Hood's most recent study of the sentencing of motoring offenders did reach the conclusion that 'very few consistent associations [were found] ... between any of the attributes describing social, political, personal background, magisterial or motoring experience and relative severity in fining or imprisoning'.[51] Nevertheless, a considerable amount of the evidence on the importance of some of the factors is conflicting, and by no means creates confidence in the validity of such explanations.

Typical examples of such conflicting evidence are to be found in those studies which have examined the importance in sentencing behaviour of judicial experience, reference groups and 'role patterns'. Thus, as early as 1933, Gaudet found no consistent relationships between many background characteristics of judges, such as length of service on the bench, and their different patterns of sentencing, so that he reached the conclusion that the sentencing tendencies of judges seemed to be largely determined before they ever sat on the bench to adjudicate and pass sentence.[52] In contrast, almost a generation later, the major hypothesis of Green's Philadelphia study was that 'certain elements of the professional role of the judge—norms rooted in law, judicial precedent, and the mores—have a restraining effect upon individual differences in penal philosophy, social background, or idiosyncrasies'.[53] Winick and his colleagues (1961) stressed that different judges might have different 'reference groups', which would directly influence their perception of their professional role; such reference groups might either increase or decrease the likelihood of sentencing disparities, as they ranged from important leaders of the judiciary, colleagues in higher courts and the ideal of justice, to the 'common man', defence lawyers and ideals of social amelioration.[54] As a final example, there is the well-known typology of judicial 'role

152

patterns', suggested by Smith and Blumberg: viz. (i) Intellec-
tual—Scholar; (ii) Routineer—Hack; (iii) Political Adven-
turer—Careerist; (iv) Judicial Pensioner; (v) Hatchet-Man; (vi)
Tyrant-Showboat-Benevolent Despot.[55] Such role patterns were seen
as deriving from a variety of factors and constraints in the sentencing
situation, including different aspects of judges' social backgrounds,
but especially from the functional requirements of the organization
and machinery of the criminal justice bureaucracy:

> Each judicial role type that has been indicated is cultivated, for
> each contributes in his own way to the total institutional arrange-
> ment, performing a systemic mission in terms of his own drives,
> need and personality.... The problem of objectivity, then, is one
> which is not only dependent upon individual social biographies, but
> also is filtered through an organisational ethos of efficiency and
> maximum production, which overrides concerns for the ideal of
> objectivity and uniformity.[56]

In view of such conflicting evidence and opinions about the
significance of specific aspects of judicial social background and
professional role constraints, it seems particularly important and
valuable that recent research, notably Hogarth's Ontario study, has
made considerable progress by investigating the human element in
sentencing along rather different lines. Instead of trying to draw rather
tenuous links between personal or professional characteristics and
decision-making, this research made a direct and explicit study of the
personal attitudes and philosophies of magistrates, which have tended
to remain merely *implicit* in most previous sentencing research.
Perhaps it should not really have come as so much of a surprise that
the main factors associated with sentencing decisions, and therefore
explaining many apparent disparities, were those attitudes and
philosophies of magistrates which relate directly to the task in
hand—the aims of a penal system, the relative roles of punishment
and treatment, the perception of the seriousness of the offences and
the potential social harm of particular offenders.[57]

In a rather unexpected and paradoxical way, Wheeler's study of
twenty-seven judges in Boston indicated how sentencing decisions
which initially appeared 'out-of-character', according to traditional

153

theories of relationships in sentencing, could be seen as entirely self-consistent and rational, if the judges' penal philosophies were closely examined and fully taken into account. Wheeler found that the judges who used institutional commitments most frequently, for the juveniles appearing before them, were those who were progressive, well-read in crime and delinquency, younger than average, less formal in court procedure, etc.—'In other words, it is just the judges whom we should think of as being permissive in attitude who take what most would regard as the more severe actions.'[58] On further analysis, it was found that the explanation of this seeming paradox lay in their view of the purposes and possibilities of institutional commitment for juvenile delinquents; whereas the general view sees institutional commitment and the length of custodial term as a measure of a judge's severity, essentially intended as a punishment, it appeared that these 'enlightened' judges stressed the positive 'treatment' aspects of institutional commitment, seeing it often as a more healthy environment for the delinquent than his own family and neighbourhood; in addition, and consistent with these views, these judges were much more sensitive to the existence of emotional disturbance among juveniles appearing before them, and correspondingly much less responsive to the perceived social harm of delinquent acts to the community.[59]

In his recent comprehensive Canadian study, John Hogarth examined the penal philosophies of Ontario magistrates in relation to the way they approached the sentencing decision. He discovered wide variations in the penal aims and beliefs held by the magistrates, including their views as to the effectiveness of different kinds of sentence, the criteria to be applied in deciding between different sentences and the ways of resolving conflicts between the needs of the offender and those of the community.[60] Interestingly, however, he found that once the personal penal philosophy of each magistrate was known, the pattern of his sentencing decisions reflected a consistent application of this set of aims and beliefs, so that magistrates were consistent within themselves while at the same time often *inconsistent* with each other.[61]

A more detailed analysis was carried out of judicial attitudes, using a variety of research techniques, to test the empirical relationship between attitudes and actual sentencing behaviour. Hogarth found that factorally derived attitude scales were better at predicting the behaviour of magistrates than were Likert scales; his analysis

154

produced five factors, around which magistrates' attitudes clustered: (i) Justice (i.e. 'just deserts', offence-oriented); (ii) Punishment corrects (i.e. individual deterrence); (iii) Intolerance (i.e. with regard to other forms of social deviance); (iv) Social defence (i.e. general deterrence); (v) Modernism (i.e. liberal permissiveness).[62] It was found that the first two factors, 'Justice' and 'Punishment corrects', were closely associated in the case of particular magistrates with patterns of sentencing behaviour, regardless of the type of offence being considered; the other three factors, on the other hand, were associated to varying degrees according to the nature of specific offences. Magistrates with high 'justice' scores exhibited relatively stern sentencing policies, although it was seen that this concern for justice incorporated an important *limiting* element with regard to the severity of punishment deemed to be warranted by an offence. High scores on the 'punishment corrects' factor were associated with a greater use of institutional commitments to reformatories, as distinct from prison or penitentiary sentences, in the belief that these institutions were more likely to provide education and training; some indirect confirmation of Wheeler's findings was provided by the fact that magistrates who frequently used reformatory sentences for this reason, also tended to commit for *longer terms,* so that the offenders could derive maximum benefit from the training facilities which were available![63]

It is impossible, in a short space, to convey adequately the range and depth of the findings deriving from Hogarth's study, which is full of valuable insights into the complex relationship between judicial attitudes and behaviour, and which lead him to describe sentencing, in the title of his book, as 'a human process', perhaps not as uniform or as impartial as many people might have hoped. The ultimate significance of the role of attitudes can only properly be considered after an examination of the role of other social and community constraints upon the sentencing process.

SENTENCING AND THE COMMUNITY

Despite the considerable emphasis in most sentencing studies upon the personal characteristics and attitudes of judges, attention has also been paid to the relationship between local community factors and

155

sentencing disparities, with or without an accompanying awareness that judicial attitudes and characteristics are often inextricably linked with their local community. Such a link is made more likely by the kind of criteria that are typically used in selecting magistrates, invariably from amongst eminent members of the community, both politically and socially. The two most recently published studies of sentencing, in England and Canada, document the strong links between the magistracy and local community affairs. In Hood's sample of English magistrates, just over half were or had been active in public service, for example as councillors or members of rent tribunals; over 60 per cent were involved in community work, such as social service organizations; and almost 90 per cent had a variety of other connexions with church affairs, charities or young people's organizations.[64] Similarly in Canada, Hogarth showed that virtually all Ontario magistrates were 'home town' people, and very much committed to membership of local organizations; less than 5 per cent had been born outside the census division where they now lived (compared to almost 40 per cent of the total adult population); nearly four fifths of them were active members of service clubs; one third held office in public service or charitable organizations, and two thirds were active participants in social and recreational clubs. Starting, then, from the plausible hypothesis that certain aspects of magistrates' sentencing behaviour may reflect the type of community in which they serve, we will survey briefly the kind of sentencing patterns which have been found to be associated with different communities. The British evidence will be considered first, followed by a selection of the findings from studies in other countries.

In his national survey of juvenile offenders appearing before the courts, Grünhut discovered that areas of the country in which the courts placed a higher than average proportion of juveniles on probation (with a correspondingly lower than average proportion fined) were usually areas with low delinquency rates (i.e. 'crimes known to the police'); conversely all the areas where there was a higher than average fining rate (and a correspondingly lower than average proportion of juveniles placed on probation) were high delinquency areas. Grünhut suggested, following the personal view of 'an experienced Chief Constable', that this was due to the essentially practical fact that in high delinquency areas the courts are so busy dealing with large

156

numbers of offenders that they have not sufficient time to give the necessary consideration to individual cases, which might in other circumstances have resulted in probation orders.[66] Grünhut's findings were confirmed by later English studies; analysis of data from Patchett and McClean's study of juvenile court decisions in the north of England, 1962–3, showed a similar, statistically significant, relationship between the use of probation and low delinquency rates;[67] and the Home Office Research Unit's survey of regional variations in the use of probation produced a perfect negative rank order correlation, showing that the greater the amount of indictable crime known to the police in a region so the smaller was the proportion of convicted persons put on probation.[68]

Hood's study of sentencing disparities in twelve selected English towns, published in 1962, provides the most interesting and important data on the links between community factors and sentencing patterns so far available for this country. The original selection of the courts had been on the basis of their differential use of imprisonment for adult offenders; when Hood examined a variety of the social characteristics of the towns served by the different courts (e.g. population density, social class distribution, extent of further education), he found that the rank order according to these social indices was almost the exact opposite to the rank order of sentencing patterns, so that those courts with a high rate of imprisonment were located in towns with better social conditions and a larger middle-class element than the courts which made less frequent use of imprisonment (see Table 4.7).[69] There was not quite such a consistent relationship between sentencing patterns and the local crime rate, but the two courts with the lowest rate of imprisonment had higher crime rates than the two courts which used imprisonment most frequently. Hood portrayed the towns with high imprisonment rates as embodying traditions of peaceful living, and 'small-town atmosphere'; they were, typically, historic cathedral towns or 'respectable' seaside resorts, with large proportions of retired people; the small size of most of these towns suggested the existence of close networks of public and private communications, in which the local press played a crucial role in reporting and commenting on the disposition of local court cases. In summary, the author felt that these towns had a greater 'consciousness of the community' than larger and more socially mixed areas, and also a

157

'common conscience' based on shared values, which included high regard for private property and a peaceful community life.[70]

It was seen, in the previous section, that the magistrates in these towns were more middle class than those on other benches, and it seems clear that there is a congruent pattern between the personal characteristics of magistrates, the type of community in which they live and their perception of their judicial responsibilities.

TABLE 4.7: *Rank order comparison of imprisonment rates and social conditions facing selected English magistrates' courts, 1951–4.*

Courts	Imprisonment rate	Density of population	% of males in social classes IV and V	% of males, aged 20–4, educated over age of 17
Nestbury	1	10	9	9
Highness	2	12	10	11
Regbury	3	6	12	5
Selbury	4	9	8	10
Monkford	5	4	2	3
Spagthorpe	6	1	4	2
Crumbledon	7	5	6	5
Rutlish	8	8	5	8
Ashlake	9	11	11	12
Tolville	10	7	7	7
Railton	11	2	1	2
Oldchester	12	3	1	1

Source: R. G. Hood *Sentencing in Magistrates' Courts* London (1962) Table 26, p. 66.

Amongst American studies, even Everson, with his great emphasis on the individual personality of judges, admitted that sentencing decisions would also reflect the temper of the communities in which the courts were situated, and he described typical communities of the time:

> In some communities, where there is a blue law conscience, the disorderly individual, the vagrant and the petty misdemeanant would be shown to fare badly in the hands of the law. In other com-

158

munities where there is more tolerance and an easygoing code of public deportment, the offenders guilty of similar infractions of the law would be found to receive light punishment, if any at all.[71]

Everson did not, however, consider the extent to which such community factors might modify the more idiosyncratic effects of the personality and temperament of judges.

Many years later, in his survey of disparities in American criminal procedure, Nagel revealed many different patterns of sentencing between urban and rural courts, and between courts in Northern states and those in Southern states. The urban and Northern courts were more likely to imprison those convicted of assault, than were the rural and Southern; but on the other hand, they were *less* likely to imprison those convicted of larceny. Nagel related the differences in handling assault cases to differences between notions of self-defence common in agricultural societies, contrasted with a reliance in industrialized societies upon public defence by professional police forces; with regard to larceny cases, agricultural societies emphasized the importance of property belonging to private individuals, whereas the emphasis in industrialized societies was upon property belonging to businesses and corporations.[72] In the light of his findings of significant disparities at various stages in the penal process, with regard to community factors such as urbanization and region, Nagel raised the question (to which we return below) of whether some of these disparities might perhaps be socially justifiable, for example whether penalties might justifiably vary from one regional culture to another.[73]

Finally, in Canada, Hogarth examined the relationship between the attitudes and penal philosophies of magistrates and the characteristics of their local communities; from this examination he was able to conclude that 'it appears that the attitudes of magistrates do, in fact, reflect the types of community in which they live', and these attitudes appeared to be those that were most appropriate to the problems they faced in their local community.[74] Thus, magistrates with high 'justice' scores, and those who attached great weight to 'social defence', were likely to live in communities characterized by a high degree of urbanization, a high crime rate and very mixed ethnic composition; magistrates who believed that 'punishment corrects' came predominantly from prosperous, high growth-rate communities, with a

159

low crime rate and mainly British population; magistrates with high 'tolerance' scores tended to come from rural, stable, French-speaking communities with a high crime rate; and, finally, magistrates who identified with liberal 'modernism' tended to come from socially and economically stable communities, where the crime rate was not particularly high.[75]

The one demographic characteristic which distinguished best among magistrates, in terms of their attitudes and beliefs, was the degree of urbanization of the community in which they lived. Urban magistrates attached less importance to reformation and more to the aims of deterrence and retribution; they were more likely to resolve conflicts between the needs of the offender and the needs of the community in favour of community protection; and, in assessing pre-sentence information, they were more likely to attach greater weight to the offence and criminal record than to the offender's social background. In actual sentencing behaviour, they were more likely to use penitentiary sentences, longer terms of ordinary imprisonment and fines; although some of these differences might be partially accounted for by differences in the types of cases appearing before them, it was also likely that the significant differences in their attitudes and penal philosophies were a major influence. In an attempt to discover whether the attitudes of the different groups of magistrates were *caused* by the social and community situations facing the courts in urban and rural areas, Hogarth further analysed the *range* of attitudes to be found amongst urban and rural magistrates. He found considerable variations, particularly within the group of urban magistrates, whereby some magistrates in urban areas were less punitive than many in rural communities, and, conversely, some magistrates in rural communities were more punitive than many in urban areas; these findings made him reject the simple hypothesis that the urban and rural situations themselves *cause* and thereby 'explain' the variations in magistrates' attitudes and sentencing behaviour.

Various aspects of the judicial role in an urban environment were examined to discover possible explanations of the wide variation in attitudes amongst the urban magistrates; it was found that although the basic influences in most urban communities encouraged the development of punitive judicial attitudes, yet it was possible for groups of magistrates to insulate themselves from these influences by social in-
160

teraction with like-minded colleagues and active participation in organizations, such as the Ontario Magistrates' Association; in addition, it seemed likely that the over-exposure of urban magistrates to various kinds of 'propaganda' for a pro-treatment approach to sentencing may well have helped to polarize the views of magistrates, making those who were initially 'anti-treatment' even more confirmed in their views.[76] The selection process and differential attractions of judicial office in urban and rural communities also seemed to go a long way towards explaining the paradoxical finding that the most punitive magistrates were the well-educated, younger, *urban* magistrates, whereas the *least* punitive were the well-educated, younger, *rural* magistrates; the status of magistrates in rural communities was very high, enjoying much more prestige than in most urban communities.

From this evidence, it is clear that the *reasons* for the connexion between community characteristics and judicial attitudes are complex, even though relationships of various kinds have been found in most research studies. There exists considerable support for two rather different interpretations: on the one hand, it can be argued that different communities contain people with distinct characteristics and personal attitudes, so that those who become magistrates simply retain pre-existing attitudes, without conscious reference to the community in their judicial decision-making; on the other hand, another interpretation, whilst accepting elements of truth in the first argument, goes further to suggest that, once magistrates have taken up appointment, they proceed to act directly on behalf of the perceived interests of their community. In terms of explaining or justifying the sentencing disparities which are associated with community characteristics, the first interpretation simply reduces the explanation to the influence of personal characteristics and attitudes, whereas the second interpretation raises important issues about the validity of magistrates and judges taking into account local community norms and values in their sentencing decisions. Smith and Blumberg were in no doubt that the judicial role has always been conditioned by and responded to the demands of a particular society or community:

In any given society, the role of a sentencing judge has been exercised in accordance with the ethos of that particular society or social order at that particular time. Over the years the judge, lawyer

161

or anyone else connected with the enforcement of laws has performed his function in accordance with the particular demands of a given society.[77]

In many of his writings, Blumberg has trenchantly attacked the American criminal justice system, which unfortunately is very vulnerable to many of the criticisms aimed against it; but, in any discussion of the sentencing process, it is much easier to point out apparent disparities and injustice, rather than to raise awkward but basic questions about the relationship between sentencing and a society's norms and values. However, at the beginning of his first study of sentencing in England, Roger Hood raised just such basic and problematic issues:

> The sociological theories of punishment rest upon the assumption that punishment for crimes should be related to the moral conscience of the community on whose behalf it is being inflicted. Unless the aims of punishment take into account the sensibility of the community, the penal system will not serve one of its primary functions, that is, to maintain communal stability.[78]

Not only does this statement raise crucial questions about how *change* can be brought about in a community's 'moral conscience', but, taken on its own terms, it raises questions about how magistrates are able to ascertain the common conscience or the strength of 'community consciousness'; as Hood says, magistrates' perceptions may be restricted to an unrepresentative section of the community, or be distorted by their own ideas and prejudices.

The main evidence which is available, from Hogarth's research, confirms some of the doubts expressed by Hood; in general terms, Ontario magistrates felt that the public was punitive and would prefer the courts to pass severer sentences on offenders; a third of the magistrates stated that they never considered public opinion in their decision-making, and most of the rest claimed to be 'guided' rather than 'controlled' by public opinion; they were equally divided on whether they agreed or disagreed with the statement that courts were the 'conscience of the community'.[79] Hogarth's general conclusion was that magistrates tend to define the constraints imposed by public opinion in ways which minimize inconsistency with their *private*

162

beliefs, and before being influenced by situational or community constraints they must not only be aware of the nature of the constraints, but must define them as part of their 'effective environment':

> The simple fact which emerges from these data is that the attitudes, definitions of constraints, and sentencing behaviour of magistrates are organised in congruence with one another. A punitive sentencing policy is associated both with punitive attitudes and with a belief that the law and the social situation demands a punitive response from the magistrate. A lenient sentencing policy is associated both with lenient attitudes and beliefs that the situation calls for a more lenient policy.... Certain reality aspects of the social environment do penetrate the consciousness of a judge resulting in a modification of his behaviour on the bench.[80]

The final question to be considered in this chapter is that of the mechanics of the process whereby information is selected and used by magistrates in reaching their sentencing decisions, and the relationship between this process and the other constraints inherent in the situation.

THE SELECTION AND USE OF INFORMATION

In most spheres of decision-making, it is becoming increasingly recognized that the availability of relevant information is one of the most important variables. As far as sentencing in England is concerned, one of the first official recognitions of the importance of information was contained in the report of the Streatfeild Committee, published in 1961.[81] The authors of this report related the need for more and different information for sentencers to the wider range of objectives gradually being pursued in the sentencing of offenders, as opposed to the former reliance on the 'tariff' system of justice; information should not just be proliferated for its own sake, but should be carefully selected according to the criteria of relevance, reliability and comprehensiveness. The Committee made detailed recommendations about ways of increasing the quality and quantity of information available to the courts before passing sentence, whilst at the same time being careful to emphasize that no amount of information *per se* can determine the relative weight that ought to be given to the various factors that can properly influence the choice of sentence.[82] This section will begin by considering the extent to which pre-sentence reports are available to English courts, and the evidence concerning the extent to which magistrates and judges appear to follow specific recommendations included in such reports.

In their early study of 400 cases of boys (aged 14–17 years, charged with theft) appearing before eight different juvenile courts in London, Mannheim and his colleagues recognized the importance of assessing the sources from which the courts obtained their information and impressions about the cases being heard, despite their awareness that magistrates differed in the way they interpreted and used the same information. They found tremendous variation in the amount of information available to the magistrates in the different courts, so that whereas Court 5 nearly always had maximum information for its decisions, Courts 2 and 3 invariably functioned with minimum information.[83] The proportion of these juvenile court cases in which probation reports were available before sentence varied from 50 per cent to 86 per cent, but with no systematic association between the availability of pre-sentence reports and different sentencing policies.

Jarvis analysed the use of pre-sentence reports from probation officers at Cornwall Quarter Sessions Courts, 1955–60.[84] Probation reports were presented in 336 (74 per cent) of the 453 cases heard during this period; 64 (20 per cent) of the reports included no specific recommendations for sentence, but the rest were divided equally between those for and those against probation. Table 4.8 shows the extent to which the recommendations were followed, and the 'success' of those cases in which probation orders were made. In only 18 (13 per cent) of the 135 cases where probation was *not* recommended did the court subsequently make a probation order, compared to 70 per cent of the recommendations *for* probation which were followed by the court; 80 per cent of the recommended cases successfully completed their period of probation, compared to only 50 per cent of those who had not been recommended, although all the 16 cases put on probation after no recommendation (for or against) had successful completions.

Hood examined the effects of an experimental local change in the procedure for providing pre-sentence reports (upon male indictable

164

offenders aged 17–21 years), following the publication of the Streatfeild Report. He carried out a survey, in Sunderland Magistrates' Courts, in which he compared the reconviction rate of 100 offenders in this category, sentenced during the two years before the change in procedure (June 1959–June 1961), with that of 100 offenders sentenced in the two years immediately following the change (September 1961–September 1963); the underlying assumption was that the provision of more pre-sentence reports should increase the 'effectiveness' of sentencing.[85] However, the overall reconviction rates of the two samples were found to be very similar, despite the fact that probation reports were available before sentence in more than three quarters of the cases in the second sample; of course, measuring 'effectiveness' by the official reconviction rate is only considering sentencing from a single point of view. Perhaps rather paradoxically, when the magistrates were asked to assess the usefulness of 259 pre-sentence reports (September 1962–September 1965), in 198 cases (76 per cent) they said that they had directly influenced their sentences, and in a further 56 cases (22 per cent) that they had been of help in other ways.[86]

TABLE 4.8: *Relationships between pre-sentence recommendations, sentences and outcome: Cornwall Q.S. Courts and Appeals Committee, 1955–60.*

	Recommendations in pre-sentence reports			No pre-sentence reports
	For probation	Against probation	No specific recommendation	
(a) Number of reports:	137	135	64	117
(b) Sentenced to probation:	97	18	16	13
(%)	(70%)	(13%)	(25%)	(11%)
(c) Successful completion of probation:	78	9	16	6
(%)	(80%)	(50%)	(100%)	(46%)

Source: F. V. Jarvis 'Inquiry Before Sentence', in T. Grygier *et al.* (eds) *Criminology in Transition* London (1965) Tables 4 and 5 p. 66.

The Home Office Research Unit's survey of regional variations in the use of probation found wide variations in the provision of pre-sentence social inquiry reports by probation officers, in cases tried at the higher courts in 1961, ranging from 33 per cent (London area) to

165

74 per cent (south of England), with an average of 58 per cent.[87] In all courts there was a positive relationship between the provision of pre-sentence reports and the extent to which the courts made probation orders on offenders, leading the authors to conclude, rather speculatively:

> Both factors may reflect the underlying relationship between justices and probation officers or the degree to which the probation service was staffed to provide a full service to the courts for both enquiries and probation supervision. However, the availability of social enquiry reports may have brought to the notice of the courts information about an offender's background which sometimes made his need of help or supervision clear in a way that the evidence of the case may not have done.[88]

An interim report of a research project, which started in 1966, studying adult males remanded for probation reports before sentence at Inner London Sessions, broadly confirmed the findings of Jarvis in Cornwall: exactly half of the first 159 reports included recommendations for probation, and 78 per cent of these offenders were placed on probation by the courts, who passed similar sentences in only 5 per cent of the cases in which the pre-sentence report recommended *against* probation; in addition, the courts followed seven out of ten of the other specific recommendations in the reports, whether for discharges, fines or imprisonment.[89]

The most recently published English study, by Peter Ford, studied 450 social inquiry reports in London, Oxford and Oxfordshire, for three separate years, 1960, 1964 and 1968.[90] Approximately four fifths of all reports each year contained recommendations for specific sentences, and approximately four fifths of all such recommendations were accepted by the sentencing courts. However, the author noted that almost two thirds of the 59 recommendations rejected by the courts were for or against probation, so that in these cases the courts apparently did not accept the probation officer's assessment of the offender's suitability for probation; in general, the rejection rate was slightly greater in the higher courts, than in the magistrates' or juvenile courts, suggesting that lay magistrates tend to follow sentencing advice more readily than judges or recorders.[91]

Some of the implications of these findings, and similar ones from studies of their own in America, were examined by Carter and Wilkins (1967), with particular reference to the problem of sentencing disparity; for if there is apparent 'agreement', in at least three-quarters of cases, between the pre-sentence recommendations of probation officers and the actual choice of sentence by magistrates and judges, then probation officers themselves must be directly implicated in any disparities which occur. They examined the relative rank order of importance attached to various factors, (a) by probation officers in their pre-sentence recommendations, and (b) by district judges in sentencing, in a sample of 500 cases from the northern district of California, 1964–5. In general there was a high degree of correlation, indicating considerable agreement between the two groups as to the significance of certain factors and characteristics for the choice of sentence.[92] In a parallel study of more than 1,200 pre-sentence recommendations in the northern district of California, 1964–7, Carter and Wilkins found that although the variation in the use of probation by different courts ranged from 78 per cent to 26 per cent, yet in all courts *at least 86 per cent* of probation officers' recommendations were accepted; in other words, the main variation occurred in the extent to which probation officers were prepared to make specific recommendations in the different courts, ranging from 14 per cent to 91 per cent.[93] The authors attributed most of the variation between probation officers to personal characteristics such as age, education and previous employment experience, particularly as disparities tended to diminish with length of service in probation work; so we are brought full circle back to one of the major explanations of *judicial* disparities, now seen to be compounded by the apparent way in which magistrates follow the recommendations of equally 'individual' probation officers!

Pre-sentence reports are only one, fairly specific, source of information available to the court; particularly in lower courts of summary jurisdiction, most information comes to magistrates more indirectly during the actual hearing, in which details of the offence will emerge and the magistrates form their own subjective opinion of the defendant; after conviction, the police are invariably asked if 'anything is known' about the defendant, and although this mainly refers to previous criminal record the police usually provide brief details of employment and family circumstances in their 'antecedents' report.

Thus in contrast to the organized presentation of information in a probation officer's pre-sentence report (often with some specific recommendation in mind from the beginning), the most common problem faced by magistrates is that of how to select relevant items from a typically much more haphazard accumulation of facts and opinion, before passing sentence; and, as the Streatfeild Committee noted, even when the information available is reasonably relevant, reliable and comprehensive, there is still the ultimate choice as to the relative weight to be given to particular aims and values in sentencing. Thus, in a discussion of the training of lay magistrates, Richard Sparks (1965) was very sceptical about the possibility of reducing disparities among magistrates, when they probably all had different objectives in mind; he claimed that it was no good giving magistrates large quantities of information, unless they were also given adequate guidance as to the correct *application* of that information in concrete cases, for 'until magistrates are told what they ought to do in cases of a given type, they cannot but go on doing a great many things for equally different reasons'.[94]

Hogarth listed eleven factors contributing to the selective interpretation of information by magistrates, ranging from the lack of agreement as to the proper principles in sentencing, and an inadequate range of sentencing alternatives, to the amount of unguided discretion in information-use given by the law and the status differences between those who provide and those who receive information.[95] He analysed the way different magistrates selected and used information in a sample of 2,354 indictable cases (February 1966–August 1967), and how their styles of 'information-search' were related to other judicial attitudes and characteristics. The magistrates who used more sources of information tended to have rather higher reformation and lower deterrence and retribution scores than average; both the number of sources and the type of information relied upon were consistent with the personal values and subjective goals of the individual magistrates:

> The selective use of information enables magistrates to maintain their original attitudes intact. Magistrates tend to seek information consistent with their preconceptions. . . . At the same time, they tend to avoid information which is likely to present a picture of the offender that may conflict with their expectations.[96]

It emerged clearly from Hogarth's research that the attitudes and penal philosophies of magistrates acted as filters through which information was allowed to pass only very selectively; however much information they were exposed to, magistrates seemed to develop characteristic ways of isolating certain 'facts' which then controlled (or reinforced) their decisions. Magistrates with high punitive scores, tended to have simple and concrete ways of organizing sentencing information, and were generally characterized by stereotyped and compartmentalized thinking. Non-punitive magistrates, on the other hand, tended to use information in more complex and subtle ways, with a more autonomous and flexible approach, and showing a greater tolerance for conflict and ambiguity. In this, as in most other aspects of his study, Hogarth found an inner consistency and logic in most magistrates' approach to sentencing, in which attitudes, social backgrounds, objectives, community norms and information-use were all organized (whether consciously or not) into a congruent whole— '*consistency appears to have been achieved through the mechanism of selectivity*' (emphasis added).[97]

Certain tentative conclusions about the sentencing process and the 'explanation' of disparities seem to be justified on the basis of the evidence reviewed in this chapter.[98] The three elements of the process, which have been examined here, all seem to contribute towards the different sentencing patterns which have been observed between different courts; viz. (i) the social background and attitudes of individual magistrates and judges; (ii) the characteristics of the communities in which the courts are situated; (iii) the extent and type of information available to the courts before passing sentence. Different researchers have emphasized one or other of these elements as being of more significance than the others; but, in this writer's view, the evidence of Hogarth's impressive study is most persuasive, according to which the most fundamental influences upon sentencing behaviour are the penal philosophies and attitudes of individual magistrates; these attitudes provide the framework through which the other social and procedural constraints are filtered, in a way which is broadly consistent with the magistrates' existing attitudes and objectives in sentencing. The implications of this view for explaining sentencing disparities are fairly clear: such disparities are to be seen as stemming mainly

169

from the way magistrates and judges selectively interpret and respond to their 'effective environment' in sentencing, resulting in a considerable degree of *self-consistency* but, as an inevitable corollary, an equal or greater degree of *inconsistency* between different sentencers. Such inconsistency must by definition, always contain an element of 'injustice' for convicted offenders appearing before different judges, but the degree to which particular sentences may also be considered 'unjustified', on their own terms, can only be assessed after a close examination of the validity not only of the individual sentencer's own penal objectives but also of the social and situational constraints to which the final sentencing decision is a response.

NOTES

1. See the interesting observations in I. S. Drapkin 'Criminological Aspects of Sentencing', in Drapkin (ed.) *Scripta Hierosolymitana: Vol. XXI, Studies in Criminology*, pp. 40ff.; also M. Grünhut *Juvenile Offenders before the Courts* Oxford (1956) pp. 8–10.
2. R. O. Dawson *Sentencing: the Decision as to Type, Length and Conditions of Sentence* Boston (1969) p. 216.
3. R. G. Hood *Sentencing in Magistrates' Courts* London (1962) pp. 14–16: e.g. 'By "equality" we do not mean that each case can be exactly compared with another, and that the decisions should be the same for cases "alike" in this sense. By "equality" we mean "equality of consideration", that is, that similar general considerations can be taken into account when a decision is made' (p. 14).
4. V. Aubert 'Conscientious Objectors before Norwegian Military Courts', in G. Schubert (ed.) *Judicial Decision-making* New York (1963) p. 201; see also Drapkin *op. cit.*
5. President's Commission on Law Enforcement and Administration of Justice *Task Force Report: the Courts* Washington, D.C.(1967) p. 23.
6. Compare the similar framework and sentencing model used by John Hogarth as the basis for his study of sentencing in Ontario: J. Hogarth 'Sentencing Research—Some Problems of Design', *Brit. Jo. Crim.* Vol. 7 (1967) p. 84; the research is fully reported in Hogarth *Sentencing as a Human Process* Toronto (1971).
7. Grünhut *op. cit.* Oxford (1956) ch. 3.
8. Grünhut *ibid.* p. 108.
9. H. Mannheim *et al.* 'Magisterial Policy in the London Juvenile Courts' *Brit. Jo. Del.* Vol. 7 (1957) pp. 13, 119.
10. Mannheim *et al. ibid.* p. 16.
11. *Ibid.* p. 136.
12. K. W. Patchett and J. D. McClean 'Decision-making in Juvenile Cases' *Crim. L. R.* |1965| p. 699.
13. *Ibid.* p. 703.

14. Hood *op. cit.*
15. *Ibid.* p. 47.
16. *Ibid.* pp. 121–3.
17. Hood *Sentencing the Motoring Offender* London (1972).
18. *Ibid.* pp. 130–5: 'Thus, the more the offence corresponded to the accepted definition of a crime in producing definite harm, or the offender showed himself to be relatively anti-social, the greater the disparity in sentencing. . . . It seems, then, that there is greater agreement among magistrates for the "easier-to-price" regulatory kind of offences than for those which more of them see as akin to crime in their seriousness.'
19. G. Everson 'The Human Element in Justice', *Jo. Crim. Law, Crimin. and P.S.*, Vol. **10** (1920) p. 90; see Tables, pp. 94–5.
20. *Ibid.* p. 97.
21. *Ibid.* pp. 98–9.
22. The findings were published in several slightly different forms, between 1933 and 1949; as the statistical bases were not always identical, the statistics used here are taken from the 1949 article; see F. J. Gaudet, G. S. Harris and C. W. St John 'Individual Differences in the Sentencing Tendencies of Judges' *Jo. Crim. Law, Crimin. and P.S.* Vol. **23** (1933) p. 811; Gaudet, Harris and St John 'Individual Differences in Penitentiary Sentences Given by Different Judges', *Jo. Applied Psychology* Vol. **8** (1934) p. 675; Gaudet *Individual Differences in the Sentencing Tendencies of Judges,* Archives of Psychology No. 230 New York (1938); and Gaudet 'The Sentencing Behavior of the Judge' in V. C. Branham and S. B. Kutash (eds) *Encyclopaedia of Criminology* New York (1949) pp. 449–61.
23. Gaudet 'Sentencing Behavior' Tables IV and V, pp. 459–60.
24. *Ibid.* p. 452; for similar conclusions see M. F. McGuire and A. Holtzoff 'The Problem of Sentence in the Criminal Law', *Boston Univ. Law Rev.* Vol. **20** (1940) pp. 423ff., at 427–8.
25. E. Green *Judicial Attitudes in Sentencing* London (1961) pp. 67–9.
26. *Ibid.* see Appendix, Tables 44–6, pp. 135–6; also R. G. Hood and R. F. Sparks *Key Issues in Criminology* London (1970) Table 5.3, p. 150.
27. Green *op. cit.* p. 62.
28. S. Shoham 'Sentencing Policy of Criminal Courts in Israel' *Jo. Crim. Law, Crimin. and P.S.* Vol. **50** (1959) p. 327.
29. *Ibid.* Table II p. 333.
30. Hogarth *op. cit.*
31. Gaudet 'Sentencing Behavior' p. 450.
32. Hood and Sparks *op. cit.* pp. 152–4; see also the comments about the non-rational aspects of 'gastronomical jurisprudence' in C. Winick *et al.* 'The Psychology of Judges' in H. Toch (ed.) *Legal and Criminal Psychology* New York (1961) p. 132.
33. *Royal Commission on Justices of the Peace 1946—8* Cmd 7463 London (1948) Table III, p. 8.
34. S. S. Nagel 'Off-the-Bench Judicial Attitudes' in Schubert (ed.) *op. cit.* p. 29.
35. *Ibid.* p. 39.
36. Nagel 'Judicial Backgrounds and Criminal Cases' *Jo. Crim. Law, Crimin. and P.S.* Vol. **53** (1962) pp. 333ff., at 339; see also Nagel 'The Relationship between the Political and Ethnic Affiliation of Judges and their Decision-making', in Schubert (ed.) *Judicial Behavior* Chicago (1964).
37. Hogarth *op. cit.* pp. 53–4.

38. *Ibid.* p. 212.
39. J. B. Grossman 'Social Backgrounds and Judicial Decision-making' *Harvard Law Review* Vol. **79** (1966) pp. 1551ff., at 1553–61.
40. Hood *Sentencing in Magistrates' Courts* pp. 76–8. For a contrary hypothesis concerning the relationship between attitudes and social class, see S. M. Lipset 'Democracy and Working-class Authoritarianism' *Amer. Soc. Rev.* Vol. **24** (1959) p. 482; compare also the comments in C. Winick *et al. op. cit.* about the unpredictable relationship between a man's parental background and his own attitudes: '. . . one judge who is the son of a conservative father may be relatively radical, whereas a judge who is the son of a radical may be relatively conservative on the bench, although both men are reacting to their father's background' (p. 129).
41. V. Aubert *op. cit.* p. 207.
42. *Ibid.* pp. 210–11.
43. Nagel 'Disparities in Criminal Procedure' *U.C.L.A. Law Rev.* Vol. **14** (1967) p. 1272.
44. *Ibid.* p. 1296.
45. Sellin 'Race Prejudice in the Administration of Justice' *Amer. Jo. Soc.* Vol. **41** (1935) p. 212.
46. H. A. Bullock 'Significance of the Racial Factor in the Length of Prison Sentences', *Jo. Crim. Law, Crimin. and P.S.* Vol. **52** (1961) p. 411.
47. *Ibid.* p. 417.
48. E. Green *op. cit.* pp. 51–63.
49. Green 'Inter- and Intra-racial Crime Relative to Sentencing' *Jo. Crim. Law, Crimin. and P.S.* Vol. **55** (1964) p. 348.
50. *Ibid.* p. 358.
51. Hood *Sentencing the Motoring Offender* pp. 140ff.
52. F. J. Gaudet *et al.* 'Individual Differences' p. 814.
53. Green, *Judicial Attitudes* p. 67.
54. C. Winick *et al. op. cit.* p. 136.
55. A. B. Smith and A. S. Blumberg 'The Problem of Objectivity in Judicial Decision-making' *Social Forces* Vol. **46** (1967) pp. 96ff., at 103–5.
56. *Ibid.* p. 105.
57. An earlier awareness of the relevance of such *specific attitudes* is to be found in Schubert 'Judicial Attitudes and Voting Behavior: the 1961 Term of the United States Supreme Court' *Law and Contemporary Problems* Vol. **28** (1963) p. 100.
58. S. Wheeler *et al.* 'Agents of Delinquency Control: A Comparative Analysis', in Wheeler (ed.) *Controlling Delinquents* New York (1968) p. 56.
59. *Ibid.* pp. 57–8.
60. Hogarth *Sentencing as a Human Process* ch. 5, pp. 68–93.
61. *Ibid.* p. 91; see also Hood and Sparks *op. cit.* p. 154.
62. Hogarth *Sentencing as a Human Process* ch. 7, pp. 103–37.
63. *Ibid.* p. 156.
64. Hood *Sentencing the Motoring Offender* p. 54.
65. Hogarth *Sentencing as a Human Process* pp. 62–3.
66. Grünhut *op. cit.* pp. 74–5.
67. L. Sebba, 'Decision-making in Juvenile Cases—A Comment' *Crim. L. R.* [1967], pp. 347ff., at 353.
68. H. Barr and E. O'Leary *Trends and Regional Comparisons in Probation* London (1966) pp. 30–4, esp. Table F, p. 31; this Home Office study also found a high

correlation between the use of probation orders by the courts and the availability of pre-sentence reports, which suggested that there might be the same underlying factors responsible for both these aspects of the decision-making process.

69. Hood *Sentencing in Magistrates' Courts* pp. 65ff.
70. *Ibid.* pp. 72–5.
71. Everson *op. cit.* p. 90.
72. Nagel 'Disparities in Criminal Procedure' p. 1292.
73. *Ibid.* p. 1296: 'Thus, it is understandable that in the frontier days of the early West, horse thieves were severely treated, but those who committed assault were not. Nevertheless, most of the disparities . . . probably cannot be logically justified in terms of societal interest.'
74. Hogarth *Sentencing as a Human Process* p. 220.
75. *Ibid.* pp. 218–20.
76. *Ibid.* pp. 222–4.
77. Smith and Blumberg *op. cit.* p. 96.
78. Hood *Sentencing in Magistrates' Courts* p. 17.
79. Hogarth *Sentencing as a Human Process* p. 220.
80. *Ibid.* pp. 209–10.
81. *Report of the Interdepartmental Committee on the Business of the Criminal Courts* Cmnd. 1289 London (1961) part B, chs. 9–11, pp. 76–118.
82. *Ibid.* p. 84: '. . . we are not concerned with the relative weight to be given to the different objectives of sentencing but with the information which is the essential basis of an informed judgment on where the right balance lies' (para 290).
83. H. Mannheim *et al. op. cit.* Table VIII, p. 32.
84. F. V. Jarvis 'Inquiry Before Sentence', in T. Grygier *et al* (eds.) *Criminology in Transition* London (1965) p. 65.
85. Hood 'A Study of the Effectiveness of Pre-sentence Investigations in Reducing Recidivism' *Brit. Jo. Crim.* Vol. **6** (1966) p. 303.
86. *Ibid.* Table 1, p. 304. A third sample of offenders sentenced between October 1963 and October 1964 had a similar overall reconviction rate to that in the first two samples, but the criminal records of the last sample were rather worse, so that 'an encouraging trend' was seen: see Hood and I. Taylor 'Second Report of the Effectiveness of Pre-sentence Investigations in Reducing Recidivism' *Brit. Jo. Crim.* Vol. **8** (1968) p. 431.
87. H. Barr and E. O'Leary *op. cit.* Table H, p. 33.
88. *Ibid.* p. 34.
89. W. McWilliams 'Pre-sentence Study of Offenders: An Interim Report', *Case Conference* Vol. **15** (1968) p. 136.
90. P. Ford *Advising Sentencers* Oxford (1972).
91. *Ibid.* p. 28.
92. R. M. Carter and L. T. Wilkins 'Some Factors in Sentencing Policy', *Jo. Crim. Law, Crimin. and P.S.* Vol. **58** (1967) p. 503; by no means all the evidence suggests that judges and probation officers consider the same factors to have the same relevance for the choice of sentence, e.g. S. Z. Gross 'The Prehearing Juvenile Report: Probation Officers' Conceptions' *Jo. Research in Crime and Del.* Vol. **4** (1967) p. 212.
93. Carter and Wilkins *op. cit.* pp. 511–12, Tables X and XI.
94. R. F. Sparks 'Sentencing by Magistrates: Some Facts of Life' in P. Halmos (ed.) *Sociological Studies in the British Penal Services* Keele (1965) p. 78.
95. Hogarth *Sentencing as a Human Process* pp. 299ff.

173

96. *Ibid.* p. 244.
97. *Ibid.*: '... magistrates choose selectively certain kinds of information, they interpret it selectively, they selectively ascribe importance to certain features of the case to the exclusion of others, and they select among purposes in sentencing those which are most consistent with their personal values and subjective ends' (p. 291).
98. For similar interpretations, see the excellent 'model of the sentencing process' constructed by Roger Hood, in Hood and Sparks *op. cit.* Figure 5.5, pp. 168–9; and particularly John Hogarth's conclusions pp. 341–4.

5 PRISON CLASSIFICATION AND PAROLE

The traditional attention which is focused on the sentencing process tends to conceal the considerable limitations upon the actual control which courts exercise over both the *nature* and the *length* of custodial sentences. The degree of this control varies according to the legal and organizational structures of different jurisdictions, but an examination of prison classification procedures and parole decisions will illustrate how the apparent power of sentencers is considerably modified in practice by the subsequent decisions made by prison and parole authorities.

AIMS OF IMPRISONMENT

A basic dilemma which surrounds any examination of the prison and parole stages of the penal process is that of the confusion and conflicts between the various objectives which influence the handling of convicted offenders. Some preliminary consideration of these aims and objectives must precede the more detailed study of the procedures involved, in order to provide the basis for subsequent interpretations. Conflict and confusion in aims exists not only *within* prison departments but *between* sentencing authorities and prison departments; although one 'solution' to the dilemma is simply to regard these two major areas of the penal process as entirely separate and unrelated in aims and organization, yet to separate them in such a way seems to be an avoidance of a critical problem in the structure of criminal justice systems, which ought to be seen as culminating and having their aims fulfilled in the post-sentence stage. Most of the scholars involved in the American Bar Foundation's programme of research into decision-making in the penal process were at pains to

175

show the essential unity of the whole process from arrest to parole revocation, whilst at the same time their research revealed the numerous conflicts at practically every stage of the same process. Thus, Dawson emphasized the need to revise the traditional view of corrections and imprisonment as separate from the earlier stages of criminal justice administration, and to recognize them as absolutely integral parts of the system:

> The stake of police, prosecutors, and trial judges in the correctional process seems as great as the importance of preconviction criminal justice administration to correctional agencies. The criminal justice system through conviction can be viewed as an elaborate intake process for corrections—as a method of selecting the persons who should be subjected to correctional control and treatment. Thus conceived, the goals of the criminal law are largely realized in the correctional process, and an ineffective correctional process can nullify the efforts of police, prosecutors, and trial courts.[1]

Accepting, therefore, the desirability and importance of viewing imprisonment as an integrated part of the penal process, what evidence is there concerning the aims of imprisonment, both at an official and 'grass-roots' level, which might help us to understand the various constraints upon classification and parole decisions?

A perusal of practically any official statement of prison objectives, in Britain or America, could easily create the impression that the aims of imprisonment are entirely non-problematic, although this fact itself is in many ways the crux of the problem. Typical of these official statements is Rule 1 of the Prison Rules (1964) for England and Wales, which states that 'the purpose of the training and treatment of convicted offenders shall be to encourage and assist them to lead a good and useful life'. However, there are some indications of a growing awareness, even in official circles, that this kind of over-simplification is no longer appropriate; so that, in an unusually honest and realistic Home Office publication, *People in Prison* (1969), we find the following discussion of aims:

> Few large organisations have only one aim, and it often obscures the real situation to try to bring all the activities of any one of them within one simple formula or slogan. Some of the confusion felt about the aims of the prison service arises from attempts to do so.

176

Those aims can best be summarised as follows. *First, it is the task of the service, under the law, to hold those committed to custody and to provide conditions for their detention which are currently acceptable to society* [emphasis added]. Second, in dealing with convicted offenders, there is an obligation on the service to do all that may be possible within the currency of the sentence to encourage and assist them to lead a good and useful life.[2]

Such an official statement of the main aims of the prison service does not, of course, indicate the way in which (or whether) the aims can be successfully combined, but simply reaffirms a belief that *security* and *rehabilitation* are not mutually exclusive, and do not vary in inverse proportion to each other. The evidence from sociological studies of penal institutions tends to confirm the importance of the aims of security and control, and at the same time casts considerable doubt on the possibility of their successful coexistence with rehabilitation.

An explicit recognition that the main conflict in prisons is between *security/control* and *rehabilitation* has been surprisingly slow to emerge and disentangle itself from the view that the main problem is the conflicting claims of rehabilitation versus *deterrence* and/or *punishment*. In fact, in England, this has mainly occurred since the watershed of the mid-1960s, when an accumulation of problems, centred around the abolition of capital punishment, prison escapes and long-term sentences of imprisonment, precipitated a crisis situation which, if nothing else, meant that certain realities about the nature of imprisonment could no longer be evaded by the prison administration and by the public at large. A fascinating historical study by J. E. Thomas (1972) has convincingly argued that many of the problems of English prison administration, particularly since the 'progressive' report of the Gladstone Committee in 1895, have been due to the existence of a latent commitment to the primacy of *control* at the 'grass-roots' prison level, which has been ignored or distorted by prison officials, penal reformers and even by many sociologists, whose commitment to the need for rehabilitation has led them to focus on the wrong issues:

Since there is an underlying assumption that the prison organisation ought to be reformative in task, reasons have to be sought as to why it is not. It is assumed that there must be blockages in the

177

achievement of this task. If reformation is not being carried out, what is it that the prison is doing? It is being punitive. Thus, like the historian, the sociologist assumes that the primary conflict in prison is between reformation and deterrence.[3]

Before the end of the nineteenth century, there had been relatively little conflict of this kind within English prisons, because measures dictated by a concern for control were usually entirely compatible with the aims and methods of a prison system whose official task was deterrence, and it is just this kind of 'compatibility' which makes it very difficult for contemporary prison authorities to avoid their basic control measures being 'misconstrued' as deriving from deterrent/punitive objectives.

By no means all sociologists have been unaware of the importance of social control in prison communities, and many of their findings can be seen to be of relevance for the examination of classification and release decisions. In his study of Trenton maximum-security prison, New Jersey, Gresham Sykes emphasized social control as perhaps the most important single factor in analysing the social structure of an institution of this kind, showing that it was a major aim in its own right, and not merely useful instrumentally as a way of punishing the inmates.[4] Similarly, in their comprehensive survey of a range of different institutions for juvenile offenders in the United States, Street and his colleagues showed that in every type of correctional institution a system of social control had been developed by the staff for purposes of inmate management:

> The system must come to terms with the fact that the inmates are involuntary members of the organization who have a high potential for disrupting activities. The system involves scheduling, monitoring, classifying, and differentiating among the inmates; defining authority and personal relations between staff and inmates; establishing rewards and sanctions over inmate behavior and the bases on which they are to be allocated; and dealing with the collective patterns that emerge among the inmates.[5]

Finally, on the basis of his international survey of corrections, Conrad (1965) diagnosed the existence of what he called the 'irrational equilibrium' in penal policy and practice, being an uneasy accom-

178

modation of the many conflicting interests in the custodial handling of convicted offenders; he reported various examples of 'advanced practice' in corrections, which suggested to him the general outlines for developing an internally consistent theory and set of objectives for prisons, but most of what he saw in the many different countries he visited was dominated by an overriding concern for control. 'Control' was the prime consideration in penal institutions, and of almost equal significance in probation and parole, so that this common denominator meant that all other humanitarian and rehabilitative activities had to be reconciled to its requirements.[6]

This increasing recognition of the centrality of control and security in prison management has important consequences for any discussion of the aims of imprisonment. From the perspective of prison authorities, the aims of rehabilitation and treatment are most likely to be weighed in the balance against considerations of security and control, and *not* against such other possible aims as deterrence or punishment. From the perspective of sentencing authorities, it is clear that the position is very different: sentencers certainly consider what weight is to be given to the aims of deterrence and punishment, as opposed to individual reformation, but for them security and control play virtually no part in their assessment of sentencing aims, except as an assumed context in which the other aims will be carried out. If this is indeed an accurate picture of the situation, a fundamental division is seen to exist between judicial aims and the aims of the prison authorities, which would seem to rule out the possibility of any real integration between these two stages of the penal process; at the same time, it would seem to go a long way towards explaining why decisions on prison classification and parole so often result in the apparent intentions of the sentencers being nullified in practice.

CLASSIFICATION IN THEORY AND PRACTICE

Definitions and purposes

In an attempt to gain a better understanding of the penal process, the very fact that the term 'classification' is used in many different ways is a signal to study the variety of its actual usage, rather than to try to put forward a personal definition of one's own choosing. To examine what prison classification is (however confused and confusing) seems more profitable in this context, than to state what it *ought* to be, as the latter can only be usefully discussed in relation to the known or desired objectives of the wider penal process of which it is a part. Leslie Wilkins has, once again, cleared the ground for our approach to this problem, by suggesting some of the important elements which must be distinguished in any discussion of the theory and practice of classification. Whilst accepting that classification is *not necessarily* the same as the separation and distribution of offenders to different penal institutions (or parts of the same institution), Wilkins recognized that in practice most prison Classification Centres are concerned with the task of allocating offenders to different institutions according to a variety of criteria.[7] He stated that, in the penal context, the purposes of classification were related to some form of action, drawing an important distinction between cases where classification serves mainly as an *administrative convenience,* and cases where it is for *treatment purposes.*

Official statements of the purposes underlying the prison classification process tend to vary from the exclusively treatment-oriented definitions, to be found in much American literature, to the typical mixture of comprehensive but potentially conflicting criteria put forward in British official publications. Thus, the following definition is from the American Correctional Association's *Manual of Correctional Standards* (1966):

> The primary objective of classification as a systematic process is the development and administration of an integral and realistic program of treatment for the individual with procedures for changing the program when indicated. . . . Classification, therefore, is neither specific training nor general treatment, but rather the process through which the resources of the correctional institution can be applied effectively to the individual case.[8]

For England and Wales, the *Prison Rules* (1964) state that prisoners shall be classified 'having regard to their age, temperament, and record, and with a view to maintaining good order and facilitating training, and, in the case of convicted prisoners, of furthering the purpose of their training and treatment as provided by Rule 1'. In the
180

more recent Home Office publication, *People in Prison* (1969), the classification and allocation process was described in rather more detail, indicating the following four aims:

(a) to obtain and record certain basic information about each prisoner, and about his family background;
(b) to attempt to identify his needs and, if possible, the factors that may have led to his criminal behaviour, as an essential to any attempt to deal with them while he is in custody;
(c) to settle his 'security' category;
(d) in the light of these factors, and of the resources available in the region, to recommend where he should serve the whole or the first part of his sentence.[9]

It seems clear that 'classification' in much contemporary American literature refers to what Mannheim and Spencer termed *internal* classification (i.e. for differential treatment *within the same institution*), whereas in Britain it usually refers to *external* classification (i.e. for allocating categories of offenders to *different types of institutions*), although we shall see (below) how classification in English prisons was originally mainly a question of internal segregation.[10] Even when the main purpose of classification is the allocation of offenders to particular institutions, this does not rule out the additional function of the investigation and diagnosis of treatment needs at the classifying stage, whether or not such investigations have a direct influence on the choice of institution.[11] However, despite the increasing official emphasis upon and the investment of specialized resources in the diagnostic/treatment aspects of the classification process, it is doubtful whether the basic administrative and management concerns, which emerge from a study of the historical development of classification, have lost much of their overriding influence on the process, even though the criteria and justifications for these concerns may have become somewhat more sophisticated with the passage of time.

English prison classification, 1777–1967

In John Howard's historic survey of English prison conditions, *State of the Prisons* (1777), the major recommendations were for 'separation' (i.e. individual cells for sleeping accommodation) and

181

'classification', by which Howard meant work and association by day in common rooms, according to a number of different classes of prisoner. Attempts were made in the last two decades of the eighteenth century to introduce the principle of complete 'separation' into the proposed new penitentiaries, and to encourage local prisons to provide separate cells for all their inmates, but the inability of the central government to enforce these discretionary provisions meant that little real progress was made in this direction. Thus, in the Prisons Act of 1823, the idea of separate cells was dropped in favour of the principle of classification, so that prisoners were to be divided into five classes, according to whether they were convicted or unconvicted, felons or misdemeanants, or came into the miscellaneous category of 'debtors and vagrants'. This first serious attempt at classification in English prisons was therefore mainly an *internal* classification, based on the desirability of *segregation* rather than differential treatment. 'Segregation' was mainly advocated to avoid the dangers of 'contamination', but it was obvious to many contemporary critics that any classification according to legal status and category of crime was a very crude way of assessing a prisoner's potential for 'contaminating' his fellows.

At about this time, in the 1820s and 1830s, information was coming from America about the rival systems of prison organization, exemplified by the Philadelphia 'Separate System' and the Auburn 'Silent System', with the former deriving from a religious commitment to the reformative value of introspection, and the latter influenced, among other things, by economic and commercial considerations of prison work. Lively public and political debate in England about the relative merits of these systems resulted in official support being given to the Separate System, particularly in view of the arguments that current 'classification' was irrelevant to the problem of contamination. A massive prison building programme was started, with the opening of Pentonville 'model' prison in 1842, followed by more than fifty similar prisons within the next ten years, all built on the basis of separate cellular confinement. The second half of the nineteenth century saw the consolidation of this system of prison organization, which not only continued to provide safeguards against contamination, but in its effects was entirely compatible with the other penal principles of this period, namely deterrence, punishment and the uniform treatment of prisoners. It could also be argued that the nature of official concern about the dangers of contamination was subtly changing during the nineteenth century, from a concern with the moral and personal dangers to fellow prisoners to a concern for its potentially undermining effects on prison discipline and the ability of staff to maintain control over prisoners; seen in this light, the separate system conveniently reduced the risks both of moral contamination and the weakening of prison discipline and control.[12]

The Gladstone Committee (1895) was anxious to introduce important reformative elements into the English prison system, and apparently saw no basic incompatibility in retaining deterrence and reformation as concurrent aims. Concern for the individual treatment of prisoners led it to recommend the early mitigation of the system of separate cellular confinement, and the introduction of elements of daily association, which formed the basis for prison development during the twentieth century. Accepting Thomas' perceptive analysis of this period of English prison history, it would seem that the Gladstone Committee was fully aware that separation and the silence rule were intended to prevent contamination and to deter, but felt that the risks were exaggerated so that, on balance, the advantages of association outweighed the disadvantages.[13]

Increased provision for association among prisoners at the turn of the century was accompanied by renewed attempts at classification; once again, the main purpose of this classification was the segregation of different categories of prisoner to avoid 'moral contamination', but the latent control function of this classification was a greater source of potential conflict within prisons because of the new official aims of rehabilitation introduced at the same time. The allocation of certain prisoners to the 'Star' class was begun in all local prisons in 1896–7 (having operated in convict prisons since 1879), with the aim of achieving 'the separation of such prisoners from those who are versed in crime and of corrupt habits'.[14] An instructive experiment was tried, by the Prisons Act of 1898, which allowed judges and magistrates direct control over the prison treatment of those whom they sentenced, by directing that they be placed in the First or Second Division; the criteria for such a direction by sentencers included evidence of 'good character', a crime due to special circumstances or 'merely temporary deviation', or, in the case of the First Division, if they were fine defaulters or 'first-class misdemeanants'.[15] In fact, so

183

very little use was made of these powers by judges that, in their Report for 1910–11, the Prison Commissioners suggested that these powers should be left entirely in the hands of the prison authorities. The prison inquiry carried out by Hobhouse and Brockway (1922) showed that there was very little difference in the conditions of the Second and Third Divisions, and sometimes the very segregation of Second Division prisoners limited the type of work which was available for them; in any case, between 1900–14, only 1–2 per cent of all prisoners were allocated to the Second Division. Similarly, witnesses giving evidence to the inquiry suggested that allocation to the 'Star' class was purely segregational, sometimes even with more *severe* treatment meted out to star class prisoners than to ordinaries by prison officers. The authors' general conclusions were that the main objects of existing prison classification were almost entrely negative:

> Appropriate treatment for the different types of criminals is the positive and more important object. This aim the prison authorities have to all intents and purposes ignored. As for individual treatment, the goal of classification, it is not even dimly hinted at under present conditions. . . . From the point of view of treatment, that is of fitting prisoners for ordinary life, it is doubtful whether specialised segregation is of value beyond a certain point. Unless special treatment demanding separation be necessary, the limitation of association to persons of the same peculiar or degraded type may be positively harmful.[16]

These sentiments expressed by Hobhouse and Brockway in many ways go further than the conventional 'reformist' viewpoint; it is easy to agree that there are 'negative' and 'positive' aims of classification, with the former characterized by administrative concern for segregation, control and the avoidance of contamination, and the latter by an overriding concern for the treatment of the individual; but, whereas it is often believed that the *same classification* can serve both aims simultaneously, Hobhouse and Brockway suggest that it is most unlikely that a prison community which is the product of a negative, administrative classification will be conducive to the more positive treatment needs of the prisoner.[17]

In fact, for most of the present century in England, up to the introduction of the Mountbatten 'security' categories in 1967, the

184

classification of prisoners serving ordinary sentences of imprisonment has been based on the most simple administrative divisions, based on the 'star' class and the 'ordinaries', and the length of prison sentence; 'treatment' considerations have only entered the process indirectly, in so far as there has been an assumption that the longer the sentence the more time there is for training/treatment to be carried out, and it is more convenient for prisoners with similar lengths of sentence to be treated together. Classification has been primarily administrative allocation, with any treatment being left very much to the individual institution with its allocated clientele. It remains to be seen whether the recent initiatives in developing regional allocation centres for long-term prisoners and the setting up of observation and classification units in all local prisons for those serving shorter sentences will really change the situation and achieve a proper integration of treatment considerations into the allocation process.[18]

A series of notorious escapes in the mid-1960s led to an official inquiry into prison security by Earl Mountbatten, who published his *Report of the Inquiry into Prison Escapes and Security* in December 1966, recommending the introduction of a four-fold classification of prisoners based on security risk:

Category A: Prisoners whose escape would be highly dangerous to the public or the police or to the security of the state.

Category B: Prisoners for whom the very highest conditions of security are not necessary but for whom escape must be made very difficult.

Category C: Prisoners who cannot be trusted in open conditions but who do not have the ability or resources to make a determined escape attempt.

Category D: Those who can reasonably be trusted to serve their sentences in open conditions.[19]

This classification system was immediately accepted and put into operation by the government, thereby re-emphasizing in an unmistakable way that security and control were of top priority in prisons, with treatment coming a very poor second, despite what many people might wish to believe and what most official statements had been proclaiming for many years. Nevertheless, despite this clear

185

reinstatement of the primacy of security and control, the Prison Department still clings to its firm belief that security and rehabilitation are not antithetical, and that progress is being made towards their 'real integration':

> Ideally all convicted prisoners would be sent to training prisons with a regime suited to their needs, and with a degree of security no greater than was necessary. We are very far from this ideal, but here too a start has been made— for example in differentiating the functions of particular institutions.[20]

The ability to reach this ideal has been put to its hardest test in dealing with long-term Category A prisoners in conditions of maximum security. The realistic but humane Report of the Advisory Council on the Penal System, *The Regime for Long-term Prisoners in Conditions of Maximum Security* (1968), fully recognized that in the classification and allocation of Category A prisoners security considerations had always to come first, although it did allow for the possibility of a prisoner being moved to a dispersal prison outside his region 'if the regime of that prison or the training available seems most likely to meet his needs'.[21] The Advisory Council's detailed discussion of the main elements of an appropriate regime for these long-term prisoners stressed the importance of fostering self-respect, choice and variety in prison life, showing a realistic focus on the *inner* life of the prison community, rather than the more usual *outward* looking aspects so often emphasized in discussions of rehabilitation: 'Clearly the aim of prison treatment must always be to change a prisoner's life for the better. *That life is to be lived first in the prison community*, and second in the world outside [emphasis added].'[22]

In fact, what seems to have been convincingly argued in this Report is the real possibility, *not* of combining security with 'rehabilitation' or 'treatment' in the normal sense, but of combining security with a humanistic concern for the self-respect and individuality of these prisoners, as major objectives in their own right, irrespective of any connexion with subsequent 'rehabilitation' prospects.

This brief historical account of how one country's system of prison classification has developed indicates clearly that the main purposes have been those of internal *segregation* and external *allocation* of

186

different prisoners to various institutions. The desire to avoid *contamination* has been a prime motive for this segregation and allocation, originally (and still to some extent) the fear of 'moral' contamination, but very soon linked with an awareness of the implications for internal discipline and control.[23] The potential conflict between administrative convenience and treatment purposes in classification was not an issue during most of the last century, as the main aims of imprisonment were punishment and deterrence, which were entirely compatible with classification for purposes of control. The official emphasis given to treatment objectives, following the report of the Gladstone Committee in 1895, while creating conflict at a certain level of political and social concern, did not change the realities of classification very much as it was still based very much on legal and administrative categories rather than on an assessment of treatment needs. This 'irrational equilibrium' continued until the Mountbatten Report recommended the introduction of new security categories, which gave official blessing to the overriding importance of security and control, to which any treatment considerations had to take second place.

Differential treatment and special sentences

A major question that was posed at the beginning of this chapter was the degree of control exercised by sentencers over the *nature* of a prisoner's custodial sentence. When a court passes a sentence of ordinary imprisonment upon a convicted offender, it has no power to direct in what kind of prison the sentence should be served or under what conditions; the attempt by the 1898 Prisons Act to give sentencers the power to direct that a prisoner should be held in the First or Second Division was a short-lived failure. Thus, the decision as to type of prison has nearly always been firmly in the hands of the prison authorities, whose classification decisions have been seen to be based largely on administrative criteria. When these criteria include such things as the previous criminal record or prison experience of an offender, or the length of his current sentence, it is clear that sentencers can theoretically exercise some degree of negative and indirect control by their awareness of the administrative category into

187

which any particular offender might be fitted; however, in such a hypothetical situation, the sentencers would be sacrificing their own aims and objectives to fit in with the potentially very different aims of the prison authorities. The important question is whether any specifically *judicial aims* are likely (or ought) to be implemented as a result of the prison classification process; the official view seems to be one of uncompromising support for the view that judicial aims are entirely separate from the objectives and methods of prisons:

> The general aims defined in the previous paragraph [viz. humane custody and rehabilitation] govern the treatment of *all* convicted offenders and do not vary according to the reasons for which the courts send any one person to custody. A court may properly pass a custodial sentence on one offender to act as a general deterrent to the commission of crime, and on another because the court believes he is in need of training that can be given to him in custody. The duty of the prison service in respect of each of them remains unaffected.[24]

Despite the questionable validity of this kind of statement about the task of the prison service in an integrated system of criminal justice, we might reluctantly accept it for ordinary prison sentences (with very mixed judicial motives underlying them), but look instead to the experience of a variety of *special sentences* to examine the degree of congruence between the aims of these sentences and the effects of the classification process upon the treatment of offenders receiving them. Once again, the historical perspective seems to provide the most useful approach to this question, drawing on English experience of borstal training and sentences for adult recidivists.

Although the origin of the special sentence of borstal training, in the first decade of this century, was clearly influenced by a desire to segregate young offenders from adult prisoners and thereby avoid the familiar dangers of contamination, yet the development of borstal training in the 1920s and 1930s was mainly based on *rehabilitative* aims of the training and treatment of young offenders specially selected with these training needs in mind. The borstal system, therefore, would seem to have been particularly appropriate for the development and implementation of exclusively *treatment purposes* in classification. Such developments were limited, in the early years, by

188

the fact that there were only two institutions for borstal trainees, although the one at Feltham did start a 'reception class' in 1920, to carry out a 'mental diagnosis' of trainees and to assess their general capacities and training needs.[25] Even when a separate Reception Centre was opened at Wandsworth Prison in 1922, staffed with psychologists, medical officers and social work staff, the considerable amount of information collected about the boys' backgrounds probably had little influence upon their actual allocation, so that in his account of the period Roger Hood concluded that 'the prime consideration was to segregate the more hardened offenders from the less criminally mature'.[26] Gradually more borstals were opened so that by 1935 there were two open institutions for 'responsible' boys (Lowdham, North Sea Camp), two for the 'intermediates' (Rochester, Camp Hill), two for the older and more criminally experienced boys (Portland, Sherwood) and one for the immature and mentally backward (Feltham)—thus providing a choice of at least two institutions for boys of similar backgrounds. The introduction of 'open' borstal institutions in the 1930s, and particularly in the early post-war period, highlighted the latent conflicts in a classification system officially based on treatment needs; not only do open institutions in any penal system raise the question of the weight to be given to public opinion and fears for the safety of the community, but they also show the underlying paradox in classification by 'treatment needs' alone, as Roger Hood observed: 'The fact that open training only existed for those boys with a good prognosis is illuminating. . . . One is drawn to the conclusion that those who were to be trained to be trustworthy were already so, and those who were considered untrustworthy were simply beyond being trusted.'[27]

The opening of a special borstal Classifying Centre at Latchmere House in 1946 seemed to mark the total acceptance of the treatment purposes of the classification process in the borstal system. Mannheim and Spencer described the process entirely in terms of training needs:

The function of the Allocation Centre may be said to be three-fold: first, to discover the kind of training which the boy requires; secondly, to provide the staff of the receiving Institution with a complete assessment of his history, personality and needs; thirdly, to prepare him for his training in the Institution.[28]

189

Paradoxically, however, the familiar problem of 'contamination' was seen to be equally (or more) important in classification for treatment purposes as in classification for administrative convenience and control purposes; it was, in fact, a reappearance of concern for 'moral contamination', but with reference to the rehabilitation prospects of borstal boys. R. L. Morrison (1957) indicated the conflicting interests involved in the process of borstal allocation: a concern for security and the avoidance of contamination results in the grouping of boys in institutions according to homogeneous categories of doubtful value for purposes of rehabilitation; and, in addition, it often involves the sacrifice of the interests of those thought to be likely 'contaminators' to the assumed benefits for other trainees, or the protection of society.[29] Following Mannheim and Wilkins' discovery that open borstals had a higher 'success' rate than closed borstals (taking into account differences in the type of boy), Wilkins suggested that this difference was probably due to the 'normative effect' of the composition of the social groups to be found in the different institutions, with important implications for the impact of classification not only on the personal identity of the prisoners being variously labelled in this way but also on the composition of the social group so classified.[30]

During the last ten years, the system of borstal training in England has experienced probably its most significant changes in terms of its aims and objectives, and its relationship with the sentencing courts. Legislation, which came into effect in 1963, provided that a sentence of borstal training should be the main custodial sentence for *all* offenders in the 17–21-year-old age group, with only certain exceptions made when a very short or very long sentence was required, or when an offender had already served a prison or borstal sentence. This meant that borstal could no longer be seen as a *special sentence,* based on judicial assessment of training needs, but became an undifferentiated sentence for an entire age group, within certain broad limits dictated mainly by the seriousness of the offence. The immediate impact of this legislative change was one of considerable confusion, particularly in the courts, and it led to an unusual spate of comments from the Court of Criminal Appeal (as it then was), which provided an interesting, if rather disturbing, insight into the perceived relationship between the courts and the prison authorities.[31] The new restrictions on the use of ordinary sentences of imprisonment for those aged

190

17–21 years, for which sentences of borstal training had now to be substituted, was not interpreted by the judiciary as an indication that all sentences for this age group were intended to have rehabilitative aims, but rather resulted in what could be seen as a unilateral redefinition of the aims and methods of borstal training by the judges of the High Court. Thus, in some early judgements, the Court of Criminal Appeal showed its willingness to uphold sentences of borstal training imposed primarily for *deterrent* purposes rather than for the purposes of training the offender, with advice to the sentencing judge in these cases to express his view to this effect 'for the information of the officer of the Prison Department who has the responsibility of allocating the offender to a particular institution'.[32] The Lord Chief Justice, Lord Parker, expressed this new judicial perception of borstal training in unambiguous terms, in the case of *Angell*:

A lot of misconception in regard to the Criminal Justice Act arises from the fact that they [i.e. the judges] are looking on the borstal training there laid down as borstal training as it was understood before the Act of 1961. Borstal training is in fact a series of institutions, forming a spectrum from pure schooling at one end to near imprisonment at the other; and as this court has only recently said, if the court in any particular case, while bound to send the youth to borstal, feel that it is a case for punishment, they can say so. At any rate, those responsible for dealing with the youth will then know what the view of the judge is.[33]

There is a clear contradiction between this judicial statement of the relationship between sentencing aims and penal treatment, and the official Home Office view as contained in *People in Prison* (1969), quoted above, where there was an equally unambiguous claim that the task of the prison service is the same for *all* offenders, whatever the aims of the sentencing court may have been. This situation, in the borstal system of the early 1960s, confirms the lack of communication between legislators, the judiciary and the prison authorities, typical of most criminal justice systems; borstal training is no longer a 'special sentence' for a group of offenders selected on the basis of their training needs, but it is a 'catch-all' custodial sentence for an entire age group, so that it has come full circle from its origins as segregating the younger from the older criminals, in which classification for treatment

191

purposes is likely to be sacrificed to administrative purposes or judicial opinion.

The other main experience of special custodial sentences in England has been with a variety of measures for adult recidivists, especially those of 'corrective training' and 'preventive detention', introduced (or modified) by the 1948 Criminal Justice Act, but abolished in 1967, when they were replaced by another special sentence of 'extended imprisonment'. Corrective training derived from the Report of the Departmental Committee on Persistent Offenders (1932), although in several important respects its eventual form departed from the recommendations of that Committee; in particular, it had been suggested that the 2–4 year sentence should be imposed not only for reformative purposes (mainly on those aged 21–30 years), but also on offenders 'for whom little in the way of positive training may be practicable, and the main object may be to provide for the control of the offender and for the protection of the public'.[34] In fact, as J. D. McClean (1964) has pointed out in an important article, the legislation which introduced corrective training in 1948 placed the emphasis almost exclusively on the *training* aspects of the sentence, with no reference to its use for those offenders from whom the public needed protection.[35]

In accordance with this emphasis on training, a special allocation centre was set up and several prisons (and parts of prisons) were set aside exclusively for use by corrective trainees; but, paradoxically, those offenders who were assessed as being the best training prospects were allocated, *not* to the special corrective training establishments, but to existing regional training prisons for prisoners serving medium or long-term sentences of ordinary imprisonment. The picture was one of the utmost confusion of aims and methods; the 1949 Prison Rules stated that the training regime in the special corrective training establishments should be the same as in other prisons 'with such modifications of method as are necessary for ensuring closer supervision and safe custody', so that presumably the main criterion for allocation to these rather than to regional training prisons was the degree of security and control required by each trainee; thus, despite the fact that a sentence of corrective training could be longer than a sentence of ordinary imprisonment for training and treatment purposes, yet the special establishments were distinguished from other
192

prisons *not* by their treatment emphasis but by their emphasis on safe custody.

The number of corrective training sentences decreased rapidly during the 1950s; by 1954 only 30 per cent of trainees were suitable for allocation to regional training prisons, and in 1960 the use of special corrective training establishments was discontinued, so that the vast majority were allocated simply according to the degree of security they required and spent their sentences in the same prisons as selected long-term 'ordinaries'.[36] Thus the brave new sentence of corrective training, which was described by Sir Lionel Fox as 'the statutory application of an existing method (i.e. the Wakefield system as it is now applied in the regional training prisons) to a category of prisoner selected not by the administrative classification system but by the courts', quickly became a sentence little different from the ordinary imprisonment for the majority of those receiving it, except that it was *longer*; and it illustrated once again how the so-called 'court selection' was little more than an empty phrase, deprived of any real significance by the subsequent decisions of prison classification and management.

It seems undeniable that, in traditional practice, prison classification has been largely influenced by the administrative and management concerns of prison authorities, focused on segregation, allocation, security and control. It is mainly for this reason that the classification process has been almost entirely independent of any judicial aims underlying particular sentences, even in the case of special sentences with clear treatment implications. Nevertheless, it would seem over-cynical to claim that there have been no gains whatsoever from the increased development of diagnosis and classification in prisons, perhaps partly at least symptomatic of changing public attitudes towards the purpose of imprisonment even if not properly integrated into existing (and ambiguous) prison systems. Hopefully, perhaps, we can agree with Conrad's assessment of the possible future direction of classification:

The new departure in classification adds to the dimension of control requirements the prospect of social restoration. . . . From the findings of social science the techniques of individualization and prediction have been added to the correctional repertory. Through these instruments *it has at last become possible to think of classification in terms of the job to be done rather than as the adjustment of the offender to correctional control* [emphasis added].[37]

PAROLE DECISIONS

The importance of parole decisions in the penal process is shown by the fact that since parole was introduced into the United States more than a hundred years ago, the proportion of prisoners released on parole has increased to an average of 60 per cent, with several states paroling virtually all their prisoners.[38] In England, where parole proper was only introduced in 1968, the most recent calculations suggest that approximately 39 per cent of eligible prisoners (i.e. those serving sentences longer than 18 months) are now being released on parole, even though in many cases the period of licence is very short.[39] This section will examine the origins and philosophy of parole, and investigate the criteria which seem to influence the parole authorities' decisions about the release date of so many prisoners.

Origins and philosphy of parole

With the ambiguity, typical of so much of the penal process, various different strands contributed to the historical origins of parole; of particular importance was the 'ticket-of-leave' system, developed alongside the use of transportation in England during the seventeenth and eighteenth century. Later, in the middle of the nineteenth century, when transportation had to be gradually phased out, a system of conditional 'licence to be at large' was introduced for those serving sentences of penal servitude, based on the same idea as the 'ticket-of-leave'; as Hawkins remarked, in his description of the historical development of parole, the main motive behind the introduction of this first example of conditional release in England was the effect it would have on easing the administrative problems created by the 'backlog' of convicts awaiting transportation.[40]

In fact, of course, it was in the United States and not in England that the parole system as such was introduced, in the last quarter of the nineteenth century, and there it was associated *not* with administrative problems of prison population but with specifically

194

reformative purposes surrounding the treatment of young offenders at the pioneering Elmira Reformatory, New York. Parole was thus first used in conjunction with indeterminate sentences at Elmira, from 1869, spreading rapidly to other states, where it was also used for adult prisoners, so that by 1900 a total of 20 states had introduced parole statutes and by 1922 only 4 states were without parole legislation of some kind.[41] The historical connexion between parole and the development of new institutional treatment methods for young offenders is particularly significant, in the light of contemporary theories underlying the use of parole; and even in those states, where it was not introduced specifically for young offenders, its development was concurrent with the spread of indeterminate sentence laws based on a similar 'reformative' orientation. This connexion explains the kind of description of parole found in the *Attorney General's Survey of Release Procedures* (1939): 'In penal philosophy, parole is an organic part of the reformatory idea and its history is inextricably part of the general trend in nineteenth century criminology in which emphasis shifted from punishment to reformation.'[42]

However, some of the early commentators in the United States were very much aware of the conflicting origins of parole, and equally conscious of the variety of purposes for which parole could be (and was being) used. For example, in 1925, Lindsey pointed out the very different functions and philosophies underlying the 'ticket-of-leave' system, as compared with the indeterminate sentence:

> Thus the ticket-of-leave or conditional liberation, which was the forerunner of our modern parole systems, arose out of experience in the care and handling of convicts and was developed by men in charge of prisoners as a practical method of dealing with them. Its origin was in practical experience rather than in theoretical reasoning and it became established because it produced results in the matter of prison discipline more favourable than had ever been secured without it. The origin of the indeterminate or indefinite sentence, on the other hand, was from theoretical considerations.[43]

By the early 1930s it was clear to many observers that whatever may have been the reformative origins of parole it had reverted to its earliest roots in the control and management of convicts, so that Lane was able to claim that parole had degenerated into 'a tool, used by the

195

institutions, to make better prisoners rather than better residents of the community'.[44] The promise or possibility of an early release was used to obtain good conduct from inmates while they were in the institution, and parole became at its worst, a bestowal of favours.

A further confusing aspect of any discussion of the historical origins of parole is that the purpose and function of indeterminate sentences are by no means clearly agreed upon or unambiguous. Although Lindsey confidently contrasted the reformative aims of indeterminate sentences with the practical administrative aims of the 'ticket-of-leave' system, it is by no means clear that this neat distinction is entirely true or useful. Among more recent discussions of this same issue, Reich examined the therapeutic implications of the indeterminate sentence, showing how its rationale was based on the assumption that imprisonment should serve a rehabilitative function, with its duration related to the response of individual offenders;[45] but Conrad, on the other hand, was aware that the actual operation of the indeterminate sentence could also lend itself to 'differential scales of retribution', and be mainly determined by internal considerations of sanctions and control.[46] Irrespective of the significance of the fact that parole originally developed in the United States at the same time as the spread of indeterminate sentence laws, the fact is that parole *introduces indeterminacy* into any system where it operates, so that the same issues and problems surround the discussion of the theory and practice of parole as of indeterminate sentences.

Contemporary definitions and justifications of parole share much of the confusion and idealism of the early years of its development. The British Government's White Paper, *The Adult Offender* (1965), which foreshadowed the introduction of parole by the Criminal Justice Act of 1967, seemed to state clearly a belief in the purely rehabilitative aim of parole:

> What is proposed is that a prisoner's date of release should be largely dependent upon his response to training and his likely behaviour on release. A considerable number of long-term prisoners reach a recognisable peak in their training at which they may respond to generous treatment, but after which, if kept in prison, they may go downhill. To give such prisoners the opportunity of supervised freedom at the right moment may be decisive in securing their return to decent citizenship.[47]

196

However, the general context of this White Paper and the subsequent parole legislation was one of concern for the rapid rise in the prison population and the increasing use of very long sentences of imprisonment by the courts; from the start, therefore, the aims of the parole system in England were confused in the minds of the public, prison staff and prisoners alike. In a recent collection of essays on parole, J. P. Martin (1972) raised the crucial issue of whether the parole decision should be seen primarily as a judicial or as a treatment decision; the former implies a balancing of the expectations of rehabilitation against the risk to the public, the latter implies a much greater involvement of the prisoner himself in the entire parole process, if real therapeutic aims are to be achieved.[48] In the same collection, Shea compared parole philosophy in England and America:

> England shares with most European countries a rather ambiguous attitude as far as the aims of punishment are concerned. While reform and rehabilitation are advocated as goals of equal standing with retribution and deterrence, none the less in practice considerable reluctance is shown to use reformative measures in any but innocuous cases. Parole yes, but not for everyone. It is granted only to those offenders whose early release runs little risk of minimising the gravity of their offence, endangering society or reducing the deterrent effect of the punishment on potential criminals. Parole therefore is by no means a measure a prisoner has a right to expect; it is a favour granted only to deserving cases.[49]

In its Model Penal Code, the American Law Institute, while still incorporating criteria relevant to traditional judicial and prison management concerns, introduced the important new principle of the *right to parole*, moving away from the idea of parole as an 'act of grace' to parole as a potentially effective means of treatment to be granted to every eligible candidate.[50] The 'ideal' definition of parole is that of the *Attorney General's Survey of Release Procedures* (1939):

> Properly conceived, parole contains none of the elements of executive clemency, as is the case of pardon. It has no connection with forgiveness, nor is it designed as a reward for good conduct in the institution. The basic purpose of parole is, or should be, to bridge the gap between the closely ordered life within the prison walls and the freedom of normal community living.[51]

197

It now remains to examine the extent to which the actual practice of parole decision-makers can be said to match this ideal.

Criteria for parole decisions

The apparently straightforward task which faces parole decision-makers is that of selecting for release those prisoners who seem likely to make a 'successful' (i.e. non-criminal) adjustment to life outside. The fact that most jurisdictions never state the manifest task in such relatively simple terms seems to be symptomatic not only of the very real difficulty of that task *per se,* but also of the fundamental ambiguities which characterize the actual operation of most parole systems. The typical kind of official 'guidance' provided for parole board members consists of a list of criteria which should be taken into account, with an emphasis on the problem of striking a balance between the different criteria and a reaffirmation of the need for 'individualization' in parole decision-making. For example, in the first Report of the Parole Board for England and Wales, 1968, the work of the Board was described as follows:

> The selection of a prisoner as one suitable for parole depends upon his history prior to the start of his current sentence, his behaviour during his current sentence, his plans for his future and the circumstances into which he will go if and when he is released. . . . The weight to be attached to these matters varies from case to case. . . .[52]

Implicit in such lists of criteria, but rarely explicit, is that each one should be considered in relation to the rehabilitation prospects of the prisoner whose case is being decided. However, even if this were to be made more explicit, parole board members would still be faced with fundamental problems concerning the practical interpretation of concepts such as 'rehabilitation prospects' and 'parole risks'; in most of their actual decisions, what is at issue is not simply *whether* a prisoner is likely to be a parole 'failure' or 'success' but what *degree of risk* is involved, both quantitatively and qualitatively. In his detailed examination of parole in the United States, Keith Hawkins isolated the 'idea of risk' as the central issue:

198

Risk is, in general, the officially acceptable basis for parole decisions. There are, however, many facets to the idea of risk. It is not simply the chance either that a prisoner will 'do it again' or that he will violate his parole. ... A board must weigh up the quantitative assessment of *likelihood of violating* with the qualitative concern for the *character of possible violative behaviour*. This is a question of values.[53]

In a rather unexpected way, English experience with the selection of preventive detainees for the special 'third stage' of the sentence highlighted an exactly similar problem, relating to the assessment of reconviction risk. Hammond and Chayen (1963) showed that this selection was based on the single main criterion of probability of further reconviction, among a group of prisoners whose overall chance of reconviction was so very high that this criterion was almost meaningless for the practical purpose of differentiating amongst them.[54] A 'qualitative' concern for any future criminal behaviour of a parolee also obviously influences parole board decisions, but it is often difficult to separate two different but overlapping concerns, both deriving from an assessment of the nature and seriousness of the prisoner's current offence. On the one hand, this assessment may affect a parole board's estimate of the kind of crime a man may commit after his release; but, on the other hand, a parole board may deny a man parole *not* in view of his probable *future* criminal behaviour, but because of their quasi-judicial concern that his sentence should reflect the seriousness with which the court viewed his *past* behaviour. Thus, in addition to the list of general criteria properly influencing the parole decision (quoted above), the first report of the English Parole Board indicated that 'consideration must also be given to whether or not there is an overriding objection to parole in the circumstances of the offence for which the prisoner is in custody, having regard to such matters as observations by the Courts'.[55] The Board returned to this same issue in its report for 1970:

The most controversial and difficult matter has always been the weight to be attached to the nature and gravity of the current offence. The problem here is, on the one hand, to avoid a tendency to re-try the case, bearing in mind that no type of offence automatically rules out a prisoner for consideration for parole; on

199

the other hand, to observe the principle that parole should not appear to be inconsistent with sentencing policy in general and, where deterrence as an exemplary element is intended in a particular sentence, to take account of the intention of the trial court.[56]

From the United States, two independent sources have commented on the conflict between the official rehabilitative aims of parole and the often overriding 'retributive' considerations underlying the operation of the California Parole Board. Reich's observations at Vacaville prison suggested that traditional considerations underlying *sentencing* policy, related to the gravity of the offence, were accorded primary significance by the Parole Board, and that the prisoners there were very conscious of this 'double-bind' situation, which inevitably negated any official treatment purposes of parole; whatever progress an individual prisoner might make during his sentence, his hopes of parole could be frustrated by the overriding concern that he should 'pay for his crime', by an appropriate length of time in custody.[57] John Irwin described the operation of the California Adult Authority Parole Board in very similar terms:

> Indications of rehabilitation, a lofty ideal, have never been the chief concern in determining a convict's sentence. Amount of time served for particular crimes has always been the primary factor, and the degree of variability of sentences because of indications of rehabilitation has always been very limited. . . . Currently, the convicts do not view the determination of sentence [by the Parole Board] as a therapeutic decision, but a judicial one.[58]

Empirical evidence provides support both for the importance attached to the risk of a serious crime being committed on parole, and for the importance of parole decisions being compatible with the wider interests of justice and, specifically, sentencing policy. Table 5.1 shows the results of a questionnaire sent to approximately 50 per cent of state parole board members in the United States by O'Leary and Glaser; it can be seen that by far the most common and important factor said to influence their parole decisions was the 'chance of a serious crime, if paroled', so that the authors concluded that 'while a variety of considerations are bound up in the decision to parole a given individual, and at times these may have little to do with the risk he
200

TABLE 5.1: *Main considerations taken into account in their previous year's decisions, by 139 state parole board members in the United States.*

Consideration	Significantly affected their decision median %	Included as one of five most important factors %
1. Chance of serious crime if paroled	79.4	92.8
2. Prisoner will *benefit* from further confinement	27.6	87.1
3. Prisoner will *worsen* with further confinement	13.6	71.9
4. Enough punishment already, to 'pay' for crime	13.3	43.2
5. Effect on relatives or dependants	9.2	33.8
6. Difficult to supervise	8.9	35.3
7. Reaction of judge, if paroled	7.5	20.9
8. Reaction of other prisoners, regarding ascribed policy	3.7	12.2
9. Reaction of press, radio, T.V. etc.	3.5	8.6
10. Reaction of local police	3.0	12.2
11. Reaction of prison officers	3.1	5.0

Source: V. O'Leary and D. Glaser 'The Assessment of Risk in Parole Decision-Making', in D. J. West (ed.) *The Future of Parole* London (1972) Table 8.1 pp. 136–7.

presents, in the great majority of cases it is the probability of failure on parole that is of most concern to the parole board member'.[59] Nevertheless, this same survey showed that parole board members would quite often take into account the fact that the prisoner had 'paid for' his crime by a long enough sentence already; similarly, Hawkins' survey of decision-making by the Commissioners of the New York State Board of Parole, showed that more than 70 per cent of them took into account the length of the prisoner's sentence, as compared to other similar cases (see Table 5.2, below), and that they exercised a general 'equalizing' policy in lengthening or shortening the actual time spent in prison.[60] Finally, the Californian opinion survey by Gottfredson and Ballard (1964) found that both 'serving the interests of justice' and the 'release of those unlikely to violate parole' were considered of equal importance in the parole decision.[61]

In view of the historical origins and conflicting theories underlying the development of parole, it is perhaps in no way surprising that empirical evidence suggests that a large variety of different factors influence parole board members; the unwillingness of most jurisdictions

TABLE 5.2: *Main factors taken into account in 623 parole decisions, by the Commissioners of the New York State Board of Parole.*

Factor	Taken into account %	Rank order	Definitely influenced decision %	Rank order
Inmate's behaviour in prison	82	1	59	8
Poor juvenile and criminal record	78	2	67	2
Stability and maturity	77	3	68	1
I.Q. score and skills	76	4	63	5
Attitude to authority	75	5=	58	10
Behaviour at hearing	75	5=	56	11=
Assume responsibilities	74	7	65	3
Proportion of sentence served	73	8	53	15
Length of sentence, compared with similar cases	72	9	47	19
Employment record	71	10	63	4
Job opportunity	69	11	59	6=
Proposed residence	69	12	59	9
Offence against the person	68	13	54	14
Need for treatment/training	68	14	55	13
Overall parole plan	66	15	56	11=

Source: Excerpted from K. O. Hawkins 'Parole Selection: the American Experience', Unpublished Ph.D. thesis, Cambridge University Library, 1971, Table 21, p. 299.

to be more explicit about the main objectives of parole obviously leaves a great deal of discretion to the parole decision-makers, so that it would seem inevitable for there to be a degree of inconsistency comparable to that found in the sentencing process.[62] In the English system the problem of inconsistency is complicated by the existence of at least three different stages at which decisions are made, viz. the Local Review Committee, the central Parole Board and the Secretary of State; and although such a system could in fact result in *greater consistency* and fairness in the final decisions, Shea has shown the more likely consequences:

Without concrete legal guidelines, the danger cannot be overlooked that all three [parole decision-making bodies] will develop their own criteria which, though probably not differing in principle, will certainly put different emphasis on different points. Two unfortunate consequences are likely to arise from this: first, the use of inconsistent criteria for assessing cases, and hence a lack of justice; secondly, a general feeling of distrust in each body regarding the appropriateness of the criteria used by the two others.[63]

202

In contrast to the attention paid to disparities in the sentencing process, there has been little research into disparities between *parole* decision-makers. Gottfredson and Ballard (1966) carried out an experimental study of the decison-making of six parole board members in more than 2,000 cases, but reached the conclusion that 'there is no support for the hypothesis that differences in parole decision outcomes may be partly attributed to the decision-makers rather than to offenders'.[64] Keith Hawkins' New York study (1971) provides the most interesting data so far available on this issue: he studied a total of 623 decisions made by the eleven Commissioners of the New York State Board of Parole, and found that the proportion granted parole varied from 30 per cent to 55 per cent.[65] The characteristics of the cases heard by each Commissioner were compared, but as the variations between the different Commissioners' cases did not reach statistical significance, Hawkins felt able to divide the Commissioners into two groups of 'liberals' and 'conservatives', i.e. as regards their parole practices, *not* their political or social views! The six 'liberal' Commissioners granted parole to more than 40 per cent of their cases, whereas the five 'conservatives' all granted parole to less than 40 per cent;[66] further analysis showed that the two groups adopted *different standards* for assessing the criminal records and other background information about the prisoners, with the liberals' assessments being interpreted as more generous, tolerant or optimistic than the conservatives', particularly with regard to the personal attributes and parole plans of prisoners.[67] It seems likely, in fact, that further investigation of parole disparities would reveal similar findings of the importance of the decision-makers' personal attitudes, concern for public opinion and approach to the use of information, as has been found in sentencing research.

Irrespective of possible differences between decision-makers, what factors seem in practice to be given most general weight by parole board members? Does the empirical evidence allow any firm conclusion to be reached about the extent to which the 'official' *rehabilitative/treatment* purposes of parole take precedence over other possible institutional *management/control* functions? Gottfredson and Ballard's opinion survey (1964) of 54 parole board members, administrative and prison staff, in California, found that one of the 'very important' factors was the release of inmates at the optimal time for

203

most probable success on parole, and that 'quite important' factors included the individual response and progress of an inmate within prison, and a concern to improve inmate adjustment in the community after release.[68] R. O. Dawson's important study of parole criteria (1969), in several major American states, found that although the principal consideration was the probability that the inmate would violate the criminal law if released, yet board members regarded the parole decision as 'an integral part of the rehabilitation process and consider the probability of recidivism to be an index of the extent to which the inmate is rehabilitated';[69] thus, the most frequent item searched for at parole hearings was evidence of 'psychological change' in the inmate's attitudes towards himself and his offence:

> The factor of psychological change is frequently expressed in terms of when the inmate has reached his peak in psychological development. The problem of parole selection becomes one of retaining the inmate until he has reached his peak and then releasing him; incarceration after this point is regarded as detrimental to adjustment on parole.[70]

The vital importance of the *availability of information* for the parole decision was incidentally shown by Dawson's finding that the Kansas Parole Board did not appear to base its decisions on the criterion of inmate change, but this was due *not* to any view in Kansas that attitude change was unimportant, but merely because information relevant to that issue was not available to the board.

Among the most important criteria in Hawkins' New York study were personality attributes relating to an inmate's stability and maturity, his attitude to authority and readiness to assume responsibilities (Table 5.2); considerable weight was also attached to a prisoner's attempt to complete prison training or treatment, indicating that such attempts were accorded as much (or more) credit by the Board as the apparently more objective *results* of such training or treatment in prison.[71] A further analysis by Hawkins of the factors actually present in cases granted parole confirmed that the two most commonly associated with actual decisions were 'good stability and maturity' (98 per cent of paroled cases) and 'good readiness to assume responsibilities' (95 per cent), whereas the two factors *least* associated with

204

favourable parole decisions were 'poor readiness to assume responsibilities' (10 per cent of paroled cases) and 'poor attitudes to authority' (9 per cent).[72]

Reference has already been made to O'Leary and Glaser's survey of 139 state parole board members, in which the most common criterion taken into account was the chance of a serious crime if paroled; the next two most important criteria were (i) that the prisoner would *benefit* from further confinement, and (ii) that the prisoner would *worsen* with further confinement, influencing the decision to defer and to grant parole respectively (see Table 5.1 above). In the same essay, the authors raised the important issue of the nature of the evidence on which parole boards base their view of the prisoner's attitude change or his response to training in prison, showing that this derives largely from staff assessments and impressions:

> If complete acceptance were given to staff impressions of inmate attitudes, several risks would be involved. In the first place, the inmate adjustment to the prison situation, and his verbal expressions there, may not be indicative of his actual interest or ability to behave in any particular fashion outside of prison. . . . Secondly, the ability of the staff to assess inmate attitudes from their expression in an institution varies tremendously. . . . A final objection to automatic acceptance of staff assessments of inmates as a basis for parole decisions, is the fact that the personal involvement of staff with inmates may interfere with their objectivity in these assessments.[73]

The significance of these considerations has also been confirmed in England, by Bottomley's study of Local Review Committee recommendations in a long-term security prison, where the main type of factor influencing the decisions was an assessment of the prisoner's personality and attitudes, in which signs of maturity and positive change were looked for, and where the basis of these assessments was mainly information available in reports by prison staff.[74] Once again, English experience with the selection of preventive detention prisoners for the 'third stage' revealed that great weight was attached by the Advisory Board to staff assessments of behaviour and attitudes in prison, although Hammond and Chayen (1963) found little correlation between staff judgements of prison behaviour and the number of offences against discipline committed by a prisoner.[75]

The cumulative evidence seems to confirm that parole decisions are significantly influenced by indications that a prisoner is attempting to profit from the treatment/training available in prison, and by evidence of the *apparent effects* of the prison experience, as indicated by staff assessments of changes in inmate attitudes and personality; to this extent, therefore, the 'official' rehabilitative purposes of parole seem to receive considerable support in actual practice. Does this mean that the importance of factors such as institutional discipline and control has been over-emphasized by critics of the parole system? On the contrary, additional empirical evidence will be seen to provide considerable support for the importance of these other factors, thereby confirming the contemporary ambiguities in both the theory and the practice of parole.

In Warner's early study of parole releases from Massachusetts Reformatory, 1912–20, he found that the item of information to which the Parole Board attached the greatest importance was the prisoner's conduct in the Reformatory, as measured by the number of marks lost for bad behaviour, so that any prisoner who had lost few or no marks during his sentence was almost certain to be paroled on his first appearance before the Board (*unless* he was a 'gunman' or sex offender!). Warner described how the Superintendent of the Reformatory continually urged the Parole Board to make parole dependent upon a prisoner's conduct in the institution:

> The reason the Superintendent keeps urging the Board to give consideration to the requirements of institutional discipline in determining questions of parole is easy to ascertain. . . . The customary methods of treating prisoners give him few favors to bestow. The hope of an early parole is the only considerable inducement he has to offer as an urge to industry and good conduct.[76]

Nearly half a century later, Dawson found that one of the major reasons for denying parole to particular prisoners, was in order to support institutional discipline, with a shift of emphasis from a concern with the future adjustment of the offender to a concern with order and control in the penal institution, within which parole became an incentive for good behaviour and a sanction against undisciplined conduct

206

by inmates; however, Dawson was aware of the difficulties of disentangling the various motives underlying decisions of parole board members:

> It is likely that even the parole board members are unable to articulate clearly their reasons for reacting as they do to inmates with disciplinary problems. . . . Treating misbehavior during confinement as an unfavorable sign for future parole success leads in most cases to the same decision which would be made if the order of the institution were the sole consideration.[77]

The questionnaire survey, carried out by Glaser and O'Leary (1972), showed that parole board members did not officially admit the importance of factors such as institutional discipline and control in their decisions; nevertheless, the authors stated their firm belief that prison conduct was often unofficially taken into account in parole decisions; parole boards were frequently expected to collaborate with prison officials in maintaining custodial control by using the granting or denial of parole as a reward or penalty for inmate conformity or nonconformity to prison rules, so much so that O'Leary and Glaser believed that the other purposes of parole were in danger of being sacrificed.[78]

The final empirical evidence comes from Hawkins' study, which also met the problem faced by O'Leary and Glaser of knowing the extent to which the New York Commissioners would admit to taking into account such factors; nevertheless, prison 'rule-breaking' was found to be a factor which influenced parole deferral, although 'average' prison behaviour was a factor favouring the granting of parole.[79] Hawkins raised many interesting points about the relationship between the criteria of institutional behaviour and parole decisions: he reaffirmed the difficulty of separating the use of such prison criteria as measures of genuine rehabilitation from their use for purposes of prison management, and emphasized the important role of parole in the motivation of inmate behaviour, and the encouragement of morale in the institution. A summary of his views is found in a recent essay:

> Remission and parole, both of which alter the extent to which an inmate is deprived of liberty, provide the two most important incentives to inmate cooperation. Both systems originated as means of

assisting prison management, partly through aiding control, partly through their capacity to adjust numbers in custody. . . . Though the first duty of parole board members is to make decisions about releasing people from prison, they must also have concern for the control of inmates in custody. While they may proclaim allegiance to the correctional ideal, they recognise that effective control and discipline are prerequisites to any rehabilitative efforts that may be made. . . . The task of parole boards, then, is seen as one of making decisions consistent with the aims of the rehabilitative approach which will at the same time aid prison management.[80]

Significantly, the American Model Penal Code included as one of the major factors which could result in the denial of parole, circumstances where 'release would have substantially adverse effects on institutional discipline'. More predictably, however, the Parole Board for England and Wales, whilst consistently accepting that an offender's behaviour in prison is an entirely appropriate criterion to take into account, have equally consistently justified its relevance solely in terms of *rehabilitation* prospects (always providing that it is not 'mere superficial conformity'!).[81] In his study of an English prison, Bottomley certainly found that those prisoners assessed as genuinely co-operative towards the staff and 'model prisoners' had a much greater chance than average of being recommended for parole both by the Local Review Committee and by the central Parole Board.[82]

In the final analysis, neither we nor parole board members are in a position to assert confidently that certain priorities always operate in the same way in every parole decision; different criteria are given varying weight in each case, but it seems equally clear that considerable weight is sometimes attached to criteria of institutional discipline and control, as well as to prospects of rehabilitation. Although the starting point for any parole decision is probably usually the board members' assessment of the risk to the community in releasing a particular prisoner at a particular time, yet many other factors play a part in the delicate balancing process, ranging from the quasi-judicial function of keeping within appropriate bounds for the offence to the likely prospects of rehabilitation, and including some attention to aspects of institutional discipline and public concern about a particular crime or criminal. It is this complex web of influences upon parole decisions that undermines the philosophy and practical utility of parole prediction tables and much of the research which links various criteria to chances of 'success' or 'failure' on parole. Such prediction tables and research are of value only to the extent that parole decisions are taken on the basis of a concern for the future behaviour of a prisoner; the concept of parole 'risk' is mainly a question of degree and social values, for which prediction tables are of limited use, as Glaser has suggested:

> Prediction tables cannot replace these [parole board] officers in serving as society's conscience. Only human beings can determine the danger—to the community and to the confined individual—that morally justifies depriving a man of his liberty. However, the tables can help officials determine, as accurately as possible, what the risks are that they must evaluate.[83]

More attention to research findings, which reveal little connexion between behaviour in penal institutions and behaviour after release from prison, might at least deprive officials of certain kinds of 'rehabilitative justifications' for decisions taken for less acceptable reasons, but it seems unlikely that the basic influences upon parole decisions would be fundamentally changed in practice—there would simply be less room for obfuscation of the real issues involved.

Parole and penal aims

It is difficult to avoid the conclusion that parole decisions are characterized by ambiguities similar to those found in the other stages of the penal process; we cannot, therefore, expect the relationship between sentencing and parole authorities to be free from conflict, and it would be entirely understandable if courts were to perceive parole boards as usurping their rightful control over the length and objectives of sentences of imprisonment. At the conclusion of his major study of sentencing and parole in the United States, Dawson was keenly aware of the need to co-ordinate the decisions of the sentencing judge and the parole board; he recognized that sentencing decisions could often be influenced by a judge's expectation of the probable parole decision;[84] and it has been seen how parole boards sometimes assume a quasi-judicial role in equalizing apparent disparities in prison sentences. Such 'reciprocal conjecture' and manipulative adjustments would not

209

seem to be the hall-marks of a just or properly integrated criminal justice system. The English Parole Board has always been concerned to encourage a degree of mutual trust and integration between the courts and the paroling bodies: 'An effective parole system must be complementary to and not in conflict with the sentencing policy of the Courts. Though the function of the Courts and of the Parole Board differ, neither should disregard the functions of the other.'[85] The suggestion that courts were increasing their sentences to take account of possible early release on parole was refuted by the Parole Board, citing highest judicial authority for the inappropriateness of any such course of action by the courts and drawing attention to the fact that many members of the board held judicial positions.[86]

One possible and positive resolution to the problems inherent in the relationship between the sentencing and parole authorities, and also to the variety of other conflicting pressures upon the decisions of parole board members, would be for a very specific *parole policy* to be developed, which would deliberately sever existing connexions, and instead create an independent role for parole which would be entirely self-justifying. Such an independent role would derive from the recognition that virtually all prisoners are released from prison sooner or later, and that the nature and timing of this release are likely to be crucial for successful reintegration into the community, thus clearly serving the interests of prisoner and community alike. Parole, therefore, should be considered with respect to its part in 'bridging the gap' between prison and community life, and the main criterion for granting it should be the *needs* of the prisoner; as Wilcox said, many years ago, it should be regarded as essential to the task of crime prevention and not regarded as leniency or a favour to those released:

> Parole is not leniency. On the contrary it is to be commended because it is at once the most severe and the safest method by which prisoners may be released.... *Every* convict who emerges from a prison should therefore be *compelled* to serve for a time under these conditions. This requirement should be enforced, not as a favor to the offender, but as a method of crime prevention adopted for the better protection of the entire community.[87]

In England, a former member of the Parole Board, Dr Donald West, has put forward radical suggestions for developing a parole policy

210

along very similar lines to those advocated here. He highlighted a major anomaly in the present parole system, whereby parole tends to be regarded as a privilege to be given to the better behaved and generally less serious offender, whereas many of those who are in greatest need of supervision are denied parole, only to be released eventually with no supervision whatsoever; part of the reason for this, perhaps, is a natural desire to avoid adverse public opinion in the early years of the operation of a new system:

> The Parole Board needs the backing of a well-informed public capable of tolerating the disasters which must occasionally ensue when serious offenders are paroled. At present the newspapers and the public show a concern for crimes committed by parolees that is ridiculously at variance with their lack of interest in crimes committed by ex-prisoners who are released without supervision.[88]

There are some hopeful signs in the latest report of the Parole Board, where this problem of the eventual release of all prisoners was recognized, so that the real question is not *whether* a man should be released but *how* he should be released. A modification of approach to certain categories of prisoners was noted, whereby petty persistent offenders were being specially considered, *not* from the point of view of their likelihood of failure (very great) but of their *need for support*.[89] The evidence reviewed in this chapter suggests that for such a new approach to make real headway, it will need great impetus to counteract the other constraints upon parole boards; as was recently proclaimed, it is not simply a question of balancing the safety of the public against the interests of the prisoner, but it involves a major redefinition of what is meant by the 'public interest':

> The public interest must include safety, but it also involves gains in human and material terms from the release of prisoners assessed as likely to respond positively during a period of parole. These must be borne in mind, together with the aspects of safety, when decisions are made at all levels.[90]

For this to be more than a unilateral 'declaration of faith', everyone connected with parole decisions must be committed to its implementation, and ultimately be guaranteed full support from an enlightened public opinion.

211

1. R. O. Dawson *Sentencing: the Decision as to Type, Length and Conditions of Sentence* Boston (1969) p. 419.
2. *People in Prison: England and Wales* Cmnd. 4214 London (1969) p. 7.
3. J. E. Thomas *The English Prison Officer since 1850* London (1972) p. 2.
4. G. M. Sykes *The Society of Captives* Princeton (1958) pp. 32–3:
   It would appear to be at least equally valid to claim that the maintenance of a quiet, orderly, peaceful institution is the dominant desire of the custodians and that the past criminality of the prisoner serves as a justification for the stringent controls which are imposed to achieve this end. The objective of eliminating incidents is not a rationalization for inflicting deprivations on the criminal within walls; *rather, the reverse is true and the prior deviance of the prisoner is a rationalization for using such extreme measures to avoid any events which would excite public indignation.*
5. D. Street, R. D. Vinter and C. Perrow *Organization for Treatment* New York (1966) p. 151.
6. J. P. Conrad *Crime and its Correction* London (1965) pp. 62–3.
7. L. T. Wilkins *Evaluation of Penal Measures* New York (1969) pp. 90ff.
8. American Correctional Association *Manual of Correctional Standards* Washington, D.C. (1966) p. 353; compare the definition of the State of California's *Inmate Classification Manual of the Department of Corrections* (1963), quoted in J. Irwin *The Felon* Englewood Cliffs N.J..Prentice-Hall (1970) p. 43.
9. *People in Prison: England and Wales* p. 69.
10. H. Mannheim and J. C. Spencer *Problems of Classification in the English Penal and Reformatory System* London (1950) pp. 1–2.
11. See the interesting discussion in A. G. Rose *Schools for Young Offenders* London (1967) pp. 43ff.
12. In general for this period see Thomas *op. cit.* pp. 30ff.
13. *Ibid.* p. 118.
14. S. Hobhouse and A. F. Brockway *English Prisons Today* London (1922) p. 214.
15. *Ibid.* p. 215.
16. *Ibid.* p. 215.
17. In a more modern context, see Glaser's conclusions on some of the ways in which the system of 'custody-grading' in penal institutions can impede rehabilitation, in D. Glaser *The Effectiveness of a Prison and Parole System* New York (1964) ch. 7, pp. 149–71. For an example of the more conventional view see the writings of Sir Alexander Paterson in S. K. Ruck (ed.) *Paterson on Prisons* London (1951) e.g. p. 25 and pp. 47–8: 'A proper system of classification meets a two-fold necessity. It has the negative advantage that it should prevent contamination—and it is of positive advantage in separating the different types of criminal, and so making it possible to give the appropriate form of treatment to each type' (p. 25).
18. *People in Prison: England and Wales* pp. 68–9.
19. *Report of the Inquiry into Prison Escapes and Security* (Mountbatten Report) Cmnd. 3175 London (1966); the proportions allocated to each category in the first few years were approximately as follows: Category A, 1 per cent; Category B, 30 per cent; Category C, 50 per cent; and Category D, 20 per cent.
20. *People in Prison: England and Wales* p. 70.

21. Report of the Advisory Council on the Penal System *The Regime for Long-term Prisoners in Conditions of Maximum Security* London (1968) p. 66.

22. *Ibid.* p. 32; the Report later emphasizes the importance of the fact that most prisoners will eventually return to the community, but that 'even if human beings remained permanently in prison it would be right for the governor and the staff of the prison to endeavour to create a liberal and constructive regime' (p. 78); see also the perceptive article by A. Gould 'Time and Training', *Howard Journal* Vol. **10** (1958) p. 50.

23. See D. Glaser *op. cit.* p. 150: 'Isolating inmates from other inmates has always been justified in penological writings primarily as a device for impeding the spread of criminal ideas among prisoners. Ostensibly it also fosters custodial control, since larger scale contraband enterprises in prison, as well as riots, require collusion among inmates.'

24. *People in Prison: England and Wales* p. 7.

25. R. G. Hood *Borstal Reassessed* London (1965) p. 112.

26. *Ibid.* p. 113: 'It can be seen that despite all the sympathetic research carried on at Wandsworth, allocation rested more on an assessment of the degree of criminality than on personal "treatment needs". However, the process of examination and allocation gave rise to the impression that the borstal system was aimed at "individualisation" of treatment' (p. 113).

27. *Ibid.* p. 120.

28. Mannheim and Spencer *op. cit.* p. 15.

29. R. L. Morrison 'Borstal Allocation' *Brit. Jo. Del.* Vol. **8** (1957) p. 95: 'Conflict may occur over the extent to which the needs of an individual may have to be sacrificed to those of other trainees as well as to the interests of society generally. Something of this is implied in the concept of "contamination" or in the question of variations in the capacity of institutions to absorb "difficult" commitments. The problem arises in its most acute form over the "untrainables".' For a further comment on the advantages and disadvantages of segregated treatment see J. Galtung 'Prison: The Organization of Dilemma' in D. R. Cressey (ed.) *The Prison: Studies in Institutional Organization and Change* New York (1961) pp. 133–44.

30. Mannheim and L. T. Wilkins *Prediction Methods in Relation to Borstal Training* London (1955) pp. 109ff; see also R. G. Hood *op. cit.* pp. 157–8, quoting from an unpublished report by Wilkins 'Classification and Contamination'. For the impact of classification on the offender himself, see Irwin *op. cit.* ch. 2 pp. 36–60; and for comments on the important 'self-fulfilling' element in penal classification see D. Street *et al. Organization for Treatment* p. 251.

31. See especially the extended article by J. E. Hall Williams and D. A. Thomas 'The Use of Imprisonment and Borstal Training for Young Offenders' *Crim. L. R.* [1965] pp. 146, 193, 273.

32. *Lowe* (17.3.64) 2194/63; 1 *W.L.R.* [1964] p. 609.

33. *Angell* (4.5.64) 468/64; *Crim. L. R.* [1964] p. 553; see Hall Williams and Thomas *op. cit.* p. 197.

34. *Report of the Departmental Committee on Persistent Offenders* Cmd. 4090 London (1932) p. 16.

35. J. D. McClean 'Corrective Training—Decline and Fall' *Crim. L. R.* [1964] p. 745.

36. *Ibid.*; see also A. E. Bottoms 'Towards a Custodial Training Sentence for Adults' *Crim. L. R.* [1965] pp. 582, 650.

37. Conrad *op. cit.* p. 181.
38. President's Commission on Law Enforcement and Administration of Justice *Task Force Report: Corrections* Washington, D.C.(1967) fig. 1, p. 61.
39. C. Nuttall 'Parole Selection' *Brit. Jo. Crim.* Vol. **13** (1973) p. 41.
40. K. O. Hawkins 'Parole Selection: the American Experience' Unpublished Ph.D. thesis, Cambridge University Library (1971) p. 25: 'Conditional release in England thus owed its origins to its capacity to go some way towards solving administrative problems of prison population pressure. This same pressure was clearly associated with the introduction of the modern parole system in this country'; see also Hawkins 'Some Consequences of a Parole System for Prison Management', in D. J. West (ed.) *The Future of Parole* London (1972) p. 98.
41. For documentation of this rapid spread of parole and indeterminate sentences in America, at the turn of the century, see E. Lindsey 'Historical Sketch of the Indeterminate Sentence and Parole System' *Jo. Crim. Law, Crimin. and P.S.* Vol. **16** (1925) p. 9, and U.S. Department of Justice *Attorney General's Survey of Release Procedures: Vol IV, Parole* Washington, D.C.(1939) ch. 6, pp. 121–35.
42. *Ibid.* p. 513.
43. Lindsey *op. cit.* p. 13.
44. W. D. Lane 'A New Day Opens for Parole' *Jo. Crim. Law, Crimin. and P.S.* Vol. **24** (1933) pp. 88ff. at p. 92.
45. M. Reich 'Therapeutic Implications of the Indeterminate Sentence' *Issues in Criminology* Vol. **2** (1966) p. 7.
46. J. P. Conrad *op. cit.* pp. 71–2.
47. *The Adult Offender* Cmnd. 2852 London (1965) p. 4.
48. J. P. Martin 'The Local Review Committee' in West (ed.) *op. cit.* p. 37.
49. E. Shea 'Parole Philosophy in England and America' in West (ed.) *op. cit.* pp. 68–9.
50. For a description of traditional 'misunderstandings' of parole, see L. E. Ohlin *Selection for Parole* New York (1951) pp. 21–2: 'Correctional authorities often reflect the same view by referring to parole as a means of "giving a fellow a break" or as a "reward for good behaviour". Their emphasis is not on its rehabilitative possibilities but on parole as a form of reward or expression of leniency.... It is thus apparent that the views held by the public, the press, professional politicians, prisoners and correctional authorities about parole have an important effect on the operation of the parole system.'
51. *Attorney General's Survey of Release Procedures* p. 4.
52. Home Office *Report of the Parole Board for 1968*, pp. 20–1; for a similar description of the work of the Parole Board for Scotland, see A. D. Smith 'The Parole Board for Scotland' *Brit. Jo. Crim.* Vol. **13** (1973) p. 46.
53. Hawkins 'Parole Selection' pp. 141–6.
54. W. H. Hammond and E. Chayen *Persistent Criminals* London (1963) pp. 163ff.
55. Home Office *Report of the Parole Board* p. 21.
56. Home Office, *Report of the Parole Board for 1970*, p. 14.
57. Reich *op. cit.* p. 10.
58. Irwin *op. cit.* p. 55.
59. V. O'Leary and D. Glaser 'The Assessment of Risk in Parole Decision Making' in West (ed.) *op. cit.* p. 138.
60. Hawkins *op. cit.*: 'It was seen that sentences which are felt to be "too short" or "light" tend to favour deferral, while those which are "too long" or "severe" tend to exert a favourable influence on the decision. This concern for equity exposes

214

the quasi-judicial role of any parole board. The general effect of the board's approach in New York would be towards standardising the length of terms actually served, which would lead to a certain elimination of sentencing disparity' (p. 318).

61. D. M. Gottfredson and K. B. Ballard *The Parole Decision: Some Agreements and Disagreements* Vacaville (1964) p. 3.
62. West 'Parole in England: An Introductory Explanation' in West (ed.) *op. cit.* p. 20: The attempt to bear in mind a multiplicity of vaguely defined indicia, some favourable and others unfavourable to the granting of parole, leads to decisions that are largely subjective, and therefore difficult to justify and liable to unexplained inconsistency.... Since it is nowhere laid down what level of reconviction risk is tolerable, what kind of offences make a prisoner unlikely to deserve parole, or what is the relative importance attached to the contradictory demands of deterrence and rehabilitation, it is impossible to know whether the system is operating a consistent policy.
63. Shea *op. cit.* p. 75; see Appendix I of the *Report of the Parole Board for 1969*, London (1970) where Table VII, pp. 44–6, gives the statistics of parole recommendations and releases from the separate prisons in England and Wales, showing considerable variation even between prisons with comparable populations.
64. Gottfredson and Ballard 'Differences in Parole Decisions Associated with Decision-makers' *Jo. Research in Crime and Del.* Vol. 3 (1966) pp. 112ff., at 119.
65. K. O. Hawkins 'Parole Selection' Table 15 p. 287, and Fig. 3 p. 288.
66. *Ibid.* p. 290 and Table 16.
67. *Ibid.* pp. 338–49; and Tables A33–A39, Appendix pp. 402–9.
68. Gottfredson and Ballard *The Parole Decision* p. 3.
69. Dawson *op. cit.* p. 263.
70. *Ibid.* p. 265.
71. K. O. Hawkins *op. cit.* p. 307.
72. *Ibid.* Table A32, Appendix pp. 400–1.
73. O'Leary and Glaser *op. cit.* p. 170.
74. A. K. Bottomley 'Parole Decisions in a Long-term Closed Prison', *Brit. Jo. Crim.* 13 (1973) pp. 26ff., at 33; for the same issue in the context of the release decision from borstal, see D. G. Longley 'An End to Borstal Training?' *Prison Service Journal* Vol. 8 No. 30 (January 1969) p. 26.
75. Hammond and Chayen *op. cit.* pp. 132ff.
76. S. B. Warner 'Factors Determining Parole from the Massachusetts Reformatory' *Jo. Crim. Law; Crimin. and P.S.* Vol. 14 (1923) pp. 172ff., at 181–2.
77. Dawson 'The Decision to Grant or Deny Parole: A Study of Parole Criteria in Law and Practice' *Washington Univ. Law Quarterly* (1966) pp. 243ff., at 278; see also Dawson *Sentencing: the Decision* pp. 291–2.
78. Leary and Glaser *op. cit.* pp. 156–60.
79. K. O. Hawkins *op. cit.* Table 26 p. 307.
80. Hawkins 'Some Consequences of a Parole System' pp. 98–9.
81. *Report of the Parole Board for 1968*, p. 21; typical ambivalence is shown in a later report: 'Those who have offended seriously against prison discipline do not inspire confidence in their ability to keep out of trouble on discharge. Moreover, to recommend the more troublesome characters for parole would have the effect of undermining discipline in the prisons, and possibly lowering the morale of better-behaved prisoners who had been refused parole on other grounds' (*Report of the Parole Board for 1969*, p. 21).

82. Bottomley *op. cit.* pp. 32, 36.
83. Glaser 'Prediction Tables as Accounting Devices for Judges and Parole Boards' *Crime and Delinquency* Vol. **8** (1962) pp. 239ff., at 241; see also N. S. Hayner 'Why do Parole Boards Lag in the Use of Prediction Scores?' *Pacific Sociological Review* Vol. **1** (1958) p. 73.
84. Dawson *op. cit.* p. 258.
85. *Report of the Parole Board for 1968*, p. 9.
86. *Report of the Parole Board for 1970*, p. 28:

> Just as sentences are passed without regard to remission, so also are they determined without regard to parole, but in the knowledge that both are features of the penal system. . . . Mutual confidence between the Board and the courts implies that the Board respects the sentencing function of the courts particularly when, for want of a better alternative, prison is regarded as the necessary sanction for the offence. The courts on the other hand respect the carefully considered conclusions of the Board that, for one or another reason, the sentence should be varied to permit early release on licence.

87. C. Wilcox 'Parole: Principles and Practice'. *Jo. Crim. Law, Crimin. and P.S.* Vol. **20** (1929) p. 345; see also W. D. Lane *op. cit.*: 'Parole is the safest way of releasing an offender from an institution. It is an extension of control beyond the walls of the prison or reformatory. . . . Parole is not based on consideration for the offender; it is based on consideration for society' (p. 89).
88. D. J. West 'Parole in England: Some Comments on the System at Work' in West (ed.) *op. cit.* p. 24; see also West 'Report of the Parole Board for 1971' *Brit. Jo. Crim.* Vol. **13** (1973) p. 56.
89. *Report of the Parole Board for 1971* London (1972) pp. 16ff.
90. *Ibid.* p. 18.

6 CONCLUSIONS: SOCIETY AND THE PENAL PROCESS

CONFLICT AND CONSENSUS IN THE PENAL PROCESS

At the end of this examination of selected decision-stages in the penal process, are we drawn to a conclusion which emphasizes the essential *unity* of the whole process, or to a conclusion which sees more value (and validity) in recognizing the essential *separateness* of the various different parts? The former conclusion receives authoritative support from the official report of the President's Commission:

> Furthermore, the criminal process, the method by which the system deals with individual cases, is not a hodge-podge of random actions. It is rather a continuum—an orderly progression of events—some of which, like arrest and trial, are highly visible and some of which, though of great importance, occur out of public view. A study of the system must begin by examining it as a whole.[1]

Although, when stated in these terms, it would seem undeniable that the penal process is *very far* from being an 'orderly progression of events', yet the equally undeniable necessity of starting by studying the system as a whole suggests that the dichotomy of 'unity' *v*. 'separateness' is rather an oversimplification. At one level, certainly, the penal process possesses the obvious *structural unity* of a conveyor belt, along which suspects are passed for 'selection' or 'rejection' as fully fledged offenders, so that even though many different things happen at various points *en route*, and many people 'leave' the process before reaching its final stages, yet the basic process continues without any interruption of the flow. The question is whether this structural unity is directed towards a *common purpose*, which makes the whole process intelligible, or whether the different stages can be better un-

217

derstood by treating them as discrete stages with their own individual purposes, which may or may not happen to coincide with purposes at any of the other stages. The major focus of the American Bar Foundation's programme of research into criminal justice administration was described, by Frank Remington, as 'the study of the process of criminal justice as *a system, one which must be studied as a whole if individual decisions and agencies are to be adequately understood*'[2] (emphasis added); important features of this 'total system' approach included an awareness that discretionary decisions made at any stage of the process could have important consequences for decisions made at other stages, so that control or elimination of discretion at one stage might simply result in 'administrative accommodation' at another; this approach also recognized the importance of effective communication between the agencies at the different stages, to avoid the nullification of the objectives of one group by another, through lack of proper information rather than deliberate intent. Thus, this usage of the term 'total system' appears to be more in the nature of a persuasive definition or statement of belief in the *desirability* of the system working in greater harmony, than an actual description of what was found to be the case in the American criminal justice system of the 1960s. However, in this context, it seems important to start by assessing the *actual operation* of the process, in terms of its apparent singleness of purpose, before attaching labels to the process which are essentially statements of personal or social *ideals* for the operation of the same process; and, when this is done, the penal process, whether in Britain or America, seems to be characterized by a lack of any overall guiding purpose.

The writings of Vincent O'Leary and his colleagues seem to reflect most closely the kind of conclusions supported by the evidence of this present examination of decisions in the penal process; in particular, O'Leary and Newman (1970) questioned the validity of treating criminal justice agencies as if they were all part of a single complex organization, held together by the network of decisions which link them:

The fact is, the criminal justice system is not an organisation, certainly not in any conventional sense. It has many sources of authority and power relationships, and its decision network does not flow along as a single process, or follow a linear chain of command, but is literally composed of many sub-processes for dealing with different types of offenses and different types of offenders.[3]

Following this perspective, greater understanding can be gained by focusing attention on the separate interests and objectives of each 'sub-process' or 'sub-system' of the penal process, rather than attempting to construct a set of broad objectives which could be claimed to influence all parts of the process. Thus, in a small but important study, the comparative analysis of agents of delinquency control carried out by Stanton Wheeler and his colleagues indicated a very fruitful line of research.[4] They started from a recognition of the 'division of labour' which had developed in the penal process, bringing with it problems of integration and co-ordination; these problems were seen to be not mainly technical problems but to derive from the multiplicity of *conflicting values*, with regard to deviant behaviour, held by each of the different groups involved in decision-making in the penal process, with no single 'authoritative resolution' of the principle objectives. In addition, the extent of structural separation in the tasks and functions of the different agencies meant that each agency saw the problems of delinquency within a different organizational context and from a different perspective, with important consequences for the perception of fairness and consistency by the delinquents being dealt with.[5] O'Leary and Newman summarized the situation as follows:

> Though the various agencies of the system work together, their formal relationship is amorphous, largely because they are structurally independent.... Likewise, while all criminal justice agencies may share some very broad objectives, like the diminution or prevention of crime, each agency has its own specific purposes, job tasks, and standards for performance evaluation as well as unique skills and methods of operation.[6]

The main sources of conflict in the penal process can be seen, therefore, to be both *ideological*, in terms of the different values of the various penal agents, and *operational*, in that each part of the process can be seen as having its own particular function, whose independence and autonomy is reinforced by the lack of communication and information-sharing between the different agents.

A final element which contributes in a significant way to this separation and fragmentation in the penal process is the *exercise of discretion*, which is officially sanctioned to a greater or lesser degree at virtually every decision-stage examined in this study. In his masterful analysis, *Discretionary Justice* (1969), K. C. Davis expressed the great potential, for good or ill, inherent in the existence of discretion in criminal and administrative justice: 'Where law ends, discretion begins and the exercise of discretion may mean either beneficence or tyranny, either justice or injustice, either reasonableness or arbitrariness.'[7] This statement would provide a perfect text for any study of decision-making in the penal process. A society's attitude towards the exercise of discretion could be said to be the basis of its evaluation of the function and tasks of the entire penal process; to accept the need for discretion rules out the possibility of a totally integrated penal process, but to eliminate the exercise of discretion would result in a system of criminal justice that would be unacceptable to the vast majority of people in society. There are, of course, various reasons and justifications for the exercise of discretion in the penal process: in our earlier analysis of police discretion in law enforcement (chapter 2), it was seen that there were some purely practical and administrative reasons for the exercise of police discretionary powers, including the difficulty of formulating laws and rules in such a way as to leave no doubt as to how they should be interpreted and implemented; however, the main contemporary justification for discretion in decision-making by the police, the courts and penal agencies, is the proclaimed need for *individualized justice*, with the consequence that not only are the individual needs and characteristics of 'clients' taken into account, but the decisions themselves are very likely to be influenced by the individual characteristics and values of the *decision-makers*. Not only, then, is the exercise of discretion inextricably linked with a commitment to the desirability of individualized justice, but, where no clear objectives exist for decision-makers, it can easily degenerate into mere 'speculation', uninformed either by any clear purpose or by information relevant to possible secondary aims of particular subsystems, as was seen in the study of bail decisions, and as is the case in many sentencing and parole decisions. Before considering some of the suggestions that have been made for controlling discretion and diminishing the conflict inherent in most criminal justice systems,

220

it may be useful to review briefly some examples of the major areas of conflict that have been found in the course of the present study.

The conflict of interests between the police and the courts shows itself in a number of ways. The wide discretion exercised by the police in the initial stages of law enforcement means that they have considerable *de facto* control over the number and type of cases that appear before the courts; the situation is further complicated by variations in local police practice with regard to formal and informal means of process against suspected offenders, so that magistrates cannot always know the extent and nature of the police 'sifting' process in the early stages prior to court appearance. One result of these variations and uncertainties is that courts may, for practical purposes, virtually ignore the existence of such wide discretionary control by the police of their 'input', and make their decisions about the cases before them *as if* they were an *unselected* group of suspected offenders, thus not only compounding the unequal effects of local variations in police practices, but also making many decisions which are unacceptable to the police, who typically select cases with certain expectations about the appropriate court dispositions. The extent to which any such police expectations are fulfilled by the courts has important implications not only for the vindication of earlier police decisions but also for the likely effects on future police practices.

Vital aspects of the relationship between the police and the courts, especially at the pre-trial stages, are illuminated by Herbert Packer's models of the criminal process, in which he contrasts the 'Crime Control' model with the 'Due Process' model, associated with a 'presumption of guilt' and a 'presumption of innocence' respectively, and reflecting important differences in value choices and systems.[8] The value system that underlies the Crime Control model is based on the belief that the repression of criminal conduct is by far the most important function to be performed by the penal process, and results in a major focus upon the efficiency and success with which this goal can be achieved, through the screening of suspects, the determination of guilt and the choice of an appropriate sentence for those convicted of crime. The Due Process model, on the other hand, emphasizes the need for greater attention to be paid to the detailed procedure and methods which are appropriate for the detection of crime and the conviction of offenders, and asserts important limits on the exercise of discretion and official powers. Although Packer put forward these alternative models as applying to the entire process of criminal justice, yet they seem particularly useful for identifying the different concerns of particular groups *within* the process; thus, a postulated police commitment to the Crime Control model would not only seem to explain much of their attitude towards the granting of bail before trial and the desirability of guilty pleas, but would also explain much of the conflict between the police and the judiciary in these matters, who in their turn are more likely to be committed to the Due Process model.

In addition to conflicts between the courts and both the earlier and later stages of the penal process, detailed analysis of sentencing disparities shows that there is a considerable degree of conflict *among* magistrates and judges, as to the appropriate aims of sentencing and the best methods of achieving any particular aim. Some of this conflict derives from a variety of *operational* constraints upon the sentencing process, including the availability of information relevant to the sentencing task and the broader influences of the community context in which courts operate; but the most important source of conflict and inconsistency in sentencing is the influence of various *ideological* factors deriving from magistrates' individual backgrounds and personal attitudes towards crime and punishment. Just as O'Leary and Newman suggested that operational and ideological factors largely contributed to the existence of conflict *between* different groups of penal agents, so it is perhaps not surprising to find that similar factors can equally contribute to the existence of *internal* conflict and inconsistencies within groups of penal agents and decision-makers at a single stage of the process; although major attention has been paid in criminological research to inconsistencies within the sentencing process, the present study has reinforced the need for and potential value of further research into other internal differences, for example between the way institutions and organizations report and handle suspected crime, between law enforcement and peace-keeping 'styles' of local police forces, between various levels of prison staff in their views about the aims of imprisonment, and between members of parole boards, in their decisions to release particular prisoners.

Finally, there are major conflicts of interest between the judiciary and the penal agencies which receive the sentenced offenders, as there seems to be no agreed view as to the extent to which judicial aims in
222

the choice of sentence should affect, for example, the nature or length of a term of imprisonment. In practice, the type of institution in which a prisoner serves his sentence is usually decided by an internal classification process based on criteria related to administrative convenience and control, which have no real equivalent in terms of judicial aims, but which clearly influence the extent to which other judicial aims (e.g. reformation, deterrence, etc.) can be successfully achieved. Although many jurisdictions seem to have accepted a compromise position, whereby decisions concerning the nature of a custodial régime are entrusted entirely to the prison administration, the situation with regard to discretionary control over the *length* of sentence seems generally to have been less satisfactorily resolved; it seems easier to incorporate Paterson's dictum, that a man is sent to prison '*as* a punishment, not *for* punishment', into a system of prison classification, than it is to maintain the importance of the 'denunciatory' or deterrent elements in any judicial pronouncement of sentence, when the actual length of sentence can vary tremendously according to the view of the subsequent paroling authorities.

To what extent is it possible for these and other conflicts in the penal process to be resolved or significantly diminished? One possibility, that has been frequently canvassed, involves greater control over the exercise of discretion. Major suggestions towards this end were made by K. C. Davis, in his *Discretionary Justice,* where he was always conscious of the need to steer a difficult but necessary course between too much and too little discretion, in any system committed to ideals of individualized justice: 'Discretionary power can be either too broad or too narrow. When it is too broad, justice may suffer from arbitrariness or inequality. When it is too narrow, justice may suffer from insufficient individualizing.'[9] The first essential step towards controlling discretion is to *recognize its existence* at certain crucial stages of the penal process, and further to recognize that the exercise of discretion often assumes an important *policy-making* role, whether in decisions taken by the police, magistrates or penal agencies. Once its existence and nature has been publicly recognized in this way, Davis suggested several important instruments for structuring or controlling discretion, including open policy statements, open rules, open reasons, open precedents and fair informal procedures, reaffirming his belief in *openness* as 'the natural enemy of arbitrariness and a natural ally in the fight against injustice'.[10] This principle of openness reflects directly upon much of what has been discussed in this study, particularly the concept of 'low-visibility', in discretionary decisions taken by the police in on-the-street encounters, and the pre-trial problems of 'negotiated justice' and plea-bargaining; similarly, the practical implications of Davis' instruments for these and other stages of the penal process are clear enough, without the need for further detailed rehearsal. Even in the apparently more visible decision-stages of the criminal courts and correctional authorities, there is a need for the introduction of more open policy statements, open rules and reasons, in sentencing and parole decisions. The exercise of discretion, therefore, certainly can and should be better controlled and structured, but in the last analysis we must agree with Davis that what we have and what we ought to retain is a 'government of laws and *of men*'; as long as this is the case, there seem bound to be inconsistencies and unfairness in discretionary decisions, deriving from the situational constraints and personal values of individual decision-makers.

The work of O'Leary and his colleagues, in the United States, directed towards the goal of 'conflict resolution' in criminal justice, takes full account of the role of 'value dissensus' among different groups of penal agents, in contributing towards existing conflicts, as does much of the research quoted in different parts of this book; however, O'Leary seems to have a confidence, not shared by the present writer, in the ability of various strategies of group discussion and education to resolve these basic value conflicts; thus O'Leary and Ryan have experimented with the problem of 'group-based dissensus' by encouraging different groups to recognize and evolve goals to supersede the goals of their own particular subsystems, by round-table discussion and the provision of systematic information and feedback about aims and methods.[11] Discussion and the provision of information can go only so far, and no further, in resolving the problem; they can help different groups to clarify their own aims and to understand the aims of others, but are unlikely to bring about major changes either in basic attitudes or practices of the decision-makers—as was seen in the analysis of the use of pre-sentence information by magistrates, where it was used selectively to *confirm* existing attitudes, rather than to bring about any significant *change*. Similarly, while accepting the basic analytical framework of the 'systems approach' to

224

policy and planning in criminal justice, the hopes and prescriptions for integrating the operation of the system seem idealistic and unreal. It is important to recognize the existence of interaction between the different parts of the system, that the 'output' of one stage provides the 'input' for another, and that for the system to be 'rational' there would need to be an overall goal towards which each and every part was directed, but in fact the complex socio-political nature of crime and society's response to criminal behaviour seems to rule out the possibility of any real integration or 'rationality' throughout the penal process.[12]

SOCIAL VALUES AND PENAL AIMS

The real crux of the matter lies in the fundmental *ambivalence* of society towards the criminal behaviour of its members; the conflicts and inconsistencies within the operation of the penal process simply reflect and are a direct product of this basic ambivalence. Many different factors could be said to contribute towards it, ranging from the deep-seated fears and fantasies of individuals about deviant behaviour, to major aspects of the social and political organization of our society; but, as no single explanation is likely to hold a monopoly of the truth in this matter, the practical problem is probably one of how to accept and come to terms with this ambivalence, rather than entertaining vain hopes of its early elimination or satisfactory resolution.

The first chapter of this book showed the crucial role played by the social attitudes of different members of the public in the defining and reporting of 'crime'; Leslie Wilkins' definition of crime was preferred, as 'something-that-the-police-ought-to-do-something-about', with its essential relativity and subjectivity, deriving from a variety of sub-cultural, institutional and practical factors, which were seen to influence the way members of the public initiated the official processes of law enforcement. From the start, therefore, different members of society are shown to have conflicting views about the nature of 'crime' and the appropriate measures to be taken against suspected 'criminals'. Throughout the subsequent stages of the process, decision-makers are directly and indirectly influenced by a variety of 'community' factors, in which the interests and pressures of a local community can be seen as a microcosm of the forces at work in society at large: the exercise of police discretion may differ according to the social characteristics of the communities in which it operates, as may the sentencing practices of magistrates' courts; decisions about the location of prisons and the allocation of prisoners to them often takes into account the views of the local community, as do many parole board decisions about the release of a prisoner to a particular locality. On many issues of penal policy public opinion exhibits a commitment to the 'Crime Control' and 'Due Process' models *at one and the same time*, demanding the successful achievement of results for the protection of society, but not supporting the necessary means to these ends.

Criminologists and penal reformers frequently suggest that public opinion can and indeed *ought* to be ignored when it is not in accord with their own 'enlightened' views, as to the way in which the penal process should operate; similarly, they often argue that apparent inconsistencies, which may be related to different community attitudes, are without any kind of justification, by discounting any possible role for community influence upon the penal process. Although it is easy to understand such a point of view, particularly if one happens to share many of the same reformers' opinions about the working of the process, yet it does seem to be based on a partial and questionable view of the relationship between a society, its definitions of 'crime' and the penal process. A proper emphasis upon the socio-political nature of crime and the 'biases' of society's methods of dealing with offenders, does not by any means imply that any single group in society, whether penal reformers, politicians or criminals themselves, can simply introduce a *unilateral redefinition* of what ought to be the guiding principles of the penal process, without fully taking into account the complex relationship between current definitions and practice, and the other groups in society. Thus, the contemporary ambivalence is arguably more true to the nature of crime in society than would be any 'authoritative resolution' of the situation, whatever the source of such a resolution. Criminological research, of the kind which forms the substance of this book, can reveal the conflicts and ambiguities inherent in the process, and at the same time question the validity of various official claims about the principles which are intended to inform the process, but the final judgement about what principles *ought* to underlie the penal process is a matter for society as a whole to work out for itself, in accordance with its values and beliefs about deviant behaviour and the appropriate response to that behaviour.

NOTES

1. President's Commission on Law Enforcement and Administration of Justice *The Challenge of Crime in a Free Society* Washington, D.C.(1967) p. 7.
2. See F. J. Remington's Editorial Foreword to R. O. Dawson *Sentencing: the Decision as to Type, Length and Condition of Sentence* Boston (1969) p. xvii.
3. V. O'Leary and D. J. Newman 'Conflict Resolution in Criminal Justice' *Jo. Research in Crime and Del.* Vol. **7** (1970) pp. 99ff., at 100; see also Reiss' discussion of criminal justice 'subsystems' in A. J. Reiss *The Police and the Public* New Haven (1971) p. 117.
4. S. Wheeler *et al.* 'Agents of Delinquency Control: A Comparative Analysis' in Wheeler (ed.) *Controlling Delinquents* New York (1968).
5. *Ibid.* pp. 33–4: 'Finally, all these problems of integration and coordination are particularly important because these groups work with human beings. Unlike a factory, where the materials passing through the system have no brain, feelings, or memory, the targets of these groups do. When youths are exposed to divergent views and interpretations of their conduct as they are passed from one agent to another, their impressions of the fairness and consistency of the entire procedure may be affected' (p. 34).
6. O'Leary and Newman *op. cit.* p. 100; see also O'Leary and E. Ryan *A Study of Conflict Resolution in Criminal Justice* Probation Management Institutes, Publication V, Washington, D.C.(1969).
7. K. C. Davis *Discretionary Justice* Baton Rouge (1969) p. 3.
8. H. L. Packer *The Limits of the Criminal Sanction* Stanford (1969) ch. 8 pp. 149–73; see also Packer 'Two Models of the Criminal Process' *U. Pa. L. Rev.* Vol. **113** (1964) p. 1.
9. Davis *op. cit.* p. 52: 'No legal system in world history has been without significant discretionary power. None can be. Discretion is indispensable for individualized justice, for creative justice. . . . The proper goal is to eliminate unnecessary discretionary power, not to eliminate all discretionary power' (p. 216).
10. *Ibid.* p. 98.
11. O'Leary and Ryan *op. cit.* pp. 7ff.:
    The kinds and sequence of interventions which appear to hold greatest promise are: (1) Facilitating the articulation of goals, such as the prevention of crime, which subsume the interests of the parties in conflict; (2) Providing feedback to increase mutual understanding and to help identify attitudes and behaviors which are discrepant with the commonly derived major goals; (3) Increasing understanding of the dynamics of inter-group conflict which blocks the successful modification of discrepant behaviors; and (4) Enhancing the problem-solving skills of the representatives [p. 40].

227

12. For one of the best recent discussions of the systems approach in criminal justice, see F. W. Howlett and H. Hurst 'A Systems Approach to Comprehensive Criminal Justice Planning' *Crime and Delinquency* Vol. **17** (1971) p. 345; see also M. W. Klein *et al.* 'System Rates: An Approach to Comprehensive Criminal Justice Planning' *Crime and Delinquency* Vol. **17** (1971) p. 355, and President's Commission on Law Enforcement *Task Force Report: Science and Technology* Washington. D.C.(1967).

SELECT BIBLIOGRAPHY

This select bibliography does not include every book and article referred to in the main text, but does include a few additional references which were found useful in the preparation of the book; those marked with an asterisk are particularly recommended.

General

S. Box *Deviance, Reality and Society* New York, Holt, Rinehart & Winston (1971).

W. G. Carson and P. N. P. Wiles (eds) *Crime and Delinquency in Britain* London, Martin Robertson (1970).

*W. J. Chambliss (ed.) *Crime and the Legal Process* New York, McGraw-Hill (1969).

D. Chapman *Sociology and the Stereotype of the Criminal* London, Tavistock (1968).

A. V. Cicourel *The Social Organisation of Juvenile Justice* New York, John Wiley (1968).

*K. C. Davis *Discretionary Justice: A Preliminary Inquiry* Baton Rouge, Louisiana State University Press (1969).

P. G. Garabedian and D. C. Gibbons (eds) *Becoming Delinquent: Young Offenders and the Correctional System* Chicago, Aldine (1970).

A. L. Guenther (ed.) *Criminal Behavior and Social Systems* Chicago, Rand McNally (1970).

*R. G. Hood and R. F. Sparks *Key Issues in Criminology* London, Weidenfeld & Nicolson (1970).

F. W. Howlett and H. Hurst 'A Systems Approach to Comprehensive Criminal Justice Planning' *Crime and Delinquency* Vol. **17** (1971) p. 345.

*N. Johnston, L. Savitz and M. E. Wolfgang (eds) *The Sociology of Punishment and Correction* 2nd edn New York, John Wiley (1970).

*M. W. Klein, S. Kobrin, A. W. McEachern and H. R. Sigurdson 'System Rates: An Approach to Comprehensive Criminal Justice Planning' *Crime and Delinquency* Vol. **17** (1971) p. 355.

V. O'Leary and D. J. Newman 'Conflict Resolution in Criminal Justice' *Jo. Research in Crime and Del.* Vol. **7** (1970) p. 99.

*H. L. Packer *The Limits of the Criminal Sanction* Stanford, Stanford U.P. (1969).

M. Phillippson *Sociological Aspects of Crime and Delinquency* London, Routledge & Kegan Paul (1971).

President's Commission on Law Enforcement and Administration of Justice *The Challenge of Crime in a Free Society* Washington, D.C., U.S. Government Printing Office (1967).

R. Quinney *The Social Reality of Crime* Boston, Little, Brown (1970).

*R. Quinney (ed.) *Crime and Justice in Society* Boston, Little, Brown (1969).

L. Radzinowicz and M. E. Wolfgang (eds) *Crime and Justice* 3 vols, London, Basic Books (1971).

N. Walker *Crime and Punishment in Britain* 2nd edn, Edinburgh, Edinburgh U.P. (1968).

S. Wheeler (ed.) *Controlling Delinquents* New York, John Wiley (1968).

L. T. Wilkins *Social Deviance* London, Tavistock (1964); reissued 1967 as a Social Science Paperback, *Social Policy, Action and Research*.

M. E. Wolfgang, L. Savitz and N. Johnston (eds) *The Sociology of Crime and Delinquency* 2nd edn, New York, John Wiley (1970).

Criminal statistics and social attitudes

D. J. Black 'Production of Crime Rates' *Amer. Soc. Rev.* Vol. **35** (1970) p. 733.

M. O. Cameron *The Booster and the Snitch* Glencoe, Ill., Free Press (1964).

J. E. Conklin 'Dimensions of Community Response to the Crime Problem' *Social Problems* Vol. **18** (1971) p. 373.

J. D. Douglas *American Social Order* New York, Free Press (1971) ch. 3–4.

P. H. Ennis *Criminal Victimisation in the United States: A Report on a National Survey* President's Commission on Law Enforcement and Administration of Justice, Field Surveys II, Washington, D.C., U.S. Government Printing Office (1967).

*P. H. Ennis 'Crimes, Victims and the Police' *Trans-Action* Vol. **4** (June 1967) p. 36.

T. C. N. Gibbens and R. H. Ahrenfeldt (eds) *Cultural Factors in Delinquency* London, Tavistock (1966).

T. C. N. Gibbens and J. Prince *Shoplifting* London, I.S.T.D. (1962).

D. C. Gibbons, J. F. Jones and P. G. Garabedian 'Gauging Public Opinion about the Crime Problem' *Crime and Delinquency* Vol. **18** (1972) p. 134.

D. Glaser 'Victim Survey Research: Theoretical Implications', in A. L. Guenther (ed.) *Criminal Behavior and Social Systems* Chicago, Rand McNally (1970).

M. Grünhut 'Statistics in Criminology' *Jo. Roy. Stat. Soc.* **Series A,** Vol. **114** (1951) p. 139.

Home Office *Report of the Departmental Committee on Criminal Statistics* (Perks Committee) Cmnd. 3448, London, H.M.S.O. (1967).

R. G. Hood *Sentencing the Motoring Offender* London, Heinemann (1972).

*J. I. Kitsuse and A. V. Cicourel 'A Note on the Uses of Official Statistics' *Social Problems* Vol. **11** (1963) p. 131.

*M. W. Klein, S. Kobrin, A. W. McEachern and H. R. Sigurdson 'System Rates: An Approach to Comprehensive Criminal Justice Planning' *Crime and Delinquency* Vol. **17** (1971) p. 355.

J. R. Lambert *Crime, Police and Race Relations* London, O.U.P. (1970).

F. H. McClintock 'The Dark Figure', in European Committee on Crime Problems, *Collected Studies in Criminological Research* Vol. **5** Strasbourg, Council of Europe (1970).

F. H. McClintock *et al. Crimes of Violence* London, Macmillan (1963).

*F. H. McClintock and N. H. Avison *Crime in England and Wales* London, Heinemann (1968).

J. McIntyre 'Public Attitudes toward Crime and Law Enforcement' *The Annals of the American Academy of Political and Social Science* Vol. **374** (November 1967) p. 34.

J. A. D. MacMillan 'The Social Pathology of Motoring Offences and Accidents' unpublished M. Phil. thesis, University of Reading (1970).

H. Mannheim *Social Aspects of Crime in England between the Wars* London, Allen & Unwin (1940).

J. P. Martin *Offenders as Employees* London, Macmillan (1962).

*D. J. Newman 'The Effects of Accommodations in Justice Administration on Criminal Statistics' *Sociology and Social Research* Vol. **46** (1962) p. 144.

M. H. Parry *Aggression on the Road* London, Tavistock (1968).

President's Commission on Law Enforcement and Administration of Justice *Task Force Report: Science and Technology* Washington, D.C., U.S. Government Printing Office (1967).

L. Radzinowicz 'English Criminal Statistics: a critical analysis' in L. Radzinowicz and J. W. C. Turner (eds) *A Modern Approach to Criminal Law* London, Macmillan (1948).

231

T. Sellin 'The Basis of a Crime Index' *Jo. Crim. Law, Crimin. and P.S.* Vol. **22** (1931) p. 335.

*T. Sellin 'The Significance of Records of Crime' *The Law Quarterly Review*, Vol. **67** (1951) p. 489.

T. Sellin and M. E. Wolfgang *The Measurement of Delinquency* New York, John Wiley (1964).

M. Shaw and W. Williamson 'Public Attitudes to the Police' *The Criminologist* Vol. **7** No. 26 (Autumn 1972) p. 18.

N. Walker *Crimes, Courts and Figures: an introduction to criminal statistics* Harmondsworth, Penguin (1971).

N. Walker and M. Argyle 'Does the Law Affect Moral Judgements?' *Brit. Jo. Crim.* Vol. **4** (1964) p. 570.

*S. Wheeler 'Criminal Statistics: A Reformulation of the Problem' *Jo. Crim. Law, Crimin. and P.S.* Vol. **58** (1967) p. 317.

*P. N. P. Wiles 'Criminal Statistics and Sociological Explanations of Crime' in W. G. Carson and P. N. P. Wiles (eds) *Crime and Delinquency in Britain* London, Martin Robertson (1971).

*L. T. Wilkins 'Criminology: An Operational Research Approach' in A. T. Welford *et al.* (eds) *Society: Problems and Methods of Study* London, Routledge & Kegan Paul (1962).

*L. T. Wilkins 'The Measurement of Crime' *Brit. Jo. Crim.* Vol. **3** (1963) p. 321.

*L. T. Wilkins 'New Thinking in Criminal Statistics' *Jo. Crim. Law, Crimin. and P.S.* Vol. **56** (1965) p. 277.

T. C. Willett *Criminal on the Road* London, Tavistock (1964).

H. D. Willcock and J. Stokes *Deterrents to Crime among Youths aged 15 to 21* London, Government Social Survey Report (1968).

M. A. P. Willmer *Crime and Information Theory* Edinburgh, Edinburgh University Press (1970).

Police discretion in law enforcement

*M. Banton *The Policeman in the Community* London, Tavistock (1964).

R. W. Balch 'The Police Personality: Fact or Fiction?' *Jo. Crim. Law, Crimin. and P.S.* Vol. **63** (1972) p. 106.

D. H. Bayley and H. Mendelsohn *Minorities and the Police: Confrontation in America* New York, Free Press (1969).

*E. A. Bittner 'The Police on Skid-Row: A Study of Peace Keeping' *Amer. Soc. Rev.* Vol. **32** (1967) p. 699.

E. A. Bittner 'Police Discretion in Emergency Apprehension of Mentally Ill Persons' *Social Problems* Vol. **14** (1967) p. 278.

D. J. Black and A. J. Reiss 'Police Control of Juveniles' *Amer. Soc. Rev.* Vol. **35** (1970) p. 63.

D. J. Bordua (ed.) *The Police: Six Sociological Essays* New York, John Wiley (1967).

D. J. Bordua 'Recent Trends: Deviant Behavior and Social Control' *The Annals of the American Academy of Political and Social Science* Vol. **369** (1967) p. 149.

M. E. Cain 'Role Conflict Among Police Juvenile Liaison Officers' *Brit. Jo. Crim.* Vol. **8** (1968) p. 366.

M. E. Cain 'On the Beat: Interactions and Relations in Rural and Urban Police Forces' in S. Cohen (ed.) *Images of Deviance* Harmondsworth, Penguin (1971).

*M. E. Cain *Society and the Policeman's Role* London, Routledge & Kegan Paul (1973).

W. J. Chambliss and J. T. Liell 'The Legal Process in the Community Setting' *Crime and Delinquency* Vol. **12** (1966) p. 310.

D. Chappell and P. R. Wilson *The Police and the Public in Australia and New Zealand* St. Lucia, University of Queensland (1969).

J. P. Clark 'Isolation of the Police: A Comparison of the British and American Situations' *Jo. Crim. Law, Crimin. and P.S.* Vol. **56** (1965) p. 307.

D. R. Cressey and E. Elgesem 'The Police and the Administration of Justice' in N. Christie (ed.) *Aspects of Social Control in Welfare States,* Scandinavian Studies in Criminology, Vol. **2** London, Tavistock (1968).

*E. Cumming, I. M. Cumming and L. Edell 'Policeman as Philosopher, Guide and Friend' *Social Problems* Vol. **12** (1965) p. 276.

T. N. Ferdinand and E. G. Luchterhand 'Inner-City Youth, the Police, the Juvenile Court, and Justice' *Social Problems* Vol. **17** (1970) p. 510.

N. Goldman *The Differential Selection of Juvenile Offenders for Court Appearance* New York, National Council on Crime and Delinquency (1963).

H. Goldstein 'Administrative Problems in Controlling the Exercise of Police Authority' *Jo. Crim. Law, Crimin. and P.S.* Vol. **58** (1967) p. 160.

J. Goldstein 'Police Discretion Not to Invoke the Criminal Process: Low-Visibility Decisions in the Administration of Justice' *Yale Law Journal* Vol. **69** (1960) p. 543.

W. F. Hohenstein 'Factors Influencing the Police Disposition of Juvenile Offenders' in T. Sellin and M. E. Wolfgang (eds) *Delinquency: Selected Studies* New York, John Wiley (1969).

J. R. Hudson 'Police-citizen Encounters that lead to Citizen Complaints' *Social Problems* Vol. **18** (1970) p. 179.

233

E. H. Johnson 'Interrelatedness of Law Enforcement Programs: A Fundamental Dimension' *Jo. Crim. Law, Crimin. and P.S.* Vol. **60** (1969) p. 509.

S. H. Kadish 'Legal Norm and Discretion in the Police and Sentencing Processes' *Harvard Law Review* Vol. **75** (1962) p. 904.

W. R. Lafave 'The Police and Nonenforcement of the Law' *Wisconsin Law Review* (1962) pp. 104, 179.

*W. R. Lafave *Arrest: the Decision to Take a Suspect into Custody* Boston, Little, Brown (1965).

J. R. Lambert *Crime, Police and Race Relations* London, O.U.P. (1967).

A. W. McEachern and R. Bauzer 'Factors Related to Disposition in Juvenile Police Contacts' in M. W. Klein (ed.) *Juvenile Gangs in Context* Englewood Cliffs, Prentice-Hall (1967).

G. Marshall *Police and Government* London, Methuen (1965).

F. W. Miller *Prosecution: The Decision to Charge a Suspect with a Crime* Boston, Little, Brown (1969).

R. I. Parnas 'The Police Response to the Domestic Disturbance' *Wisconsin Law Review* (1967) p. 914.

D. M. Petersen 'Informal Norms and Police Practice: The Traffic Ticket Quota System' *Sociology and Social Research* Vol. **55** (1971) p. 354.

I. Piliavin and S. Briar 'Police Encounters with Juveniles' *Amer. Jo. Soc.* Vol. **70** (1964) p. 206.

President's Commission on Law Enforcement and Administration of Justice *Task Force Report: The Police* Washington, D.C., U.S. Government Printing Office (1967).

*A. J. Reiss *The Police and the Public* New Haven, Yale U.P. (1971).

H. Sacks 'Notes on Police Assessment of Moral Character' in D. Sudnow (ed.) *Studies in Social Interaction,* New York, Free Press (1972).

L. W. Shannon 'Types and Patterns of Delinquency Referral in a Middle-sized city' *Brit. Jo. Crim.* Vol. **4** (1963) p. 24.

M. Shaw and W. Williamson 'Public Attitudes to the Police' *The Criminologist,* Vol. **7** No. 26 (Autumn 1972) p. 18.

*J. H. Skolnick *Justice Without Trial: Law Enforcement in Democratic Society* New York, John Wiley (1966).

J. G. Somerville 'A Study of the Preventive Aspect of Police Work with Juveniles' *Crim. L. R.* (1969) pp. 407, 472.

D. J. Steer *Police Cautions—A Study in the Exercise of Police Discretion* (Oxford University Penal Research Unit, Occasional Paper No. 2) Oxford, Blackwell (1970).

A. Stinchcombe 'Institutions of Privacy in the Determination of Police Administrative Practice' *Amer. Jo. Soc.* Vol. **59** (1963) p. 150.

D. C. Sullivan and L. J. Siegel 'How Police use Information to make Decisions—An Application of Decision Games' *Crime and Delinquency,* Vol. **18** (1972) 253.

*R. M. Terry 'The Screening of Juvenile Offenders' *Jo. Crim. Law, Crimin. and P.S.* Vol. **58** (1967) p. 173.

*R. M. Terry 'Discrimination in the Handling of Juvenile Offenders by Social Control Agencies' *Jo. Research in Crime and Del.* Vol. **4** (1967) p. 218.

L. L. Tifft and D. J. Bordua 'Police Organisation and Future Research' *Jo. Research in Crime and Del.* Vol. **6** (1969) p. 167.

N. L. Weiner and C. V. Willie 'Decisions by Juvenile Officers' *Amer. Jo. Soc.* Vol. **77** (1971) p. 199.

E. P. Wenninger and J. P. Clark 'A Theoretical Orientation for Police Studies' in M. W. Klein (ed.) *Juvenile Gangs in Context* Englewood Cliffs, Prentice-Hall (1967).

W. A. Westley 'Violence and the Police' *Amer. Jo. Soc.* Vol. **49** (1953) p. 34.

*W. A. Westley *Violence and the Police: A Sociological Study of Law, Custom and Morality* Cambridge, Mass., M.I.T. Press (1970).

*S. Wheeler *et al.* 'Agents of Delinquency Control: A Comparative Analysis' in S. Wheeler (ed.) *Controlling Delinquents,* New York, John Wiley (1968).

B. Whitaker *The Police* Harmondsworth, Penguin (1964).

B. Whitaker 'Conflict in the Role of the Police' in P. Halmos (ed.) *Sociological Studies in the British Penal Services* Keele, University of Keele (1965).

C. Williams 'A Chief Constable's View' in C. H. Rolph (ed.) *The Police and the Public* London, Heinemann (1962).

*J. Q. Wilson 'The Police and the Delinquent in Two Cities' in S. Wheeler (ed.) *Controlling Delinquents* New York, John Wiley (1968).

*J. Q. Wilson *Varieties of Police Behavior* Cambridge, Mass., Harvard U.P. (1968).

Bail and remands in custody

C. E. Ares and H. J. Sturz 'Bail and the Indigent Accused' *Crime and Delinquency* Vol. **8** (1962) p. 1.

C. E. Ares, A. Rankin and H. J. Sturz 'The Manhattan Bail Project: An Interim Report on the Use of Pre-trial Release' *N.Y.U.L. Rev.* Vol. **38** (1963) p. 67.

A. K. Bottomley 'The Granting of Bail: Principles and Practice' *Modern Law Review* Vol. **31** (1968) p. 40.

*A. K. Bottomley *Prison Before Trial* (Occasional Papers on Social Administration, No. 39) London, Bell (1970).

C. Davies 'Pre-trial Imprisonment: A Liverpool Study' *Brit. Jo. Crim.* Vol. **11** (1971) p. 32.

S. Dell *Silent in Court* (Occasional Papers on Social Administration, No. 42) London, Bell (1971).

P. Devlin *The Criminal Prosecution in England* London, O.U.P. (1960).

*C. Foote (ed.) *Studies on Bail* University of Pennsylvania (1966).

C. Foote, J. P. Markle and E. A. Woolley 'Compelling Appearance in Court: Administration of Bail in Philadelphia' *U. Pa. L. Rev.* Vol. **102** (1954) p. 1031.

D. J. Freed and P. M. Wald *Bail in the United States: 1964* Washington, D.C., U.S. Dept of Justice (1964).

*M. L. Friedland *Detention Before Trial* Toronto, University of Toronto (1965).

E. Gibson *Time Spent Awaiting Trial* (Home Office Research Unit Report) London, H.M.S.O. (1960).

R. L. Goldfarb *Ransom: A Critique of the American Bail System* New York, Harper & Row (1965).

Granting Bail in Magistrates' Courts: Proposals for Reform London, Howard League for Penal Reform (1972).

* M. King *Bail or Custody* London, Cobden Trust (1971).

F. E. Mostyn 'Bail and the Presumption of Innocence: England and America—A Comparison' *Law Society's Gazette* Vol. **61** (1964) p. 799.

H. L. Packer 'Two Models of the Criminal Process' *U. Pa. L. Rev.* Vol. **113** (1964) p. 1.

*A. Rankin 'The Effect of Pre-trial Detention' *N.Y.U.L. Rev.* Vol. **39** (1964) p. 641.

J. W. Roberts and J. S. Palermo 'A Study of the Administration of Bail in New York' *U. Pa. L. Rev.* Vol. **106** (1958) p. 685.

R. F. Sparks 'The Decision to Remand for Mental Examination' *Brit. Jo. Crim.* Vol. **6** (1966) p. 6.

H. J. Sturz 'The Manhattan Bail Project and its Aftermath' *Amer. Jo. Corr.* Vol. **27,** No. 6 (1965) p. 14.

T. G. Tennant 'The Use of Remand on Bail or in Custody by the London Juvenile Courts—A Comparative Study' *Brit. Jo. Crim.* Vol. **11** (1971) p. 80.

United States Department of Justice *Bail and Summons: 1965* Washington, D.C., U.S. Government Printing Office (1965).

P. M. Wald 'Pre-trial Detention and Ultimate Freedom: A Statistical Study' *N.Y.U.L. Rev.* Vol. **39** (1964) p. 631.

D. J. West and J. S. Bearcroft 'The Choice of Bail or Custody for Offenders Remanded for a Psychiatric Report' *International Jo. Soc. Psychiatry* Vol. **6** (1960) p. 34.

*M. Zander 'Bail: A Reappraisal' *Crim. L. R.* (1967) pp. 25, 100, 128.

*M. Zander 'A Study of Bail/Custody Decisions in London Magistrates' Courts' *Crim. L. R.* (1971) p. 191.

Guilty pleas

A. W. Alschuler 'The Prosecutor's Role in Plea Bargaining' *Univ. Chic. Law Rev.* Vol. **36** (1968) p. 50.

*Association of Chief Police Officers of England and Wales 'Trial by Jury' *New Law Journal* Vol. **116** (1966) p. 928.

*A. S. Blumberg *Criminal Justice* Chicago, Quadrangle Books (1967).

A. S. Blumberg 'Lawyers with Convictions' in A. S. Blumberg (ed.) *The Scales of Justice* Chicago, Aldine (1970).

*A. Davis 'Sentences for Sale: A New Look at Plea Bargaining in England and America' *Crim. L. R.* (1971) pp. 150, 218.

S. Dell *Silent in Court* (Occasional Papers on Social Administration, No. 42) London, Bell (1971).

A. Enker 'Perspectives on Plea Bargaining', in President's Commission on Law Enforcement and Administration of Justice *Task Force Report: The Courts*, Washington, D.C., U.S. Government Printing Office (1967), Appendix A.

H. Kalven and H. Zeisel *The American Jury* Boston, Little, Brown (1966).

*S. McCabe and R. Purves *By-passing the Jury* (Oxford University Penal Research Unit, Occasional Paper No. 3) Oxford, Blackwell (1972).

S. McCabe and R. Purves *The Jury at Work* (Oxford University Penal Research Unit, Occasional Paper No. 4) Oxford, Blackwell (1972).

*D. J. Newman 'Pleading Guilty for Considerations: A Study of Bargain Justice' *Jo. Crim. Law, Crimin. and P.S.* Vol. **46** (1956) p. 780.

D. J. Newman 'Official Inducements to Plead Guilty: Suggested Morals for a Marketplace' *Univ. Chic. Law Rev.* Vol. **32** (1964) p. 167.

*D. J. Newman *Conviction: the Determination of Guilt or Innocence Without Trial* Boston, Little, Brown (1966).

A. Rosett 'The Negotiated Guilty Plea' *The Annals of the American Academy of Political and Social Science* Vol. **374** (November 1967) p. 71.

D. Sudnow 'Normal Crimes: Sociological Features of the Penal Code in a Public Defender Office' *Social Problems*, Vol. **12** (1965) p. 255.

P. Thomas 'An Exploration of Plea Bargaining' *Crim. L. R.* (1969), p. 69.

P. Thomas 'Plea Bargaining and the Turner Case' *Crim. L. R.* (1970), p. 559.

D. R. Vetri 'Guilty Plea Bargaining: Compromises by Prosecutors to Secure Guilty Pleas' *U. Pa. L. Rev.* Vol. **112** (1964) p. 865.

R. G. Weintraub and R. Tough 'Lesser Pleas Considered' *Jo. Crim. Law, Crimin. and P.S.* Vol. **32** (1942) p. 506.

Yale Law Journal 'The Influence of the Defendant's Plea on Judicial Determination of Sentence' *Yale Law Journal* Vol. **66** (1956) p. 204.

Sentencing

H. Barr and E. O'Leary *Trends and Regional Comparisons in Probation* London, H.M.S.O. (1966).

H. A. Bullock 'Significance of the Racial Factor in the Length of Prison Sentences' *Jo. Crim. Law, Crimin. and P.S.* Vol. **52** (1961) p. 411.

R. M. Carter 'The Pre-sentence Report and the Decision-making Process' *Jo. Research in Crime and Del.* Vol. **4** (1967) p. 203.

*R. M. Carter and L. T. Wilkins 'Some Factors in Sentencing Policy' *Jo. Crim. Law, Crimin. and P.S.* Vol. **58** (1967) p. 503.

R. O. Dawson *Sentencing: the Decision as to Type, Length and Conditions of Sentence* Boston, Little, Brown (1969).

I. S. Drapkin 'Criminological Aspects of Sentencing' in I. S. Drapkin (ed.) *Scripta Hierosolymitana: Vol. XXI, Studies in Criminology* Jerusalem, Hebrew University (1969).

G. Everson 'The Human Element in Justice' *Jo. Crim. Law, Crimin. and P.S.* Vol. **10** (1920) p. 90.

P. Ford *Advising Sentencers* (Oxford University Penal Research Unit, Occasional Paper No. 5) Oxford, Blackwell (1972).

F. J. Gaudet 'The Sentencing Behavior of the Judge' in V. C. Branham and S. B. Kutash (eds) *Encyclopaedia of Criminology* New York, Philosophical Library (1949).

F. J. Gaudet, G. S. Harris and C. W. St John 'Individual Differences in the Sentencing Tendencies of Judges' *Jo. Crim. Law, Crimin. and P.S.* Vol. **23** (1933) p. 811.

*E. Green *Judicial Attitudes in Sentencing* London, Macmillan (1961).

E. Green 'Inter- and Intra-racial Crime Relative to Sentencing' *Jo. Crim. Law, Crimin. and P.S.* Vol. **55** (1964) p. 348.

238

S. Z. Gross 'The Prehearing Juvenile Report: Probation Officers' Conceptions' *Jo. Research in Crime and Del.* Vol. **4** (1967) p. 212.

J. B. Grossman 'Social Backgrounds and Judicial Decision-making' *Harvard Law Review* Vol. **79** (1966) p. 1551.

M. Grünhut *Juvenile Offenders before the Courts* Oxford, O.U.P. (1956).

J. E. Hall Williams 'Sentencing in Transition' in T. Grygier *et al.* (eds) *Criminology in Transition* London, Tavistock (1965).

J. Hogarth 'Sentencing Research—Some Problems of Design' *Brit. Jo. Crim.* Vol. **7** (1967) p. 84.

*J. Hogarth *Sentencing as a Human Process* Toronto, University of Toronto Press (1971).

Home Office *Royal Commission on Justices of the Peace 1946–8* Cmd. 7463, London, H.M.S.O. (1948).

*Home Office *Report of the Interdepartmental Committee on the Business of the Criminal Courts* Cmnd. 1289, (Streatfeild Committee) London, H.M.S.O. (1961).

*R. G. Hood *Sentencing in Magistrates' Courts* London, Stevens (1962).

R. G. Hood 'A Study of the Effectiveness of Pre-sentence Investigations in Reducing Recidivism' *Brit. Jo. Crim.* Vol. **6** (1966) p. 303.

*R. G. Hood *Sentencing the Motoring Offender* London, Heinemann (1972).

R. G. Hood and I. Taylor 'Second Report of the Effectiveness of Pre-sentence Investigations in Reducing Recidivism' *Brit. Jo. Crim.* Vol. **8** (1968) p. 431.

F. V. Jarvis 'Inquiry before Sentence' in T. Grygier *et al* (eds) *Criminology in Transition* London, Tavistock (1965).

S. H. Kadish 'Legal Norm and Discretion in the Police and Sentencing Processes' *Harvard Law Review* Vol. **75** (1962) p. 904.

M. F. McGuire and A. Holtzoff 'The Problem of Sentence in the Criminal Law' *Boston Univ. Law Rev.* Vol. **20** (1940) p. 423.

W. McWilliams 'Pre-sentence Study of Offenders: An Interim Report' *Case Conference* Vol. **15** (1968) p. 136.

H. Mannheim 'Comparative Sentencing Practice' *Law and Contemporary Problems* Vol. **23** (1958) p. 557.

*H. Mannheim, J. C. Spencer and G. Lynch 'Magisterial Policy in the London Juvenile Courts' *Brit. Jo. Del.* Vol. **7** (1957) pp. 13, 119.

S. S. Nagel 'Judicial Backgrounds and Criminal Cases' *Jo. Crim. Law, Crimin. and P.S.* Vol. **53** (1962) p. 333.

*S. S. Nagel 'Disparities in Criminal Procedure' *U.C.L.A. Law Rev.* Vol. **14** (1967) p. 1272.

*L. E. Ohlin and F. J. Remington 'Sentencing Structure: Its Effect upon

239

Systems for the Administration of Criminal Justice' *Law and Contemporary Problems* Vol. **23** (1958) p. 495.

K. W. Patchett and J. D. McClean 'Decision-making in Juvenile Cases' *Crim. L. R.* (1965) p. 699.

President's Commission on Law Enforcement and Administration of Justice *Task Force Report: The Courts* Washington, D.C., U.S. Government Printing Office (1967).

A. G. Rose 'An Experimental Study of Sentencing' *Brit. Jo. Crim.* Vol. **5** (1965) p. 314.

G. Schubert 'Judicial Attitudes and Voting Behavior: the 1961 term of the United States Supreme Court' *Law and Contemporary Problems* Vol. **28** (1963) p. 100.

*G. Schubert (ed.) *Judicial Decision-making* New York, Free Press (1963).

G. Schubert (ed.) *Judicial Behavior* Chicago, Rand McNally (1964).

L. Sebba 'Decision-making in Juvenile Cases—A Comment' *Crim. L. R.* (1967) p. 347.

T. Sellin 'Race Prejudice in the Administration of Justice' *Amer. Jo. Sociol.* Vol. **41** (1935) p. 212.

S. Shoham 'Sentencing Policy of Criminal Courts in Israel' *Jo. Crim. Law, Crimin. and P.S.* Vol. **50** (1959) p. 327.

A. B. Smith and A. S. Blumberg 'The Problem of Objectivity in Judicial Decision-making' *Social Forces* Vol. **46** (1967) p. 96.

R. F. Sparks 'Sentencing by Magistrates: Some Facts of Life' in P. Halmos (ed.) *Sociological Studies in the British Penal Services* Keele, University of Keele (1965).

D. A. Thomas 'Sentencing—the Basic Principles' *Crim. L. R.* (1967), pp. 455, 503.

D. A. Thomas *Principles of Sentencing* London, Heinemann (1970).

*N. D. Walker *Sentencing in a Rational Society* rev. edn, Harmondsworth, Penguin (1972).

*L. T. Wilkins and A. Chandler 'Confidence and Competence in Decision Making' *Brit. Jo. Crim.* Vol. **5** (1965) p. 22.

C. Winick, I. Gerver and A. S. Blumberg 'The Psychology of Judges' in H. Toch (ed.) *Legal and Criminal Psychology* New York, Holt, Rinehart & Winston (1961).

H. Zeisel 'Methodological Problems in Studies of Sentencing' *Law and Society Review* Vol. **3** (1969) p. 621.

Prison classification

F. A. Allen 'Criminal Justice, Legal Values and the Rehabilitative Ideal' *Jo. Crim. Law, Crimin. and P.S.* Vol. **50** (1959) p. 226.

240

A. E. Bottoms 'Towards a Custodial Training Sentence for Adults' *Crim. L. R.* (1965) pp. 582, 650.

*R. A. Cloward *et al.* *Theoretical Studies in Social Organization of the Prison* New York, Social Science Research Council (1960).

J. P. Conrad *Crime and its Correction* London, Tavistock (1965).

D. R. Cressey 'Contradictory Directives in Complex Organisations: the Case of the Prison' *Administrative Science Quarterly* Vol. **4** (June 1959) p. 1.

F. E. Emery *Freedom and Justice within Walls* London, Tavistock (1970).

J. Gittins *Approved School Boys* London, H.M.S.O. (1952).

D. Glaser *The Effectiveness of a Prison and Parole System* New York, Bobbs-Merrill (1964).

J. E. Hall Williams *The English Penal System in Transition* London, Butterworth (1970).

*J. E. Hall Williams and D. A. Thomas 'The Use of Imprisonment and Borstal Training for Young Offenders under the Criminal Justice Act, 1961' *Crim. L. R.* (1965) pp. 146, 193, 273.

*S. Hobhouse and A. F. Brockway *English Prisons Today* London, Longman, Green (1922).

Home Office *Report of the Departmental Committee on Persistent Offenders* Cmd 4090 London, H.M.S.O. (1932).

Home Office *Preventive Detention* (Report of the Advisory Council on the Treatment of Offenders) London, H.M.S.O. (1963).

Home Office *Report of the Inquiry into Prison Escapes and Security* (Mountbatten Report) Cmnd. 3175 London, H.M.S.O. (1966).

Home Office *The Regime for Long-term Prisoners in Conditions of Maximum Security* (Radzinowicz Report) (Report of the Advisory Council on the Penal System) London, H.M.S.O. (1968).

*Home Office *People in Prison: England and Wales* Cmnd. 4214 London, H.M.S.O. (1969).

*R. G. Hood *Borstal Reassessed* London, Heinemann (1965).

J. Irwin *The Felon* Englewood Cliffs, Prentice-Hall (1970).

A. N. Little 'Penal Theory, Penal Reform and Borstal Practice' *Brit. Jo. Crim.* Vol. **3** (1963) p. 257.

*J. D. McClean 'Corrective Training—Decline and Fall' *Crim. L. R.* (1964) p. 745.

*H. Mannheim and J. C. Spencer *Problems of Classification in the English Penal and Reformatory System* London, I.S.T.D. (1950).

H. Mannheim and L. T. Wilkins *Prediction Methods in Relation to Borstal Training* London, H.M.S.O. (1955).

*R. L. Morrison 'Borstal Allocation' *Brit. Jo. Del.* Vol. **8** (1957) p. 95.

A. H. Papps 'Control—Treatment' *Prison Service Journal* Vol. **8** (n.s.) (1972) p. 6.

L. N. Robinson 'Contradictory Purposes in Prisons' *Jo. Crim. Law, Crimin. and P.S.* Vol. **37** (1947) p. 449.

A. G. Rose *Schools for Young Offenders* London, Tavistock (1967).

S. K. Ruck (ed.) *Paterson on Prisons* London, Muller (1951).

D. Street, R. D. Vinter and C. Perrow *Organization for Treatment* New York, Free Press (1966).

G. M. Sykes *The Society of Captives* Princeton, U.P. (1958).

J. E. Thomas 'The Prison Officer's Role' *The Criminologist* Vol. **8** (May 1968) p. 7.

*J. E. Thomas *The English Prison Officer since 1850* London, Routledge & Kegan Paul (1972).

M. Q. Warren 'Classification of Offenders as an Aid to Efficient Management and Effective Treatment' *Jo. Crim. Law, Crimin. and P.S.* Vol. **62** (1971) p. 239.

*L. T. Wilkins *Evaluation of Penal Measures* New York, Random House (1969).

Parole

A. K. Bottomley 'Parole Decisions in a Long-Term Closed Prison' *Brit. Jo. Crim.* Vol. **13** (1973) p. 26.

*R. O. Dawson 'The Decision to Grant or Deny Parole: A Study of Parole Criteria in Law and Practice' *Washington Univ. Law Quarterly* (1966) p. 243.

R. O. Dawson *Sentencing: the Decision as to Type, Length and Conditions of Sentence* Boston, Little, Brown (1969).

D. Dressler *Practice and Theory of Probation and Parole* 2nd edn, New York, Columbia University Press (1969).

V. H. Evjen 'Current Thinking on Parole Prediction Tables' *Crime and Delinquency* Vol. **8** (1962) p. 215.

D. Glaser 'Prediction Tables as Accounting Devices for Judges and Parole Boards' *Crime and Delinquency* Vol. **8** (1962) p. 239.

D. Glaser *The Effectiveness of a Prison and Parole System* New York, Bobbs-Merrill (1964).

D. M. Gottfredson and K. B. Ballard *The Parole Decision: Some Agreements and Disagreements* Vacaville, Institute for the Study of Crime and Delinquency (1964).

D. M. Gottfredson and K. B. Ballard 'Differences in Parole Decisions Associated with Decision-makers' *Jo. Research in Crime and Del.* Vol. **3** (1966) p. 112.

J. E. Hall Williams 'Alternatives to Definite Sentences' *The Law Quarterly Review* Vol. **80** (1964) p. 41.

W. H. Hammond and E. Chayen *Persistent Criminals* London, H.M.S.O. (1963).

H. Hart 'Predicting Parole Success' *Jo. Crim. Law, Crimin. and P.S.* Vol. **14** (1923) p. 405.

'Indeterminate Sentence Laws—the Adolescence of Peno-correctional legislation' *Harvard Law Review* Vol. **50** (1937) p. 677.

*K. O. Hawkins 'Parole Selection: the American Experience' unpublished Ph.D. thesis, Cambridge University Library (1971).

K. O. Hawkins 'Parole Procedure: An Alternative Approach' *Brit. Jo. Crim.* Vol. **13** (1973) p. 6.

N. S. Hayner 'Why Do Parole Boards Lag in the Use of Prediction Scores?' *Pacific Sociological Review* Vol. **1** (Fall 1958) p. 73.

Home Office *The Adult Offender* Cmnd. 2852 London, H.M.S.O. (1965).

Home Office *Reports of the Parole Board for 1968–71* London, H.M.S.O. (1969–72).

D. R. Jaman, R. M. Dickover and L. A. Bennett 'Parole Outcome as a Function of Time Served' *Brit. Jo. Crim.* Vol. **12** (1972) p. 5.

W. D. Lane 'A New Day Opens for Parole' *Jo. Crim. Law, Crimin. and P.S.* Vol. **24** (1933) p. 88.

*E. Lindsey 'Historical Sketch of the Indeterminate Sentence and Parole System *Jo. Crim. Law, Crimin. and P.S.* Vol. **16** (1925) p. 9.

M. Lopez-Rey 'Release and Provisional Release of Sentenced Prisoners' *Brit. Jo. Crim.* Vol. **6** (1966) p. 236.

C. Nuttall 'Parole Selection' *Brit. Jo. Crim.* Vol. **13** (1973) p. 41.

L. E. Ohlin *Selection for Parole* New York, Russell Sage Foundation (1951).

M. Reich 'Therapeutic Implications of the Indeterminate Sentence' *Issues in Criminology* Vol. **2** (1966) p. 7.

J. P. Shalloo 'Legal and Social Concepts of Parole' *Federal Probation* Vol. **11** (1947) p. 37.

A. D. Smith 'The Parole Board for Scotland' *Brit. Jo. Crim.* Vol. **13** (1973) p. 46.

P. A. Thomas 'An Analysis of Parole Selection' *Crime and Delinquency* Vol. **9** (1963) p. 173.

*United States Department of Justice *The Attorney General's Survey of Release Procedures: Vol. IV, Parole* Washington, D.C., U.S. Government Printing Office (1939).

243

S. B. Warner 'Factors Determining Parole from the Massachusetts Reformatory' *Jo. Crim. Law, Crimin. and P.S.* Vol. **14** (1923) p. 172.

*D. J. West (ed.) *The Future of Parole* London, Duckworth (1972).

D. J. West 'Report of the Parole Board for 1971' *Brit. Jo. Crim.* Vol. **13** (1973) p. 56.

C. H. White 'Some Legal Aspects of Parole' *Jo. Crim. Law, Crimin. and P.S.* Vol. **32** (1942) p. 600.

C. Wilcox 'Parole Principles and Practice' *Jo. Crim. Law, Crimin. and P.S.* Vol. **20** (1929) p. 345.

INDEX OF AUTHORS

Ahrenfeldt, R. H. 9, 32n
Alschuler, A. W. 127n, 128n
Ares, C. E. 127n
Argyle, M. 33n
Aubert, V. 132, 147, 170n, 172n
Avison, N. H. 24, 25, 26, 34n, 64, 65, 66, 73, 81n, 82n

Balch, R. W. 78n
Ballard, K. B. 201, 203, 215n
Banton, M. 79n
Barr, H. 172n, 173n
Bauzer, R. 73, 82n
Bayley, D. H. 54, 80n
Bittner, E. A. 50, 60, 79n
Black, D. J. 52, 57, 79n, 80n
Blumberg, A. S. xv, 106, 109, 110n, 111, 116, 117, 123, 127n, 128n, 129n, 153, 161, 162, 172n, 173n
Bordua, D. J. 69, 70, 73, 80n, 81n, 82n
Bottomley, A. K. 89, 91, 92, 99, 101, 125n, 126n, 127n, 205, 208, 215n, 216n
Bottoms, A. E. 213n
Box, S. 32n, 42, 58, 77n, 78n, 80n, 82n
Branham, V. C. 140n, 171n
Briar, S. 36, 52, 53, 54n, 55, 56, 77n, 79n, 80n
Brockway, A. F. 184, 212n
Bullock, H. A. 149, 150, 172n

Cain, M. E. 80n
Cameron, M. O. 33n
Carson, W. G. 32n
Carter, R. M. 167, 173n
Chapman, D. 15, 33n
Chayen, E. 199, 205, 214n, 215n
Christie, N. 78n
Cicourel, A. V. 4, 5, 32n, 80n

Cohen, S. 80n
Conrad, J. P. 178, 193, 196, 212n, 214n
Cressey, D. R. 38, 78n, 79n, 213n
Cumming, E. 45, 46n, 78n
Cumming, I. M. 45, 46n, 78n

Davies, C. 89, 91, 125n
Davis, A. 128n, 129n
Davis, K. C. xv, 220, 223, 224, 227n
Dawson, R. O. xiv, 131, 170n, 176, 204, 206, 207, 209, 212n, 215n, 216n, 227n
Dell, S. 117, 118, 126n, 127n, 129n
Devlin, p. 10, 33n
Douglas, J. D. 32n
Downes, D. M. 79n
Drapkin, I. S. 170n

Edell, L. 46n, 78n
Elgesem, E. 38, 78n, 79n
Ennis, P. H. 19, 33n, 34n
Everson, G. 138, 139, 143, 158, 159, 171n, 173n

Ferdinand, T. N. 67, 69, 81n, 82n
Foote, C. 88, 125n, 126n
Ford, P. 166, 173n
Fox, L. 193
Friedland, M. L. 87, 89, 91, 125n, 126n

Galtung, J. 213n
Gaudet, F. J. 138, 139, 140, 143, 152, 171n, 172n
Gibbens, T. C. N. 9, 17, 32n, 33n, 34n
Gibson, E. 121n, 125n, 126n, 127n, 129n
Glaser, D. 20, 33n, 34n, 200, 201n, 205, 207, 209, 212n, 213n, 214n, 215n, 216n
Goldman, N. 63, 66, 69, 72, 80n, 81n, 82n

245

Goldstein, J. 35, 77n, 78n
Gottfredson, D. M. 201, 203, 215n
Gould, A. 213n
Green, E. 140, 141, 143, 150, 151, 152, 171n, 172n
Gross, S. Z. 173n
Grossman, J. B. 146, 172n
Grünhut, M. 2, 32n, 82n, 133, 156, 157, 170n, 172n
Grygier, T. 173n
Guenther, A. L. 33n

Hall Williams, J. E. 213n
Halmos, P. 173n
Hammond, W. H. 199, 205, 214n, 215n
Harris, G. S. 171n
Hart, H. L. A. 10, 33n
Hawkins, K. O. 194, 198, 201, 202n, 203, 204, 207, 214n, 215n
Hayner, N S. 216n
Hills, S. L. 127n
Hobhouse, S. 184, 212n
Hogarth, J. 102, 126n, 142, 145, 153, 154, 155, 156, 159, 160, 162, 168, 169, 170n, 171n, 172n, 173n, 174n
Hohenstein, W. F. 68, 81n
Holtzoff, A. 171n
Hood, R. G. 17, 33n, 57, 80n, 82n, 131, 136, 137, 143, 144, 146, 152, 156, 157, 158n, 162, 164, 170n, 171n, 172n, 173n, 174n, 189, 212n
Howard, J. 181
Howlett, F. W. 32n, 228n
Hudson, J. R. 78n, 79n
Hurst, H. 32n, 228n

Irwin, J. xvi, 200, 212n, 213n, 214n

Jackson, R. M. 129n
Jarvis, F. V. 164, 165n, 166, 173n
Johnson, E. H. 78n, 83n

Kalven, H. 119, 120n, 127n, 129n
King, M. 96n, 99, 125n, 126n
Kitsuse, J. I. 4, 32n
Klein, M. W. 32n, 82n, 228n
Kutash, S. B. 140n, 171n

Lafave, W. R. xiv, 47, 77n, 78n, 79n, 80n, 125n

Lambert, J. R. 25, 34n, 39, 78n, 79n, 81n
Lane, W. D. 195, 214n, 216n
Lindsey, E. 195, 196, 214n
Lipset, S. M. 172n
Longley, D. G. 215n
Lopez-Rey, M. 9, 32n
Luchterhand, E. G. 67, 69, 81n, 82n

McCabe, S. 108, 111, 113, 118, 123, 127n, 128n, 129n
McClean, J. D. 65, 66, 73, 81n, 82n, 135, 136n, 157, 170n, 192, 213n
McClintock, F. H. 11, 12, 14, 22, 23, 24, 25, 26, 32n, 33n, 34n, 64, 65, 66, 73, 81n, 82n
McEachern, A. W. 73, 82n
McGuir, M. F. 171n
MacMillan, J. A. D. 13, 33n
McWilliams, W. 173n
Mannheim, H. 10, 11, 22, 31n, 34n, 134, 143, 164, 170n, 173n, 181, 189, 190, 212n, 213n
Martin, J. P. 12, 16, 33n, 197, 214n
Mendelsohn, H. 54, 80n
Morrison, R. L. 190, 213n
Mountbatten, Earl 184, 187, 212n

Nagel, S. S. 144, 145, 147, 159, 171n, 172n, 173n
Newman, D. J. xiv, 4, 6, 32n, 75, 83n, 106, 109, 113, 115, 120, 123, 124, 127n, 128n, 129n, 218, 219, 222, 227n
Nuttall, C. 214n

Ohlin, L. E. 214n
O'Leary, E. 172n, 173n
O'Leary, V. 32n, 200, 201n, 205, 207, 214n, 215n, 218, 219, 222, 224, 227n

Packer, H. L. 124n, 126n, 221, 222, 227n
Palermo, J. S. 125n, 126n
Parnas, R. I. 49, 50, 79n
Parry, M. H. 33n
Patchett, K. W. 65, 66, 73, 81n, 82n, 135, 136n, 157, 170n
Paterson, A. 212n, 223
Perrow, C. 212n
Piliavin, I. 35, 52, 53, 54n, 55, 56, 77n, 79n, 80n
Prince, J. 17, 33n, 34n

Purves, R. 108, 111, 113, 118, 123, 127n, 128n, 129n

Quinney, R. 37, 38, 40, 42, 45, 54, 77n, 78n, 79n, 80n, 128n, 129n

Radzinowicz, L. 2, 31n, 34n
Rankin, A. 92, 126n
Reich, M. 196, 200, 214n
Reiss, A. J. 33n, 44, 49, 53, 56, 57, 77, 78n, 79n, 80n, 82n, 83n, 227n
Remington, F. J. 218, 227n
Roberts, J. W. 125n, 126n
Rock, P. 49, 79n
Rose, A. G. 212n
Ruck, S. K. 212n
Ryan, E. 224, 227n

Sacks, H. 80n
St John, C. W. 171n
Schubert, G. 170n, 171n, 172n
Sebba, L. 82n, 172n
Sellin, T. 2, 29, 30, 31, 32n, 34n, 70, 81n, 149, 172n
Shannon, L. W. 62, 80n
Shaw, M. 15, 33n, 79n
Shea, E. 197, 202, 214n, 215n
Shoham, S. 141, 142, 171n
Siegel, L. J. 53, 80n
Skolnick, J. H. 48, 55, 78n, 79n, 80n
Smith, A. B. 153, 161, 172n, 173n
Smith, A. D. 214n
Somerville, J. G. 65, 73, 81n, 82n
Sparks, R. F. 17, 33n, 57, 80n, 82n, 143, 168, 171n, 172n, 173n, 174n
Spencer J. C. 181, 189, 212n, 213n
Steer, D. J. 66, 68, 71, 81n, 82n
Sterling, J. W. 73, 82n
Stinchcombe, A. 37, 38, 78n
Stokes, J. 33n
Street, D. 178, 212n, 213n
Sudnow, D. 80n, 112, 129n

Sullivan, D. C. 53, 80n
Sykes, G. M. 178, 212n

Taylor, I. 173n
Terry, R. M. 63, 76, 80n, 82n, 83n
Thomas, D. A. 122, 129n, 213n
Thomas, J. E. 177, 183, 212n
Thomas, P. 129n
Toch, H. 171n
Turner, J. W. C. 31n

Vinter, R. D. 212n

Wald, P. M. 126n
Walker, N. D. 18, 31n, 33n
Warner, S. B. 206, 215n
Weiner, N. L. 64, 67, 81n
Welford, A. T. 32n
Werthman, C. 55, 80n
West, D. J. 210, 214n, 215n, 216n
Westley, W. A. 48, 78n, 79n, 82n
Wheeler, S. 6, 7, 28, 32n, 71, 79n, 82n, 83n, 153, 154, 155, 172n, 219, 227n
Whitaker, B. 40, 71, 78n, 82n
Whitlock, F. A. 33n
Wilcox, C. 210, 216n
Wiles, P. N. P. 7, 14, 32n, 33n
Wilkins, L. T. xiv, 3, 4, 6, 9, 11, 30, 32n, 34n, 53, 167, 173n, 180, 190, 212n, 213n, 225
Willcock, H. D. 33n
Willett, T. C. 33n
Williamson, W. 15, 33n, 79n
Willie, C. V. 64, 67, 81n
Wilson, J. Q. 7, 32n, 52, 57, 58, 59, 60, 61, 72, 79n, 80n
Winick, C. 152, 171n, 172n
Wolfgang, M. E. 29, 30, 31, 32n, 34n, 70, 81n

Zander, M. 99, 102, 126n, 127n
Zeisel, H. 119, 120n, 127n, 129n

INDEX OF SUBJECTS

Acquittal
  bail and 88–90
  directed by judge 113, 124
  pleas and 119–20
Advisory Council on the Penal System 186, 213n
American Bar Foundation xiv, 131, 175, 218
American Correctional Association 180, 212n
Arrest 43–58 *passim*
Association of Chief Police Officers 106, 119, 127n, 129n

Bail 85–105 *passim*
  acquittal rates and 88–90
  Cobden Trust survey on 86, 94–6, 99, 101–2
  criteria 93–8
  discretion and 102–3
  Home Office Working Party on 103–4
  information and 98–105
  judicial process and 88–93
  legal representation and 90, 99–104, 126n
  Manhattan Bail Project 99n, 104
  pleas and 89–90, 125n
  police objections to 94–7, 99, 101–3, 126n
  preventive detention and 97, 104, 127n
  right to 103, 126n
  sentences and 90–3
  statistics 85–6, 93
Borstal training
  classification and 188–92, 212n, 213n
  judicial aims and 190–2

Cautioning 64–6, 68, 72–3, 81n, 82n
Charge reduction 109–12, 121, 128n

Clear-up rate 23–6, 57, 73–4
Cobden Trust 86, 94–6, 99, 101–2
Community
  parole and 208, 211
  police and 14–15, 42–3, 45–7, 58–61, 72–3, 79n, 226
  reporting crime and 11–12, 14–15, 225–6
  sentencing and 135, 137, 149–51, 155–63, 226
Corrective training 192–4, 213n
Crime
  clear-up rate 23–6, 57, 73–4
  classification 27, 30, 34n
  'dark figure' of 2, 11–13, 21
  employers and 12–13, 16–20
  index 29–31
  'institutional immunity' and 15–18
  recording by police 21–4
  reporting of 8, 12, 14, 18–21, 27–8, 34n, 42–3, 61
  social attitudes and xvii, 8–9, 11–13, 16, 28, 225–7
  statistics 1–8, 22–31, 57–8
  subcultural toleration of 11–13
  'taken into consideration' 25
  victim studies 19–20
Criminal statistics 1–8, 22–31, 57–8
  (see also *Crime,* above)

Decision-stages in the penal process xiii–xvi, 3–8, 28, 31, 35–6, 71–7, 123–4, 217–25
Discretion xv, 4, 6, 218–25
  bail and 102–3
  individualization and 124, 223
  parole decisions and 202
  penal process and 218–25
  police 35–6, 78n; need for, 37–43; in

Discretion (*contd.*)
    arrest decisions 43–58; in disposition decisions, 61–73
    sentencing and 130–1
Domestic disturbances 22, 49–50, 81n
Drunks 50–1, 53, 79n

Elmira Reformatory 195

Gladstone Committee 177, 183, 187

Holloway prison survey 117–18, 126n, 129n
Home Office Research Unit 91, 106, 119, 121, 125n, 126n, 157, 165
Howard League for Penal Reform 103, 127n

Indeterminate sentence 195–6, 214n
Individualization
    discretion and 124, 220, 223
    judicial acquittals and 124
    parole and 198
    plea-bargaining and 109–10, 112–13
    police and 38–9, 69–70
    sentencing and 130–2
Information use in decision-making xv, 28, 31, 53, 98–105, 135, 164–70, 173n, 203–4, 220, 224

Jury trial 105–8, 111, 116, 118–20, 122–4, 127n
Juveniles
    cautioning and 64–73
    police and 52–6, 59–60, 62–73
    sentencing of 133–6, 154, 156–7, 164

Law
    morality and 10
    public opinion and 10–11
Legal representation
    bail and 90, 99–104, 126n
    pleas and 115–18, 123
    sentencing and 147

Manhattan Bail Project 99n, 104
Model Penal Code 197, 208
Motoring offenders 12–13, 15, 18, 22, 61, 137–8, 152, 171n
Mountbatten Report 184–7

National Opinion Research Centre 19, 20

Parole 194–211 *passim*
    concepts of 194–8
    criteria 198–209
    disparities 203
    history of 194–8
    indeterminate sentence and 195–7, 214n
    policy for future 210–11
    prediction tables and 208–9
    preventive detention and 199, 205
    prison management and 194–7, 206–8, 214n, 215n
    rehabilitative aims of 195–8, 203–6, 208–11
    risk 198–200, 208–9
    sentencing aims and 199–201, 209–11, 214n, 216n
    statistics 194, 203, 215n
    'ticket-of-leave' system and 194–6
Penal process
    bail and 85, 88–93
    conflict resolution in 83n, 175, 210–11, 223–5, 227n
    conflict within 71–7, 175–6, 187–8, 190–2, 209–10, 217–25
    control of discretion in 223–4
    'Crime Control' model 124n, 221–2, 226
    'Due Process' model 124n, 221–2, 226
    parole and 209–11
    pleas and 105–6, 108–15, 123–4
    police and 35–6, 71–7
    prison aims and 175–6, 187–8, 190–2
    sentencing and 130–2
    social values and xiii, xvi, xvii, 225–7
    study of xiii–xvii, 35
    systems approach to xiv, 6, 218, 224–5, 228n
Perks Committee on Criminal Statistics 26–30, 34n
Pleas 105–24 *passim*
    acquittal rates and 119–20
    bail and 89–90
    bargaining 108–24
    charge reduction and 109–12, 121, 128n
    individualization and 109–10, 112–13
    judicial process and 108–15, 122–4

250

Pleas (*contd.*)
  legal representation and 115–18, 123
  police and 117–18
  reasons for 115–19
  recidivists and 115–16, 122–3
  sentences following 119–22, 128n
  sentencing structure and 113–15
  statistics 106–7
Police
  arrest decisions 43–58
  attitudes to the courts 41, 70–7, 221–2
  bail 87–8
  cautioning 64–6, 68, 72–3, 81n, 82n
  clear-up rate 23–6, 57, 73–4
  community and 15, 42–3, 45–7,
    58–61, 72–3, 79n, 226
    discretion 35–6, 78n; need for
    37–43; in arrest decisions 43–58; in
    disposition decisions, 61–73
  disposition decisions 36, 61–73
  domestic disturbances and 49–50, 81n
  drunks and 50–1, 53, 79n
  ethos and 'styles' 41–2, 58–61
  guilty pleas and 117–8
  individualization and 38–9, 69–70
  'judicial' role of 56–8, 70–2
  juveniles and 52–3, 56, 59, 60, 62–73
  law enforcement role of 44–52, 60, 78n
  'moral character' and 52–6, 68–70,
    81n
  objections to bail 94–7, 99, 101–3,
    126n
  organizational influences upon 40–1,
    58–61, 72–3
  peace-keeping role of 44–52, 60
  penal process and 35–6, 41, 71–7
  race and 14, 52, 55–9, 66–9
  recording of crime 21–4
  'social support' role of 45–7, 50–1, 78n
  subcultures and 14, 15
  summons and 86–7, 125n
  working philosophy and stereotypes
    54–8
Prediction tables 141, 208–9
Presentence reports 164–7, 173n, 224
President's Commission on Law Enforcement and Administration of Justice
  xiv, 6, 17, 32n, 33n, 40, 77n, 78n, 107,
  112, 114, 127n, 128n, 129n, 132,
  170n, 214n, 217, 227n, 228n

Preventive detention 97, 104, 127n, 192,
  199, 205
Prison
  aims 154, 175–9, 187–8, 193–4
  classification 179–94, 212n, 223
  community and 189, 226
  contamination 182–3, 187, 190, 212n,
    213n
  corrective training 192–4
  Gladstone Committee on 177, 183,
    187
  management and parole 194–7, 206–8,
    214n, 215n
  Mountbatten Report and 184–7
  preventive detention 97, 104, 127n,
    192, 199, 205
  security and control 177–9, 183–7,
    192–3, 212n
  sentencing aims and 175–6, 179,
    187–8, 190–2, 222–3
  Separate System 182–3
  Silent System 182–3
  'Star' class 183–5
Probation officers 147, 164–7, 173n

Race
  police and 14, 52, 55–9, 66–9
  sentencing and 147–51
Research
  penal reform and xvii, 226–7
  social values and xvii, 225–7
  theory and empiricism in xiv, xvi, xvii
Royal Commission on Justices of the
  Peace 144

Sentencing
  aims of imprisonment and 175–6, 179,
    187–8, 190–2, 222–3
  bail and 90–3
  community characteristics and 135,
    137, 149–51, 155–63, 226
  discretion in 130–1
  disparity: concept of 131–3;
    explanations of, 146, 149–51,
    161–3, 167–8, 222; statistics of,
    133–43, 147–51
  human element in 135–6, 138–41,
    143–55, 159–61
  individualization and 130–2
  information use in 135, 163–70, 173n
251

Sentencing (*contd.*)
    judicial attitudes and 136, 139–41, 144–6, 152–5, 159–61, 169–70, 173n
    judicial 'role patterns' and 152–3, 160–1
    juveniles 133–6, 154, 156–7, 164
    legal representation and 147
    motoring offenders 137–8, 152, 171n
    parole and 199–201, 209–11, 216n
    penal process and 130–2
    pleas and 113–15, 119–22, 128n
    presentence reports and 164–7, 173n
    social background of judges and 143–7, 152, 158, 172n, 222
Sexual offences 18–19, 21, 38, 81n, 149–50
Shoplifting 17, 18, 20
Streatfeild Committee 163–5, 173n
Summons 86–7, 125n

Vera Institute of Justice 87
Victim studies 19–20